BECOMING A
TWO-JOB FAMILY

BECOMING A
TWO-JOB FAMILY

Jane C. Hood

PRAEGER

PRAEGER SPECIAL STUDIES • PRAEGER SCIENTIFIC

New York • Philadelphia • Eastbourne, UK
Toronto • Hong Kong • Tokyo • Sydney

Library of Congress Cataloging in Publication Data

Hood, Jane C.
  Becoming a two-job family.

  Bibliography: p.
  Includes index.
  1. Married people—Employment—Social aspects—United
States—Longitudinal studies. 2. Married women—
Employment—Social aspects—United States—Longitudinal
studies. 3. Sex role—United States—Longitudinal
studies. 4. Negotiation—Longitudinal studies.
5. Family—United States—Longitudinal studies. I. Title.

HQ536.H64   1983   306.8′7   83-21150
ISBN 0-03-063638-8

Published in 1983 by Praeger Publishers
CBS Educational and Professional Publishing,
a Division of CBS Inc.
521 Fifth Avenue, New York, NY 10175 USA

3456789   052   987654321

Printed in the United States of America
on acid-free paper

"It's more of a fifty/fifty deal. We're both providers and we're both homemakers and we're both parents."

James Mooney
Machinist, Age 31 (1976)

FOREWORD

Professor Hood has given us a study in the theoretical tradition of Georg Simmel, one of the founding lights of sociology. Although this tradition once predominated the discipline, it subsequently fell into a period of neglect. Studies such as Hood's are giving this tradition a contemporary flavor, and restoring it to a position of eminence.

The Simmelian perspective pinpoints the unique province of sociology as being the dynamic processes between persons. Those processes are constrained by social or contextual forces which, in turn, give rise to the organization of relationships, which subsequently become the forces influencing later dynamics, and so forth.

Hood applies this general model to sixteen families. Her aim is to try to show how and why the families change or develop as a result of the wife's entering the paid labor force. Covering a wide range of important issues, the book makes a meaningful contribution to our understanding of the nature of the paid-work housework intersection. Hood gathered qualitative data from the couples in 1976, and based on those data she provides insightful analyses regarding what the families were like prior to the wife's labor force entry, why they entered, and what the consequences were for the family. While the study is rich in fascinating descriptions, Hood does not remain merely at that level. Instead, she significantly extends our theoretical thinking regarding husband-wife equality, power, bargaining, conflict, and the sharing of both domestic and provider roles.

Some six years after the initial data-gathering, Hood contacted her sixteen families once again to try to determine the intermediate-term effects of the changes she had previously documented. Those particular reports make for some of the most illuminating reading in the entire volume.

Hood freely acknowledges that her work is aimed chiefly at hypothesis-formulation, and not hypothesis-testing. Keeping that criterion in mind, it is clear that her study has been exceptionally successful. Future quantitative research, as well as conceptualizations of the work-family interplay, will surely need to take her suggested hypotheses into account. That is because Hood has substantially enlarged our understanding of the nature of husband-wife dynamics in the midst of continuing changes from traditional to emerging family patterns. Given that those types of changes are likely to continue, Hood's book becomes required reading for students and professionals alike—whether their interests are applied or research-oriented.

John Scanzoni
University of North Carolina-Greensboro

PREFACE

BACKGROUND

From the 1975–1976 taped interviews to the 1982–1983 follow-up letters and telephone conversations, the two-job family study has gone through several stages. Many of the ideas presented here were developed in convention papers and presentations done between 1976 and 1979, and the draft upon which this book is based was written in 1978 and 1979 (Hood, 1980). At about the same time, several books and articles began to appear that made important contributions to the understanding of power, conflict, division of labor, and negotiation in families. The work most closely related to mine includes Ralph LaRossa's *Conflict and Power in Marriage* (1977), John Scanzoni's *Sex Roles, Women's Work and Marital Conflict* (1978), John Scanzoni and Maximiliane Szinovacz's *Family Decision Making* (1980), and several articles by Linda Haas on role sharing in Sweden and America. In addition, Anselm Strauss published a valuable book on negotiations in general in 1978.

In this book, I have tried to take into account much of this recent work as well as that of many other researchers who have been writing about dual-worker families in the past few years. Thus, although much of the material in Chapters 2 through 5 remains as it was written in 1979, Chapters 1, 6, and 7 are new, reflecting not only what I have learned from my colleagues but also what I have learned from the families themselves both in the follow-up interviews and from their comments on portions of the manuscript.

Were I to start such a study again knowing what I have learned from this one, I would, of course, do it differently. Given the willing cooperation of the families I worked with, I would be less hesitant to ask for time diaries or permission to interview children. I would also combine formal self-administered questionnaires with open-ended interviews. For all its shortcomings, however, insofar as this book helps to deepen our understanding of how families change when wives return to work, it has succeeded.

ACKNOWLEDGMENTS

Many people have helped with this project since I began it in 1974. At the University of Michigan, James Brown, Roy Hansen, Anne Joachim, and David Scheffler helped with transcriptions and coding of the 1975–1976 interviews. Their insightful comments on over 2000 pages of notes and transcriptions were invaluable. At this stage, the research was partially supported by a grant from the Horace H. Rackham School of Graduate Studies.

As I made the first leap from field notes to theory construction, I had helpful conversations with Roxanna Balay, Stan Bernstein, Rafe Ezekiel, Andre Modigliani, Jacquelynne Parsons, and Charles Tilly. In the early stages of this research, I also received guidance from the late David Street, Lawrence Redlinger, and Lois W. Hoffman.

As the analysis progressed, members of a study group on work and family roles (Joseph Pleck, Susan Golden, and Chaya Piotrkowski) read chapter drafts and responded to pieces of theory as they developed. Joseph Pleck helped to broaden my knowledge of the literature by sharing citations, bibliographies, and copies of unpublished manuscripts. His enthusiastic support of my work has helped it over many temporary snags.

Charles Tilly's incisive comments on earlier drafts of this manuscript helped me to create coherence out of chaos. Without his help as well as that of my other colleagues at the University of Michigan, the two-job family study might have remained a few file drawers full of field notes and cassette tapes.

Bill Sell typed the 1980 manuscript and Debbie Ritchie-Kolberg helped with charts and diagrams. My husband, John Krogman, copyedited the entire 300 pages, relentlessly imposing consistency upon the author. In the preparation of the 1983 manuscript, Linda Sharp, Barbara Leffel, and the editorial staff at Praeger have taken over John's job, and Linda has, in addition, offered suggestions, encouragement, and reassurance along the way. I am also indebted to John Scanzoni, Maximiliane Szinovacz, Linda Haas, Ralph LaRossa, Elam Nunally, Charles Tilly, Bill Maryl, and Nan Blyth for their useful comments on the draft. To the extent that I have been able to address the questions they have raised, this is a better book. Donna Bennett made time in her schedule to enter Chapters 1 and 6 into the word processor as well as to make minor editorial revisions, and Elizabeth Earnest, Steve Swetlik, Zona Selensky, and Monica Shafer all helped in the preparation of revisions. In addition, Linda Haas, Eleanor Hall, and John Dorosz provided valuable editorial assistance.

In addition to all of this intellectual and technical help, I have had the benefit of colleagues, friends, and family who have cheered, goaded, and pushed me along the way. Mary Frank Fox helped to convince me that I had indeed written a book and not "just a dissertation." My family, Otis, Frances, and Nancy Hood; Lucy Allen, and Betsy and Huntington Thompson all read and responded enthusiastically to the 1980 manuscript. Bill and Mary Krogman, who have seen many Krogman books to completion, took an active interest in this one as well. More recently, members of a writing support group have kept me focused on writing in spite of a variety of other academic demands. These include: Margaret Atherton, Cecilia Barron, Jane Bowers, Eleanor Hall, Eleanor Miller, Juliette Redding, Anne Robertson, Linda Haughton, and Mary Ann Steger.

My husband, John Krogman, deserves special mention. In addition to copyediting, he has done nearly all of the cooking, all of the shopping, most of the laundry, and billpaying and has given far more emotional support than he received during the times I worked intensively on this project. As John and I continue to work through the feelings such role reversals inevitably arouse, my respect for his sensitivity and courage continues to grow. As did many of the couples in this book, we have also found that those who can live through the pain role change produces are rewarded with an expanded relationship and new appreciation of each other.

Lastly, the families who participated in this study should be considered coauthors. Their willingness to answer my questions, reply to my letters, and read and comment upon portions of the manuscript has continued to surprise and delight me. Their experiences and their words provide the basis for this book.

CONTENTS

LIST OF TABLES

LIST OF FIGURES

OVERVIEW: PLAN OF THE BOOK

Chapter 1 sketches out the central components of the role bargaining model. Here I define role bargaining and role sharing, discuss the relationship between conflict and equity, and raise some questions about the definition of marital equality. Chapter 2 describes how the families were selected and how the interviews were done and then briefly discusses the method of data analysis. A more detailed description of qualitative data analysis is included in the appendix. Chapters 3 and 4 are devoted to the findings of the 1975-76 interviews. Here I discuss the wives' motivations for returning to work, their husbands' reactions and how the definitions of each spouse's provider, companion, parent and housekeeper roles were affected by the wife's return to work. Chapter 5 goes back to Chapter 1 and fleshes out the role bargaining model using concepts developed in Chapters 3 and 4 as well as data from the case studies. This chapter concludes with eight hypotheses derived from the theory presented up to this point. Chapter 6 then procedes to "test" these hypotheses against the data collected in the 1982-83 follow-up study, and in the spirit of "grounded theory," (Glaser and Strauss, 1967) to suggest some refinements of the theory. In Chapter 7, I evaluate the implications of the role bargaining model for family research and theory and conclude with a few recommendations for policy makers, family counselors and two-job families themselves.

BECOMING A
TWO-JOB FAMILY

1
ROLE BARGAINING
AND ROLE SHARING

The family process is thus perceived as an ongoing peace-making effort which may result in a negotiated order, a state of affairs which remains, however, open to renegotiation. (Sprey, 1969:702)

INTRODUCTION

As wives and mothers have entered the labor force in steadily increasing numbers, family scholars have followed one step behind with their analyses of this trend and their predictions of its probable impact on family structure. By far the most popular theme in this literature is what I call the marketwork/housework bargain. If the wife goes to work outside the home, how much, if any, of the household work will the husband take on in exchange? The answers to that question have varied from "no more than he did before she went to work" (Walker, 1970) to "more than he used to, especially with regard to child care" (Pleck, 1983).[1] In contrast to studies designed to measure *how much* housework and child care husbands do, this book focuses on *how* husbands and wives renegotiate family roles. Based on the experiences of 16 lower and upper-middle-class couples, this book describes how the terms of the marketwork/housework bargain changed after the wives went back to work.

Between 1970 and 1980, the proportion of husband-wife families supported by one male earner decreased from 34% to 24%, whereas the proportion of such families supported by both husband and wife increased from 46% to 52% (U.S. Deptartment of Labor, 1979; 1980; 1982). By 1980, the U.S. Bureau of Census was no longer assuming that the male was head of the family. Family sociologist Jesse Bernard (1981:9) refers to that

1

change as "the death knell of the good provider role" and suggests that although the good provider role may be disappearing, "its legitimate successor has not yet appeared on the scene." In this book, I will describe three emerging alternatives to the good provider role. These are main, secondary, and coprovider roles. Furthermore, I will be demonstrating that the redefinition of the provider role is one of the central tasks involved in becoming a two-job family. Only after this redefinition has taken place is it possible to clearly renegotiate responsibility for the marital relationship, parenting, or household work.

THE HOLLINGS AND THE MOONEYS: TWO SKETCHES

Before explaining the role bargaining model and its components, I would like to illustrate the marketwork/housework bargain with sketches of two couples who arrived at very different answers to the pivotal question, "Who is the provider now?". Bess Holling went back to work temporarily in mid-life, becoming a *secondary provider* in order to put her children through college. Jill Mooney reentered the labor force when her children were much younger, and within a year her husband James had begun to think of her as a *coprovider* whose income was essential to the household.

Martin and Bess Holling

At age 52, Martin was in a middle management position in a large engineering firm. His wife, Bess, had earned a B.A. and had done some work in journalism before raising their three children. During the child rearing years, the couple moved several times as Martin made his way up the ladder. Bess characterized Martin as "more involved with his children" than most men, and Martin described parenting as a "joint venture." When the children were young, he was active in the PTA and the Cub Scouts. However, he said that Bess was with them more and that as the children became teenagers they become less close to him: "I'm sure you see that with other father-children relationships. The mother probably retains the day to day communication."

Throughout their marriage, the Hollings' social life has centered around Martin's work and Bess' club memberships. Before she returned to work, Bess typically belonged to the company wives' club, a university women's group, a book review club, and perhaps a hospital guild. Preferring outside activity to housework, Bess usually became president of the organizations she worked with. In spite of her club activities and a variety of hobbies (sewing, bridge, bowling, and interior decorating), Bess feels "lazy" in comparison to an old friend who is now a college trustee.

However, feeling lazy has not prompted Bess to seek a career. She would never think of having a career in the same way that her husband does or of having a job that she could not leave when Martin had to move. In fact, she has enjoyed her work with organizations far more than she does her job as a secretary. She hates the word "secretary" as much as she hates the word "housewife."

Nonetheless, Bess went back to work part-time when her younger son was 14, another was in college, and a daughter was graduating from high school. As she explained it, "We always said that I was the kids' scholarship to college." When interviewed in 1976, Bess was making about 25 percent of the family income at her full-time job as an administrative secretary. She had applied for and gotten a promotion since the previous interview. However, she did not see her job as essential to her family: "It isn't as if we were going to starve. We're not dependent upon my salary for living expenses. With two in college in the fall semester, we would have had to take out a loan. It would have been more of a strain if I weren't working."

When asked how he had adjusted to Bess' return to work, Martin said: "Basically, I think that we've adjusted to it fairly well. She's made a greater adjustment than I have and I respect her for it." Martin does do some more things around the house now, such as helping to set the table and helping with some cleaning, but, as he said, "the dishwasher and fixing dinner have always been ladies' work and that's continued to be."

Bess concurred with her husband's view that their division of labor had not changed much. She explained that when the children were younger it was "accepted that the wife did these things." She said that perhaps if she had gone to work when the children were younger, she would have put more pressure on Martin to help, but now, with two in college and one graduating from high school, she doesn't need much help and so chooses not to make an issue of it, even if, as she confided, she does sometimes resent having all the load.

Because Martin has ulcers, Bess told me she doesn't like to ask him to do anything that will "get him really upset". Instead, she "lets him do the things he likes to do". This strategy prevents Bess's feelings of resentment from disturbing what she describes as a very harmonious marriage. She and Martin enjoy being together in the evenings talking about their work, their friends, the children and politics. Since both Bess and Martin have a strong investment in keeping things the way they are, Bess' work has had relatively little impact on either their marital or household roles. Moreover, whatever impact it has had is viewed as temporary because, as Martin pointed out, Bess will stop working as soon as "their high income needs have been satisfied".

James and Jill Mooney

Jill Mooney, a high–school educated wife of a machinist, did not like housework any more than Bess Holling did. However, in contrast to Bess, Jill had few social outlets. Married to a second–shift worker whom she described as a "loner". Jill felt trapped in the house with her two small boys. The 2 year-old and hyperactive 4 year-old were making her nervous, she explained. The doctor told her she needed to get out of the house. Her husband, James, had taken little household responsibility before Jill went back to work. Although he was not very much involved with his children, he was, however, devoted to Jill. Anything she wanted badly enough, he was willing to try. For this reason, he agreed to care for the two boys during the day while Jill was at work. He took them to a babysitter before he left for work and Jill would pick up the children on her way home.

Because the Mooneys had two preschool children when they became a two–job family, they, unlike the Hollings, had to agree on some sharing of child care as a precondition to the wife's return to work. Furthermore, because Jill enjoys working, she continues to look for more challenging jobs. For her, "work is a haven from home and home is a haven from work". Since James was more invested in his marriage than in his work, he gradually relinquished part of his provider role to Jill and took on half of the parenting responsibility in its place. By 1982, Jill was earning 42 percent of the household income. Even when Jill earned only 30 percent of the family income, however, James described their relationship as a "50/50 deal" in which they share provider and parenting roles. Jill thinks that she still does most of the housework but, while James is home, he does laundry, some shopping, and picks up after the children.

For Jill and James Mooney, becoming coproviders was easier than it is for some couples. Jill and James have been able to renegotiate their roles and agree to share them because they have complementary rather than competing interests. Jill wants to work and James, now that he has discovered them, enjoys his children. In fact, he feels sorry for men who have not had the opportunity: "Yeah, I see situations like that, where the wife doesn't work. It seems the wife is 'the parent'. Whereas, the situation we have . . . I never really thought . . . it might be just the way the situation was out of necessity . . . I was brought closer to my kids".

The Hollings and the Mooneys became two–job families for different reasons at different stages of the family life cycle and with very different results. By comparing and contrasting their experiences as well as those of fourteen other lower–and upper–middle class dual–worker couples, this book provides a detailed analysis of how husbands and wives negotiate family roles after the wife returns to work.

ROLES AND ROLE SHARING

Role sharing in the family literature can mean anything from the proportion of tasks shared equally by husband and wife (Blood and Wolfe, 1960:51) to the extent to which husband and wife share the responsibility for performing the role of homemaker (Lein et al., 1974:39; Lein 1979; Grønseth, 1975:9; Haas, 1982). Because most studies of division of labor in the family have focused on who does what rather than on who decides what should be done (exceptions are Hoffman, 1958; Herbst, 1952; Nye et al., 1977), it has been difficult to make an empirical distinction between actual task performance and responsibility for the task. However, as one of the families in the Cambridge Work and Family Life Project explained,

> There are enormous differences among families in which a husband occasionally helps his wife with the dishes but both believe it is her job, families where both take the responsibility for the dishes and it is their job together or at different times, and those where the role of "home-maker" is shared and both take responsibility for many home-related tasks. (Lein et al., 1974:39)

In this study, role sharing refers to the sharing of responsibility for a major household area such as cooking, shopping, and dishwashing; housecleaning; parenting and child care; providing and financial management; and maintenance of the marital relationship. Furthermore, family roles are defined as *mutual expectations negotiated by the actors that define each actor's responsibility to other family members in a given context.* When a husband and wife agree that a responsibility such as housekeeping or parenting is not to be compartmentalized into husband's and wife's responsibilities but shared between the two of them, this is termed role sharing, whether or not the responsibilities or tasks are shared equally. If roles were totally shared in parenting, for example, each partner would be interchangeable for the other. Although few couples had developed equal role sharing in any area, those who had begun to share several major responsibilities within an area were judged to be "role sharing." Except for providing, role sharing generally meant that the husband had begun to share responsibilities that were previously his wife's. This was the case because of the very small proportion of household work and child care normally done by husbands. Thus, since mothers are generally the primary care givers for their children whereas fathers play the role of distant "overseer" and occasional playmate, fathers who took over areas of day-to-day care and planning of children's activities were judged to be sharing the parental role.[2]

ROLE BARGAINING

Goals

Role bargaining is the process that results in such a redivision of family roles.[3] Although it might commonly be expected that as wives become coproviders, husbands will become coparents and cohousekeepers, this exchange took place in only some of the 16 families. Some husbands were more eager than others to give up part of the responsibility to provide, and some wives were more eager than others to take it on. Thus, as we shall see, the resulting role redefinitions depend, to some extent, upon how invested each spouse is in his/her present role. I will refer to this investment as *role attachment*. In his essay on "role distance," Goffman (1961:89) describes role attachment in the following terms:

> The self-image available for anyone entering a particular position is one of which he may become affectively and cognitively enamored, desiring and expecting to see himself in terms of the enactment of the role and the self-identification emerging from this enactment. I will speak here of the individual becoming attached to his position and its role . . .

Given a strong role attachment, a person may nonetheless be willing to give up all or part of the valued role provided that the cost of retaining the role is greater than the desire to keep it. In that case, *commitment* to the role (Goffman, 1961:88) will decline in spite of one's subjective *attachment* to it. For example, a machinist who grew up in a home in which his mother always had a hot meal on the table when his father returned from work may dream of similar hot meals waiting on the table for him. He may even tell the interviewer that this is indeed the way it *should* be. However, if he cannot support his family without working overtime and if working overtime makes him too tired to enjoy the family he is providing for, his need for relief from the responsibility to provide for his family may outweigh his desire to be waited upon by his wife. The higher the cost of retaining the sole-provider role, the more willing he will be to relinquish part of that role (role relinquishment) and its privileges in exchange for an expansion of his household roles. Role attachment and commitment are, therefore, important determinants of each spouse's *goals* in the role bargaining process.

Although each spouse's goals are determined by his or her needs and wants, the bargaining process itself is shaped by the extent to which these goals are *complementary* or *competing*. A wife such as Bess Holling who enjoys being provided for will have little need to bargain with a man such as Martin Holling who enjoys being the sole provider and considers his wife's working to be a temporary measure "to help out for a while." Since neither of them wants a permanent redefinition of provider roles, what bargaining that does take place will concern how long the wife will be expected to work rather than what she should get in exchange for working. On the other hand, a wife who is seeking financial autonomy and insulation from household demands will need to bargain with a husband who prefers to be sole provider and who also wants to avoid additional household responsibility. Likewise, a husband who does not want to remain sole provider must bargain with a wife who prefers being provided for. James Mooney did not have to bargain because Jill *wanted* to share the provider role. Given competing goals, however, the outcome of the role bargaining process will depend upon the relative amounts of bargaining power possessed by each spouse.

Bargaining Power

In this book, bargaining power is defined as *the ability to get another person to cooperate in or to allow the achievement of one's goals.*[4] Bargaining power is determined both by the external resources at one's command and by the internal resources available to one in the form of self-esteem and personal autonomy (cf. Scanzoni and Szinovacz, 1980:28–31). It is also affected by the mutually recognized right or authority to exercise power in a given area. As Bahr (1982) has found, the authority over a decision area often comes with the responsibility for tasks in that area. Thus, the authority to decide whether or not to buy a car may come with the responsibility to provide, the responsibility for car maintenance, and/or the responsibility for keeping the family budget. Given the relationship between division of marital roles and the distribution of authority, role bargaining may result not only in agreements about *who will do* what and who *ought to do* what but also in new understandings about *who has the right to decide* about what. When a couple bargains about the redefinition of family roles, therefore, they are bargaining about the ground rules governing their relationship to each other and the household. To the extent that these ground rules form what LaRossa (1977:128) describes as the procedural rules that are the most important element in the marital relationship, redefinitions of them may have profound effects on that relationship. In fact, as the follow-up interviews for this research revealed, efforts to change such procedural rules pushed some relationships beyond their limits to dissolution and revolutionized others, resulting in greater equality between the spouses.

CONFLICT AND EQUITY

Although a more equal balance of power is the outcome of some of the bargaining described in this book, I conceive of the role bargaining process as a circular one in which some redistribution of resources must precede the bargaining process both in order for bargaining to occur in the first place and in order for a more equitable division of labor to result from it. Leaving aside, for the moment, the definition of "equality" in the marital relationship, let us consider how exchanges between unequals differ from exchanges between equals.

In a marriage in which one spouse already possesses a much larger share of the power and resources than the other (often referred to as either *partriarchal* or *matriarchal*), there may be a lot of domination but little or no conflict. To the extent that the subordinate spouse accepts his or her subordination, conflict is unlikely to result (Walster and Walster, 1975:38). Futhermore, even if the subordinate resents the authority of the dominant spouse, conflict is still unlikely to surface, because, as Jean Baker Miller (1976:13) has noted, within such a relationship not only are the means to engage openly in conflict absent but the very existence of the conflict is denied. However, in order to change his or her status in the relationship, the subordinate must induce the dominant to engage in what Miller terms *productive conflict*. For some wives, the money earned after returning to work and the self-esteem derived from accomplishment make productive conflict possible.

If Miller is right, we should expect the most rancorous conflict in marriages in which subordinates are just beginning to question their subordinate status and the least rancorous conflict in marriages in which couples have attained a more equal balance of power. As Blood has argued, "only in egalitarian marriages may concessions from one partner be expected to trigger similar concessions from the other" (Blood, 1972:425). Given a very lopsided power balance, there is no need for the powerful spouse to enter into bargaining, let alone make concessions (cf. Sussman, 1975:567).

EQUITY AND THE EGALITARIAN MARRIAGE

What, then, is an egalitarian marriage? In the land of equal opportunity "with equality and justice for all," a clear definition of marital equality is hard to find. Definitions vary, with their emphases upon (1) division of labor, (2) balance of power, or (3) a more general balance of contributions and rewards in the marriage. In addition, even those based on division of labor or power vary according to how much role specialization within a task or decision-making area is allowed before a marriage no longer qualified as egalitarian. Linda Haas (1982:749), for example, specifies that task specialization within roles is compatible with role sharing as long as the specific tasks are not assigned to the spouse on the basis of gender. Given these differences in criteria, the egalitarian marriage discussed in the family literature may be one in which the husband and wife share household, income-producing, and decision-making roles in roughly equal proportions (Haas, 1982) or one in which the wife does all the housework and does not work outside the home but, due to the nature of urban life, has sufficient personal autonomy to guarantee her equal decision-making power (Burgess and Locke, 1953:110).

Built into most definitions of marital equality are one or more biases that can be classified as feminist, patriarchial, and/or middle class. Although I cannot claim to have avoided all of these biases in the writing of this book, I would like to identify what I consider to be the most prevalent ones and then let the reader beware.

Feminist Biases

Feminist biases stem from the observation that in a sexist society what women do is valued less than what men do. Although I have no quarrel with this, I am not sure that it then follows that because housework is valued less than marketwork in society as a whole, it is done by the least powerful spouse and, conversely, whichever spouse is responsible for the housework is least powerful (Ericksen et al., 1979:304). I also doubt that it can be assumed that because marketwork earns one more prestige than does housework, women who work outside the home have "won the right" to work and have, therefore, already exercised more marital power than do those who stay at home (Scanzoni; 1978:83). Assuming a link between power and division of labor makes it unnecessary to empirically examine the relationship between the two.

The case studies in this book suggest that a woman's reasons for working and her husband's attachment to his provider role affect the way in which her marketwork is valued in the marriage. Furthermore, the woman's own attachment to provider and household roles determines how she chooses to use whatever power she gains from her marketwork. Thus, a woman who is working because she has to and who would prefer to stay home may use a combination of putdowns and threats in order to shame her husband into finding a way to earn more money so that she can afford to stay home. In this case, reassuming the role of full-time housewife will be the result of a successful use of the wife's role bargaining power. Feminist conceptions of marital equality leave little room for even thinking of such a possibility.

Patriarchal Biases

Although feminist sociologists assume a necessary link between power and housework, Chicago sociologists of the 1930s erred in the other direction by explaining housework away altogether. Burgess, Locke, and Mowrer assumed that the urban woman would have little housework to do in her small city apartment and that what little there was left could be done by maids (Mowrer, 1932:98; Burgess and Locke, 1953:10). The liberated woman in Burgess and Locke's (1953:110) prototypical egalitarian family is able to attend to all her household duties and have enough time left over so that she can have several club affiliations and attend meetings and lecture programs. It is these outside activities that allow her to develop enough personal autonomy to share decision-making power equally with her husband.

Although this definition may be more correctly called *urbanist* than patriarchal, it does allow husband-centered upper-middle-class marriages to be classified as egalitarian. A woman whose outside activities were built around her husband's work would probably still be seen as autonomous according to Burgess and Locke's criteria.

A more recent example of a bias that is both patriarchal and middle class is Blood and Wolfe's operational definition of the companionate marriage. Although Blood and Wolfe (1960:12–21) base their definition of egalitarianism on their measure of power and decision making, the extent of marital companionship is determined by (1) the number of organizations to which spouses jointly belong, (2) the frequency with which the husband tells the wife about events at work, (3) the frequency of getting together with the husband's colleagues, and (4) the proportion of the husband's friends the wife knows quite well (Blood and Wolfe, 1960:151–157). Given that definition, it is not surprising that Blood and Wolfe find the companionate marriage to be a middle-class phenomenon. Strangely enough, however, the wife's satisfaction with companionship is not strongly related either to social class or to the intensity of companionship by each of the four measures. Perhaps this is because a husband who never listened to his wife talk about her work and knew none of her friends could be classified on the high end of Blood and Wolfe's companionship scale and still have a wife who was unsatisfied with his companionship.

Middle-Class Biases

All the definitions discussed so far also contain a middle-class bias. It is, after all, only middle- and upper-middle-class women who can afford not to work and who, therefore, can be spoken of as having either the *option* or the *right* to work. Many lower-middle-class and poor women have the *duty* to work outside the home (cf. Scanzoni 1978:38–40). Burgess and Locke's egalitarian woman could afford to have a maid and a laundress as well as not to be employed in income-producing activity and Blood and Wolfe's (1960:168) companionate marriages involved people who were active in organizations and husbands who socialized with their co-workers, patterns that the authors themselves acknowledge are more common for upper-income groups.

I suspect that the primary source of the middle-class bias is the reasoning that education leads to enlightenment, which in turn produces a sense of fairness that will somehow be translated into marital equality. As the reader will see in Chapter 6, the empirical support for this chain of reasoning is, at best, mixed. Nonetheless, many researchers continue to operate as if each link were proven fact. For example, since most family researchers use individuals rather than couples as the unit of analysis, they are left guessing about which kinds of people marry which other kinds. Noting that wives who earn the most money are also most likely to think that their incomes have an impact on the family's life-style, Scanzoni (1978:62) comments

> And it is gender-modern wives who both earn more and also have more substantially increased their incomes over the past several years. Such women do not work primarily for money to meet family expenses. Instead, they have a history of long term work involvement with career overtones, including defining work as their right. What complicates their impact on family lifestyle is that they tend to be married to *egalitarian* men who also earn more money.

Although it may indeed be true that gender-modern women seek and find those few husbands who are both egalitarian and earn high incomes, most time-budget studies show a negative relationship between husbands' income and household work (Pleck, 1983). Furthermore, Mason et al. (1976) find that although for both men and women education is positively related to such egalitarian values as "women should get as equal pay for equal work," income does not predict such values for husbands. In fact, men with the highest incomes were significantly less likely to subscribe to the idea that men should help with the housework than were men with the lowest incomes. Some of this apparent discrepancy may be explained by the fact that it is quite possible to agree with values farther from home such as equal pay for equal work while objecting to those closer to home such as "men should share housework with women".

Among the husbands discussed in this book are several examples of upper-middle-class men who, like sociologist S. M. Miller, are more egalitarian in thought than in deed:

> I guess what dismays me and makes me see my marriage and family as unfortunately typically upper middle class, collegial, pseudo-egalitarian American — especially in light of my own continuing commitment to an egalitarian, participatory ethos — is that I assume no responsibility for

major household tasks and family activities. (S.M. Miller in Pleck and Sawyer, 1974:48)

Given what I consider to be class-biased and value-laden connotations of the words *modern* and *traditional* when applied to gender roles, I have tried as much as possible to avoid using such words in this book. Because these words have come to mean both too much and too little, I prefer instead to use words with more direct referents such as *family oriented* or *work oriented*, and *husband centered* or *couple centered*.

A WORKING DEFINITION OF MARITAL EQUALITY

Deference in American society has this as its root; a calculation that someone else's time is more valuable than your own, which seems to give that person the right to command your time in accordance with his needs. (J. Cobb in Sennet and Cobb, 1973:264–265)

My own biases are more feminist than anything else. Providing the income gives one the title of "head of household," whereas raising children does not. If the things men do outside the house for money are valued more highly than the things women do inside the house for love, then, in effect, women's time is worth less than men's time. It is this relationship which prompts Gillespie to write:

It is not because of individual resources or personal competence, then, that husbands obtain power in marriage, but because of the discrimination against women in the larger society. Men gain resources as a class, not as individuals. (in Freeman, ed., 1975: p. 85)

Although I agree with Gillespie that discrimination against women by men as a class has direct bearing on the balance of power within marriages, I am reluctant to define marital equality solely in terms of division of labor. Does a man who has negotiated with his wife the right to be a househusband, lose bargaining power in comparison to a man who would like to have such a right but whose wife will not stand for it? Perhaps. However, the man who can negotiate such a role reversal probably has more bargaining power than the man who cannot at *the time at which he makes such a bargain.* Similarly, a woman who uses her bargaining power to induce her husband to agree to her decision to stop working has more bargaining power than a similar wife who would also prefer to stay home but cannot get her husband to agree that he should be the sole provider. However, after the bargain is struck, I would argue that the non-providing spouse will lose some of the provider role rights which go with provider role responsibilities. Will the househusband lose more rights or fewer rights than the housewife? If the force of patriarchal tradition adds to the bargaining power of those who want to operate within its confines, then we would expect the answer to be "yes." This book does not answer that question, but does offer some of the tools for others to use in seeking such an answer.

Meanwhile, I have chosen a working definition of marital equality which is based upon bargaining power rather than upon the division of labor:

An egalitarian marriage is one in which each spouse has roughly the same capacity to get the other to cooperate in order to allow the attainment of his/her goals.

SUMMARY

In this chapter, I have defined the central components of the role bargaining model. Role bargaining is described as a series of negotiations that may result in a redivision of role responsibilities. Although all family process may be thought of as continuous negotiation (Sprey, 1969), the role bargaining described in this book occurs in the context of the wife's decision to return to work. It is through role bargaining that husbands and wives come to new understandings about role sharing. Increased role sharing, however, is only one possible outcome of role bargaining. Depending upon the nature and strength of each spouse's role attachments and the relative bargaining power of each partner, role bargaining may result in a wife leaving the labor force, a husband taking on more household duties in exchange for his wife's newly acquired coprovider role, a wife retaining all her former household roles while adding an outside job, or a stalemate in which neither spouse is able to get the other to cooperate in the achievement of his/her goals. After a description in Chapter 2 of how this study was done, the remainder of this book elaborates upon the framework just outlined.

NOTES

1. Because several excellent reviews of the literature on division of labor in the family have appeared recently, no attempt is made to review it here. The most thorough review is Pleck's article on men's family work (Pleck, 1983). See also Berk and Berk (1979) and Miller and Garrison (1982).

2. This definition emphasizes the *existence* of shared responsibility rather than the *equal* sharing of it or the equal sharing of household tasks. See Haas (1982) for a definition of role sharing based on equal task performance. Even in Haas' study of egalitarian couples, however, the handyman role was not shared.

3. Role bargaining could be described as "conglomerate decision making" in that role bargaining outcomes are usually the result of several separate decisions. For a recent treatment of family decision making, the reader is referred to Scanzoni and Szinovacz (1980).

4. Maximiliane Szinovacz points out that power may be used to stop someone from blocking the achievement of one's goals and that if coercion is the strategy used, cooperation is not likely to be the result. (Also see Sprey; 1969; 1971; 1975). I am assuming that negotiation takes place only when each partner *is willing* to enter into negotiation. This means that coercive strategies are less likely to be used in bargaining contexts than in other kinds of conflicts. However, going on strike (discussed in Chapters 4 and 5) may be seen as a unilateral action (a coercive strategy) which A may use to induce B to bargain. In this sense bargaining power is conceived of as one type of power which overlaps with but does not include all kinds of decision-making power.

5. Although not much survey research has been done on the wife's duty to provide, there is some evidence that black wives and wives whose husbands earn least are most likely to reject the idea that husbands have all or most of the duty to provide (cf. Haas, 1982; Huber and Spitze, 1981; Scanzoni, 1978).

2
THE FAMILIES
AND THE INTERVIEWS

It has been said of Marx's *Capital* that he did not begin with a definition of "capital" because the entire book was such a definition (Braverman, 1974:25). Because the development of theory from data is the goal of this book most of Chapters 3 and 4 are, in effect, a discussion of methods as well as of substance. This chapter then deals primarily with issues not fully addressed in the analysis itself. Here I will be discussing (1) how the families were selected and how they compare with other dual-worker families, (2) how the interviews were conducted, and (3) limitations on generalizing from case studies. Although I have also included a brief note about analyzing field notes, much more detailed information on the development of grounded codes may be found in the appendices.

SELECTING FAMILIES

Because the main purpose of this research was the development of new theory rather than the testing of existing ones, I did not start with a detailed study design. I chose instead the methods outlined in Glaser and Strauss's (1967:45) description of theoretical sampling:

> Theoretical sampling is the process of data collection for generating theory whereby the analyst jointly collects, codes and analyses his data and decides what data to collect next and where to find them, in order to develop his theory as it emerges.

I began, therefore, with a problem statement and criteria for selecting respondents and, in the course of the study, refined both the problem statement and the sampling frame.

Having decided to do an intensive study of a limited number of dual-worker couples, I then chose to focus on a population likely to be most representative of all dual-worker couples. Since in 1970 only 10% of working couples included two professionals (U.S. Bureau of Census, 1976:38), the couples selected for this study include primarily nonprofessional women, some of whom are married to professional men. Although it would have been ideal to find women who were about to return to work or who had all returned to work within six months of the interview, this was not possible. However, since I wanted to document the changes in household roles that took place when a woman returned to work after having been a full-time housewife for several years, I did want to interview women who had reentered the labor force.

Because of the intensive nature of the study and the limited number of couples to be included, I decided to hold constant or limit the range of several variables previously found to be related to the division of labor in the home. These were

1. Wife's education
2. Husband's employment status
3. Race
4. Age of children at the time of wife's return
5. Hours of wife's work

Thus, couples in the study have wives who, with two exceptions, do not have college degrees, have husbands who are employed full-time, are white, had at least one child 14 years old or younger at the time of the wife's return, and who work full-time during the day.

Because the original focus of the study had been "changes in the wife's self-concept and friendship network upon her return to work," husbands had not been included in the first round of interviews. However, analysis of the first wife interviews made it clear that changes in the division of family roles were central to changes in the wife's self-concept. Role bargaining, therefore, became the central focus of the study, and husbands were interviewed separately at the time of the second wife interviews. Sampling stopped at 16 couples. Furthermore, because women who could afford to stay out of work for several years were likely to be married to men earning decent incomes, the sample selected included eight professional or managerial husbands with most of the remainder being skilled workers. In contrast to the families Lillian Rubin interviewed for *Worlds of Pain*, the blue collar families in this study were not "just up from poverty" or making do with hand-me-downs (1976:17). With two exceptions, the husbands were earning incomes above the median for a family of four *even before* their wives returned to work. I therefore refer to them as "lower-middle-class".

In addition, although all women had children school aged or younger at the time of their return, half had children under 12, most of whom still required continuous adult supervision, and half had children 12 and over, who were more likely to be on their own for substantial parts of the day. These variables do not control in the general population, because the lower the husband's income, the sooner the wife returns to work after childbirth (Sweet, 1974:5). However, in this sample they are statistically independent with four couples in each category as shown in Table 2.1. The only qualification to be added is that all women who reentered the labor force while they still had preschool children were married to nonprofessionals, so that I could not analyze the effects of having preschool children and husband's occupation separately. Demographic characteristics of each couple are listed in Table 2.2.

TABLE 2.1: Husband's Occupation and Life Cycle Status in the 16 Couples

Husband's Occupation	Life Cycle Status		
	All Children under 12	One or More Children Over 12	Total
Professional, managerial, or sales	4	4	8
Craft, operative, or service	4	4	8
Total	8	8	16

One of the most difficult parts of the study proved to be finding couples who fit the requirements described in the sampling frame. Thus, a variety of strategies were employed. Two women were part of a series of pilot interviews which I did in preparation for the study and were later chosen to be reinterviewed along with their husbands. Seven were chosen from 200 respondents to a screening questionnaire distributed to 424 women employees at a large data processing firm, which I shall call Datan. Four reponded to an advertisement in a hospital workers' bulletin or were referred by others who responded to it, and three answered a screening questionnaire sent home with school children in the first through third grades of a public school system.

Table 2.2: Demographic Characteristics of Respondents

Pseudonyms	Husband's occupation	Wife's occupation	Husband's education	Wife's education	Wife's age at return	Time elapsed between return and first interview	# of children	Youngest child at return	Religion	Time out	Husband works late shift	Additional information on wife's work history
Professional/Managerial Husbands: (Older Families)												
Maria and Joe Correlli	engineer; self-employed	secretary	BSE	12	46	2	3	12	Cath	17	No	
Jane and John Devore	doctor	staff benefits clerk	MD	GED	43	3	6	11	Cath	14	No	Worked putting husband through school when children were small.
Bess and Martin Holling	engineer	secretary	BSE	BA	48	5	3	14	Meth	20	No	Part-time at first.
Paula and Harold Reade	engineer	secretary	BSE	12+	45	.25	2	11	Luth	17	No	
Professional/Managerial Husbands: (Younger Families)												
Joan and Ted Collins	engineer	title editor	BSE	13+	29	2	3	6	Cath	7	No	Was in school before returning.
Anne and Bob Dooley	professor	finance analyst	PhD	MBA	32	0.5	2	7	Cath	10	No	Was in school and/or working for husband during parts of time out.
Gisela and Peter Marx	vaccum cleaner dealer	vacuum cleaner dealer	12	12	27	0.5	2	3	Cath	3	No	Worked part-time previously.
Linda and David Meyers	hospital administrator	secretary/ customer service	BA+	15	30	4	3	6	----	10	No	Returned to school prior to work.

Table 2.2: Demographic Characteristics of Respondents (continued)

Pseudonyms	Husband's occupation	Wife's occupation	Husband's education	Wife's education	Wife's age at return	Time elapsed between return and first interview	# of children	Youngest child at return	Religion	Time out	Husband works late shift	Additional information on wife's work history
Blue Collar Husbands: (Older Families)												
Mary and Bill Anderson	factory worker, electrician	data analyst	12+	11	35	5	6	6	Prot	10	Yes	Was out two five-year periods with a five-year gap in between.
Roberta and Tom Hutchins	factory foreman, cannery super-visor	receiving clerk (library)	12	12	36	9	4	.5	Cong	19	Yes	
Billie and Forrest King	firefighter and factory worker	clerk	GED	GED	34	3	4	3	Bapt	13	Yes	
Nancy and Don Williams	factory foreman	switchboard operator	11	11	36	4	5	10	Bapt	16	Yes	Worked part-time driving school bus before this year.
Blue Collar Husbands: (Younger Families)												
Cynthia and Mike Davis	factory stores clerk	hospital housekeeper	14	12	24	6	2	1	Prot	2	Yes	
Theo and Richard James	factory worker	secretary	12+	12+	25	2	2	3	Prot	6	No	
Jill and James Mooney	factory machinist tool clerk	clerk	12+	12	23	4	2	2	Cath	4	Yes	
Cathy and Mike Schultz	machinist "set up man"	word processor	12	12+	26	4	2	3	Prot	6	Yes	

THE INTERVIEWS

Interviews were arranged by telephone and usually held at the family's home. In the course of the study, all homes were visited at least once, most wives interviewed twice and husbands once, and in most cases spouses were interviewed separately. A year lapse between the first interviews with the wife in 1975 and subsequent interviews with both spouses allowed time for both data analysis and refinement of hypotheses. In addition, the couples' responses to new developments in their lives such as layoffs, job changes, promotions, or a child's entering school deepened my understanding of their coping strategies. Interviews were tape-recorded, and field notes taken on physical surroundings and interactions. The 1976 case record for each couple includes (1) the first interview with the wife, (2) analysis notes for this interview and a list of specific questions to be asked in the second interview, (3) second interview with the wife, (4) interview with the husband around the time of the second wife interview, and (5) field notes taken on all telephone calls, interview settings, and any chance meetings with respondents outside of formal interviews. For each couple there is an average of six hours of taped interviews and 60 or more typed pages of field notes and transcriptions.

Added to this are each spouse's responses to a 1982 follow-up questionnaire and notes taken on telephone interviews done in late 1982 and early 1983. Some participants volunteered to read the manuscript, and their comments have been incorporated in my revisions. The follow-up study itself is the basis for Chapter 6.

Interviews were unstructured but followed a life-history format focusing on the events leading up to the wife's return to work, her and other family members' feelings about her working, marital division of labor before and after her return to work, and changes in her self-image attributable to her new status. In order to get the respondent's own construction of the event, questions were open-ended, such as, "Tell me what it was like when you (your wife) first went back." To assure comparability of the interviews, I used a checklist of topics that I consulted before ending the interview (see Appendix A). In the second interview, care was taken to fill any gaps in case records.

ANALYZING FIELD NOTES

Because the analysis of qualitative data is more cumbersome than the analysis of quantitative data, sociologists have established fewer conventions for making sense out of case study material than they have for the statistical analysis of survey responses. Although good field researchers adopt rigorous methods of extracting meaning from their notes, not all of them have taken the time to tell us just how they did it. Those who have taken the time (e.g., Glaser and Strauss, 1965; Komarovsky, 1940) have taught the rest of us a great deal about building theory from seemingly insurmountable piles of information.

For those of you who want to know just how my research assistants and I got from the interviews to the typologies developed in this book, I have included several methodological appendices. Using Appendices B, C, and F thru I, the reader can follow the development of what Glaser and Strauss refer to as "grounded categories" (1965:36–43) from the transcriptions of the interviews to the construction of categories. Then, using Appendix D, the reader may examine our method for dealing with inconsistencies in coding and assessing the reliability of the categories we constructed. To those who choose not to make their way through the appendices, let me say that typologies such as coprovider, secondary provider, and ambivalent coprovider should be considered hypotheses about the order of social reality as well as heuristic devices for understanding it. If it appears that the data must be forced to fit the categories constructed, then the categories are not well made and need to be revised. For me, one of the best tests of the theory presented here has been the reaction of several of the study participants to an earlier version of this manuscript. Some found themselves nodding in response to my interpretations as they read, whereas others frowned and wondered whether or not I was really writing about them. For the latter, I have taken a fresh look at the data and included their comments in this revision.

GENERALIZING FROM CASE STUDIES

Before introducing the reader to the 16 families, I would like to say a few things about how the families to be described in this study compared with other dual-worker families in 1973–1977. How typical are they and how may we apply what we learn about them to dual-worker couples in general? Given the criteria established for selecting respondents, it should be clear from the start that findings cannot be generalized without qualification to other populations. For example, I studied only families who added a second earner after having lived as a one-job family for two or more years. My findings, therefore, do not apply to spouses who have both worked full-time continuously since they were married. I am also talking about white families and about families in which the husband and wife both work full-time, year-round. My findings may or may not be applicable to black families and have qualified application to families in which either the husband or the wife work part-time or part of the year. Furthermore, the study families live within commuting distance of a heavy industrial center. This means that I interviewed more late-shift workers than would be expected in a cross section of blue-collar workers (Appendix E, Table A-1).

It is also important to recognize at the outset that, with the exception of two couples (see Table 2.2), the couples in this study are either two-job or one-job/one-career couples. They are, therefore, much more representative of dual-worker couples in general than are couples involving two professional or managerial workers. The families in this study are also stable dual-worker families in that the wives had all been working for at least a year and a half by the time of the second interview. They are, therefore, more similar to families that have learned to cope with two full-time jobs than to those that were not able to.

Given all these qualifications, it is incumbent upon the reader to take into account the characteristics of each family discussed when considering how far to generalize findings. Glaser and Strauss (1965:191–192) refer to this as "the discounting process." For example, readers may know from a variety of sources that the more educated a woman worker is, the more household help she expects from her husband. Knowing this, they will realize that Bess Holling, a college-educated wife of an engineer, is not representative of college-educated women in general because she expects little help from her husband. Readers may, however, wonder if Bess might not be typical of college-educated wives of engineers. Indeed she may be, and this is an example of one testable hypothesis that can be derived from this study, i.e., college-educated wives of professionals will expect less help from their husbands than will college-educated wives of nonprofessionals. Several such hypotheses are listed at the end of Chapter 6.

I have just described the ways in which the 16 families compare with dual-worker families in general. In the next chapter, I will begin to lay the groundwork for a general theory of role bargaining by describing some of the ways in which the families differed from each other at the time the wives returned to work.

3
RETURNING TO WORK

Before the wives returned to work, all 16 husbands worked outside the home to provide the income, whereas the wives worked inside the home doing full-time child care and family work. Although husbands were described as having helped when asked, when laid off from their own work, or when the children were very young, their own family work was usually limited to "men's work" such as car maintenance, repairs, and yard work. Most wives did not expect them to do more than this. Thus, even though some husbands helped with child care and household work more than others, none of the couples were sharing the daily responsibility for the overall running of the household before the wives returned to work.

In addition to differences in how much help husbands gave their nonworking wives, the 16 families differed according to (1) the relative emphases placed on husband-family, parent-child, or husband-wife bonds (family bond type), (2) the wives' reasons for returning to work, (3) husbands' attitudes toward their wives' working, (4) the husbands' orientations to their own work, and (5) the husbands' work/family priorities. Furthermore, as the reader knows already from Chapter 2, the families varied in life cycle status and, therefore, in how much child care help was needed, as well as in income and, therefore, in how much outside help they could afford. As we shall see in Chapters 4 and 5, these differences helped to determine each couple's goals or bargaining positions as well as to shape their bargaining strategies. In this chapter, 1 will begin to elaborate upon the framework developed in Chapter 1 by describing how husband-centered, child-centered, and couple-centered families differ from each other; how *self*-motivated wives differ from *family*-motivated ones; why some husbands responded more positively than did others to their wives' decisions to return to work; and how husbands' orientations to their own work and the relative importance of their work and family obligations (role attachments) affected their feelings about having working wives. At the end of the chapter, I will give the reader a "sneak preview" of what is to come by telling the stories of two couples who are at opposite ends of the continuum on nearly all of the dimensions discussed.

FAMILY BOND TYPE

Probably the best measure of family bond type would be a diagram showing who is most important for whom in the family. Although I did not construct such a measure and did not even interview the children, I have been able to make educated guesses about the relative priority of husband-family, parent-child, and husband-wife bonds in each family before and after the wife returned to work. Using information about how families spend their time together and the respondents' own constructions of role hierarchies, I found three distinct combinations of family bonds and some mixed types. Husband-centered families organized themselves around the husband/father's schedule and needs. Child-centered families focused on the mother-child and sometimes the father-child bond while paying less attention to the husband-wife relationship, whereas couple-centered families did the reverse, giving the couple relationship a place of its own with each spouse paying attention to the other's needs. Although there may be families in which the wife's needs come first, I did not find any. Only after they returned to work did the wives in this study start to compete with their husbands and children for "first place." And even then, as we shall see, the competition was very much disguised, because being a good wife and mother, after all, means serving others *before* and not *after* oneself.

Husband-Centered Families

In husband-centered families the wives have almost total responsibility for the children with husbands assuming the role of provider and distant educator. The wife typically provides support for her husband's work either by actually participating in it on a nonpaid basis or by being a hostess for his co-workers. Because of the central part played by the husband's career, husband-centered families are from the middle or upper middle class.

Anne and Bob Dooley (MBA and PhD in business administration, respectively) had a relatively husband-centered marriage before Anne went back to work. Anne worked with Bob in his accounting practice and then ran the household while he studied for his PhD. After he got a job as an assistant professor, she became treasurer of the Faculty Wives Club. Having moved from their hometown, Anne's social contacts were limited to

Bob's co-workers and their spouses. Although Anne had an MBA, her life with Bob had centered around his career and his work until Anne took a full-time job herself.

Jane Devore had also worked closely with her husband John, a physician. Lacking Anne Dooley's formal education, she had taught herself how to read John's medical journals and keep the books for his private practice. As we shall see later in this chapter, John's participation in the family was limited to bringing home the paycheck and exposing his children to the proper cultural influences. He described taking them to museums and on trips to Europe. Jane, however, spoke of having raised the children by herself.

Since husband-centered families are distinguished from husband/child-centered families primarily by the amount of attention the wife gives to the children in comparison to that given to the husband (see Figure 3.1), it is difficult to tell them apart without having interviewed the children. In the rest of the analysis, therefore, I group the two together.

Child-Centered Families

Families that are primarily child centered are held together by the parent-child bond with the wife as the primary parent and the husband as provider and playmate for the children. Although the family sometimes does things as a family, the husband and wife rarely spend time together without the children. Couples in child-centered marriages often do not know what to do with each other when the children are not around. For example, when Ted and Joan Collins decided to spend some of their second income on a vacation for themselves in San Francisco, they missed the children so much that they came home early, and while they were away, the children were the focus of their conversation.

The Schultzes are also a child-centered family, but before Cathy went back to work, Mike was less involved with his children than Ted Collins had been with his. When he came home from work, Mike would sit in front of the television, and on weekends he would get involved in projects around the house. He and Cathy didn't talk much and spent time instead with same-sexed friends outside the house. Meanwhile, Cathy would fantasize about taking the children and leaving or wonder whether if it were not for the children she would stay married. Before Cathy Schultz went to work, her children were her life.

In child-centered families, the husband-father is first a provider, second a father, and last a husband. Because the husband and wife do little to maintain their relationship with each other, the children are the major link between them. When the husband does not have much relationship with the children either, he becomes an outsider who brings home the

Figure 3.1 Family Bond Types

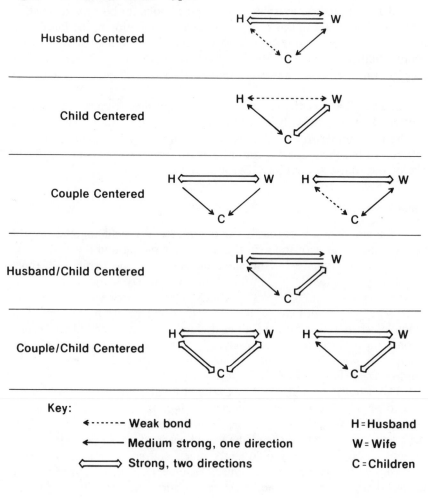

Husband Centered

Child Centered

Couple Centered

Husband/Child Centered

Couple/Child Centered

Key:

◀······ Weak bond

◀——— Medium strong, one direction

⟺ Strong, two directions

H = Husband

W = Wife

C = Children

paycheck but has little connection with his family otherwise. Bill Anderson, for example, worked two factory jobs and spent almost all his time at home either sleeping or rebuilding antique gas engines in the barn. Most of his contact with his children occurred as they helped him work on the engines. He cooked dinner on Saturday nights but became famous for falling asleep on the couch as soon as people finished eating. Like Bill Anderson, many husbands in child-centered families keep themselves busy with a second job, a time-consuming hobby, or both. The choice point in these marriages comes when there is no longer a family to provide for and only each other to talk to.

Couple-Centered Families

In couple-centered and couple/child-centered families, the couple bond is important for both husband and wife. Ideally each spouse tries to meet the other's needs. In contrast to husband-centered relationships, couple-centered ones are more symmetrical, and recreational activities are likely to involve friends the couple met together or neighbors rather than the husband's workmates. The husband and wife typically describe each other as best friends and say that there is nothing they cannot talk about with each other. The wives describe their husbands as supportive and devoted to them, and the husbands value their wives' thinking and support. Some couples clearly gave precedence to the couple bond over the parent-child relationship whereas others tried to balance the two. However, both kinds of couples stressed the importance of having their own time together away from the children.

One couple-centered pair, Peter and Gisela Marx, told me that they were not "in love" when they married but decided that they could make a good marriage. Love grew along with companionship, and finally it was the need to have more time together that made them decide to open a vacuum cleaner dealership together. The children were not the center of attention that they are in child-centered families but instead were encouraged to participate in adult activities along with their parents both at home and at the store.

In Figure 3.2, I have placed the families into five categories. In the rest of the analysis, I group husband- and husband/child-centered families together into a single category and couple and couple/child-centered families into another, leaving child-centered families as the third. I also talk about degrees of husband-centeredness or couple-centeredness in families regardless of which category they fit into. For example, both Paula Reade and Bess Holling were in husband-centered relationships before they went back to work. However, Paula Reade held several important community positions unrelated to her husband's work and already had a busy schedule

FIGURE 3.2 Family Bond Types before the Wives Returned to Work

Category	Description
Husband	
1. Husband centered	Husband's needs come first. Wife is more a companion to the husband than he is to her. She is hostess to his workmates. Wife also has nearly all parenting responsibility.
2. Husband/child centered	Same as no. 1 with the exception that husband participates more in parenting on a daily basis.
Child	
3. Child centered	Spouses have little to do with each other except in household and parent roles. They have no joint recreation outside the house that does not involve the children.
Couple	
4. Couple/child centered	Husband-wife relationship is as important as parent-child bond. Couples spend time alone as well as *en famille*.
5. Couple centered	The couple relationship takes priority over the parent-child relationship.

of nonfamily activities before she took a full-time job as a secretary. Bess Holling, on the other hand, had just moved to a new community because of her husband's job. She belonged to an organization for wives of employees and to some women's book discussion groups, but none of these activities were hers alone. All were part of being "Mrs. Martin Holling, wife-of-an-engineer-in-a-managerial-position." Thus, even though Harold Reade's electrical engineering research gave him the right to peace and quiet when he came home at night with a locked briefcase full of work, the Reade family was less husband centered than were the Hollings because Paula Reade had competing activities of her own. The dimensions of husband-, child-, or couple-centeredness, therefore, are useful both for grouping families into the categories shown in Figure 3.2 and for making comparisons within those categories.

The priority given to husband-family, parent-child, and husband-wife bonds within each family helped to shape both the wife's decision to work and the effects of that decision on the family. It was all right for Bess Holling to go back to work to help with the children's college expenses, but it soon became clear that it would not be all right with her husband Martin if he had to make major adjustments in his own life because Bess was working. In a husband-centered marriage, it is the wife who is supposed to adjust to changes in the family's life-style. Don Williams, on the other hand, a factory foreman in a couple/child-centered marriage, did not mind helping more when his wife Nancy took a job as switchboard operator at Datan. However, he did not like it when he worked afternoons and she worked days so that they saw each other only on weekends. What was the point of being married if you never saw each other awake, he wondered? Differences among the 16 families in the structure of family bonds before the wives returned to work, therefore, mediated their adjustment to becoming two-job families.

WHY THEY WENT TO WORK

Another variable that affected family adjustment was the wife's motivation for returning to work. Some women went back to work to get away from the children or the housework or because they were bored or depressed and needed either to have a challenge or to break their isolation. Many also thought that they would feel better about themselves if they were contributing some money to the family income. Women who went back to work for these kinds of reasons were motivated primarily by their own needs for self-improvement and not by their family's need for money or their husband's need to work less. Because the women selected for this study had to have remained out of the labor force for two years or more, those who could not afford to stay home during the early child-rearing years were not interviewed. It is, therefore, not surprising that 11 of the 16 women gave "self" reasons for returning to work. However five women went back to work primarily because their families needed the money and although they also mentioned "self" reasons for returning, they stressed that they would not have gone to work had it not been necessary at the time.

In considering the reasons women gave for working, we must keep in mind that they are speaking retrospectively. Since their reasons for working changed over time, it is quite possible that their recollections of why they first went back to work may have changed also. In addition, added rapport in the second interview sometimes allowed information not given in the first to surface. Paula Reade, for example, had just begun her new secretarial job when first interviewed. At that time, she stressed self reasons for returning. However, a year later, after the job had become more routine and after she and I knew each other better, she added that her husband's job had been insecure for some time prior to her return to work and that this too had been "in the back of her mind."

Because women often mentioned both self and family reasons for working, it was not always immediately clear which reasons were most important. However, by separating reasons given for going back to work in the first place from reasons given for continuing to work, I was able to distinguish between those women who were primarily financially motivated from those who originally went to work to satisfy personal needs. In Table 3.1, I have listed the reasons each woman gave both for returning to work and for continuing, and whether she was self or family motivated.

Self-Motivated Women

Paula Reade had reached a point in her life when she needed something more to define herself. Her two boys were 11 and 14 years old and she had already done a great deal of volunteer work in political campaigns and for her church. She said

> I just felt like, you know, what are we all here for, you know, who am I? But, people suggested going back to work, and I said, "I don't know. Why would I want to do that?" So, uh, I felt like, volunteerwise, I had done everything else there was to do. So, this summer, I got to thinking, why not.

Why not something that would both be more focused and earn money? In the first interview she also mentioned being depressed due to her father's death and not liking housework, and in the second, as I said earlier, she let it slip that, yes, she had also been concerned about what would happen if her husband lost his job as an engineer. Like most women in this study she thought that she should be prepared to "pinch hit" should the time come. However, now she was working because of the satisfaction it brought her.

Like Paula Reade, Jill Mooney went back to work because she needed something else in her life. She had been at home full-time for four years and had boys aged 2 and 4 at the time she found a job as a clerk in a hospital. She said

> I had two children, one right after the other, something like fifteen months apart . . . I started breaking out. . . . Do you know what eczema is? Sometimes it's a nervous reaction. I just couldn't stand staying in the house with my kids. . . . The doctor told me, "You're going to have to get out and start doing things."

Table 3.1 : Why They Went to Work: Family vs. Self Reasons

	Self Reasons								Family Reasons			
	Dislike Housework	Bored	Need Challenge	Depressed	Isolated	Get Mind off Family	Money for Self	Total Self Reasons	Money for Family	Husband's Health	Husband's Job Insecure	Total Family Reasons
Family												
Davis								0	x	x		2
King		x	x			x		3	x			1
Holling				x				1	x			1
Williams			x		x			2	x	x		2
Self												
Anderson		x	x					2			x	1
Collins[a]	x	x	x	x	x			5	x			1
Correlli	x			x		x		3				0
Devore	x	x	x	x		x		5		x		1
Dooley	x	x	x		x			4				0
Hutchins		x		x				2	x			1
James	x	x		x		x	x	5				0
Marx		x	x	x	x			4	x			1
Meyers	x	x	x	x			x	5				0
Mooney		x	x	x		x	x	5				0
Reade	x		x	x				3			x	1
Schultz	x	x	x	x			x	5				0
Total mentions of each reason	8	10	11	11	5	5	4		7	3	2	

[a]Initially worked for family reasons but continued to work for self reasons.

Because Jill's children were not school aged when she went back to work, her decision had more implications for the family than did Paula Reade's. Perhaps this is why a doctor's prescription was necessary to relieve her of some of the responsibility for making the decision. If Jill Mooney needed "doctor's orders" to get out of the house, then it may not be coincidental that Theo James, who like Jill returned to work for self reasons before her youngest child entered school, also had a doctor's prescription to "get out of the house." Women who were working full-time just because they wanted to, after all, had to have some justification for any inconvenience they might cause their families. What could be better than an excuse from the doctor?

Family-Motivated Women

The five women who returned to work primarily to meet family needs went back either because of temporary increases in the family's expenses or because their husbands' health would no longer tolerate overtime work. All five of them would rather have been spending their time doing something other than working 40 hours a week at the time they went back to work. Joan Collins would have liked to continue at the university where she had been enrolled the previous year, but since she and her husband owed money to her husband's parents she postponed returning to school in order to earn money to repay the debt. In fact it was her mother-in-law who suggested that she work and *earn money* rather than *spend money* going to school! Joan, therefore, went back to work for family reasons. However, she was fortunate enough to find a job that was intrinsically rewarding and offered the opportunity for on-the-job training and advancement. After the debt was repaid, therefore, Joan decided to continue working because of the gratification it brought her.

Cynthia Davis, whose story is told in more detail at the end of this chapter, may be the only woman in the study who is working only because her family needs her to work. When her husband Mike got pneumonia, they both realized that he could no longer work overtime at his poorly paid job as a general stores clerk in a factory. Although Cynthia was on medication for a heart disorder and although her children were not yet in school, she decided that it would be better for each of them to work full-time than for Mike to continue working time and a half. However, Cynthia made it very clear that she was not working by choice:

> I liked being there and taking care of Mary and Mikey when they were small. I was glad I didn't have to go out and work. . . . But then [when they decided to buy a house], I just knew that I needed to work to have more income . . . and when you feel that you have to do something, you just do it. As long as Mike was willing to help me, I didn't really have any complaints.

She is also the only woman who does not give self as well as family reasons for remaining at work.

As they prepared to reenter the labor force, then, the 16 women faced a variety of common and individual problems. Five had no children over 6 years old at the time, and two others had at least one child under 6 (see Table 2.2) whereas the remaining eight all had children aged 6 or older. Although all of them had husbands who worked full-time, two were concerned about the future of their husbands' jobs and two others were worried about the effect of overtime work on their spouses' health. Although most of the women went back to work to expand their worlds and/or to escape from their homes and families, some like Cynthia Davis and Joan Collins went back primarily because their families needed the money. After they had been working for awhile, however, some women's reasons for working changed. Joan Collins continued to work after the money was no longer necessary because she enjoyed her work, whereas other women who went back to work for their own enjoyment continued to work after they had lost interest in their jobs because their families had become dependent on their incomes. As I will argue in Chapter 5, both their original motivations for working and their reasons for continuing to work helped to determine their bargaining positions.

THEIR HUSBANDS

What about their husbands? Since husbands' attitudes toward wives' working affect both the likelihood that a woman will enter the labor force and the chances that she will stay in it once she gets there (Shea et al., 1970:48), I asked both the women and their husbands how the men had reacted when first told that their wives intended to go back to work. Since it soon became clear that their feelings about their wives' decisions depended upon how their own work and family lives would be affected by having wives who worked full-time, the husbands' orientations to their own work and their work/family priorities are an important part of the following discussion.

Supportive Husbands

Only 4 of the 16 husbands had expected their wives to go back to work. For years, Bess and Martin Holling had planned that when the children were ready for college Bess would be "the kids' scholarship." Although Martin earned over $30,000 a year at his job in an engineering firm, neither his income nor the stock market could cover the $10,000 a year he and Bess paid in college expenses. Martin and Bess, however, made it clear that Bess was working only temporarily while Martin continued to do whatever he could to advance up the corporate ladder. However, for a man in his early fifties, moving up may already have become a closed option:

M.H.: I'm not any big comer that is going to be head of the company. I would have liked to be an officer, but I would have had to have gotten further in the business than I am today to make it. My age is a negative factor.

J.C.H.: Do you have this feeling that you've gone as high up on the ladder as you can?

M.H. God, I hope not [emphatically]!

Martin, after all, has worked hard to get as far as he is now and in the process has moved his family several times. At the time that Bess went back to work, he was still heavily invested in his work and did not expect that to change anymore than he expected life at home to change for him. Although his family has always been important to him, he has often had to put work first. Therefore, when he and Bess agreed that Bess would go back to work, they had a tacit understanding that she, and not Martin, would make the adjustments necessary at home.

Mike Davis is another husband who was not at all surprised when his wife went back to work. In fact, he encouraged her to get a job because his health had gotten so bad that he realized he could no longer work two jobs in order to support his family. However, in contrast to Martin Holling, Mike Davis gets his major satisfaction from his family and not from his work. It was, therefore, not a hardship for him to take over more of the child care and housework when Cynthia began working full-time.

In addition to Martin Holling and Mike Davis, two other husbands reported having been in favor of their wives' return to work. Tom Hutchins encouraged his wife Roberta to go to work because he wanted her to be happy. David Meyers was in favor of Linda's working because they needed the money at the time.

Tom Hutchins had been in construction sales and had traveled a lot while Roberta brought up two sons, one of them blind. He didn't care for children that much but had developed a close companionship with his wife. When I interviewed him, I was impressed with his devotion to her and with the way his eyes watered when he told me that he would do anything rather than lose her. When she went to work, he was in the canning business. During the 60-day season, he worked 12-hour shifts and she had to prepare three different dinners. As Tom said, "It was rough for her, I know it was." At the time, they had one son in college, another on the way to college, and had added an 8-year-old son, and an infant girl.

Tom and Roberta had been talking for some time about the possibility that Roberta might return to work. In fact, she felt that it was a "foregone conclusion" that she would. But Tom's moving from one community to another and his traveling made it difficult for her to think about working. Finally, Tom was asked to move again and decided to give up the job and look for something more settled. As he put it, "I didn't want to get that involved anymore."

Confined with a new child while Tom was working 12-hour shifts in the canning business, Roberta thought more about working. There was a neighbor down the street who could care for the baby, and the library had a job open on the bookmobile. An ardent reader, Roberta told Tom, "Gee, I'd like that job." She remembers his saying, "Well, go ahead and get it, if you want to."

It is hard to know how attached Tom Hutchins was to his work when he was in construction sales, but when I asked him how work fit into his life in general, he said

T.H.:　　I think it's very low, too low, in fact for any kind of success.

J.C.H.:　What is success?

T.H.:　　I don't know. Money, prestige, this sort of thing. If someone would say, here's a salary of $100,000 a year, this would be fine, but I probably wouldn't put any more effort into it than into a $15,000-a-year salary.

Like Tom Hutchins, David Meyers was putting his family before his work at the time that Linda got her job:

I've always turned down opportunities to work overtime, turned down opportunities that would involve moving the family . . . I'm concerned with my kids . . . who they are, where they are . . . what they're doing. . . . I have lots of time . . . five weeks vacation. I don't punch a clock. All I have to do is managerial . . . getting things done. If I had to punch a clock, I wouldn't work.

According to David, what motivated Linda's return to work was money:

D.M.:　We both understood why she went back to work. . . . We needed the money.

L.M.:　That wasn't the only reason. I wanted to go to work. I was going stir crazy.

> D.M.: Partly, but what motivated it was the money. We decided that if we wanted to continue living the way we expected to that Linda would have to work. Linda wanted to work and got a good job at Datan.

Although Linda stressed psychological reasons for returning to work, her husband emphasized financial ones. This pattern repeated itself several times during my interviews and surprised me each time. I had thought it would be the other way around. However, except for husbands who were adamant about not needing the second income, most husbands mentioned money as one of the motivations for their wives' return to work, whereas most wives stressed nonfinancial reasons. Were they saving face for each other or did each have difficulty imagining that the other was not entirely happy in his or her traditional role? I am not sure. In any case, husbands and wives had different explanations of why the wives were working, and the differences were not in the expected direction.

The four men just described all supported their wives' decisions to return to work and three of the four placed greater emphasis on family than on work in their own lives at the time their wives returned to work. They were the exception, however. The 12 other husbands were all surprised and needed time to get used to the idea before they could be supportive.

Surprised Husbands

Surprised husbands can be divided into two categories. First there were men whose pride was hurt. They were afraid that having a working wife reflected poorly on their own abilities as providers. They, however, were working only to provide for their families, and after they got used to the idea that their wives actually wanted to work, they began to appreciate what some described as "a load off their backs." The second kind of men also experienced wounded pride but were much more invested in working than were the "job-oriented men" first mentioned. They, like Martin Holling, gave work top priority in their lives and were not about to change this. If their wives' work meant that they would have to make adjustments in their own priorities, then they had mixed feelings about their wives working.

Job-Oriented Men

Whereas the three family-oriented men discussed earlier were supportive of their wives' decisions to work, three others did not welcome the idea at first, at least if we accept their wives' version of the story. In general, wives were more likely than their husbands to report that the men had felt uncomfortable when first confronted with a working wife. Jill Mooney, for example, remembers that when she and James were first married, James wanted to be the provider and would not allow her to work. As she said, "My husband is the type to say, 'My wife won't work.'" James reported having been "mixed-up" when Jill first went back to work but then added that it was not really all that bad even though he did have to care for the two preschool children during the day. Some time after Jill returned to work, it seems, James decided that, since he was not the kind of guy who could get "really caught up" in his job, having Jill work full-time was not a bad idea. As it later turned out, James Mooney so enjoyed his new relationship with his two boys that, in retrospect, he would not have it any other way.

Like James Mooney, Mike Schultz and Richard James were surprised when their wives went back to work, but like him they also got used to the idea and welcomed both the extra income and their newly discovered relief that providing was now not entirely up to them.

Superproviders

With the exception of David Meyers who was a hospital administrator, job-oriented men were blue-collar workers. However, not all blue-collar workers were job oriented. Forrest King, Bill Anderson, and Don Williams had been superproviders. Superproviders had regularly worked more than one job while their families were growing. In this study, the superproviders each had four or more children, making it necessary for them to work overtime. However, two of these men continued to work at both jobs even after their wives returned to work, and the one who did not had already had to reduce his work hours due to a heart attack.

Forrest King is a born-again Christian who believes that a man's position as head of his family is God-given:

> To me, I believe in the Bible and this sort of thing. First of all, the woman's place is in the home taking care of the children, I think, as long as the children are of the age that they need to be taken care of. Billie is not working right now because of the kids. They're home for the summer and they have no supervision, and this is why she wanted to take the summer off.

Although Billie agrees with Forrest, she and he decided that it would make sense for her to work for awhile to help finance the family's new home and pay for the children's parochial school. Billies remembers that when she first started to work, Forrest felt guilty about it. "He never wanted me to work," she said. Forrest, like most husbands, remembered it a little differently:

At that particular time that we [sic] went to work, I hadn't had a raise in almost two years. It seemed like the economy was way up there and it was costing way up there and we were way down here [gesturing]. The purpose of her going back to work at the time was just to help out; I didn't have any objections because at the time I was working two jobs and we still weren't [making it].

As a possible consequence of heavy involvement in providing, superproviders often feel inadequate in their other family roles. Forrest King, when asked how his role as father had developed over the years, answered, "Poorly."

J.C.H.: What do you mean by that?

F.K.: Personally, I haven't spent the time with the kids that I should. Course, a lot of people say I can't spend all my time, but I should spend more. I've put work over being with the kids and it shows.

Bill Anderson, another superprovider, had similar feelings about his performance as a father, and his wife Mary remembers that when she first went back to work, he was afraid that she might get too independent and leave him, since "women who start to make money sometimes get ideas." When I interviewed him five years after Mary had gone back to work for the second time, Bill had forgotten these objections. After all, Mary had worked for two different five-year periods and had not left him yet. Perhaps she would stay with him whether or not he was supporting her.

Like Forrest King and Bill Anderson, Don Williams had regularly worked two jobs while the children were growing up, but unlike them, he had a close relationship with his wife and took every opportunity he got to spend time with his children. It is hard to say what would have happened if he had not had to reduce his work hours after a heart attack. However, by the time I interviewed him, he was enjoying being laid off for the summer and told me that since his heart attack he had learned to live at a slower pace. Nonetheless, he insisted that his wife Nancy was not providing but "just helping" for awhile. Men who were superproviders did not easily relinquish this role, especially when, as for Forrest King and Bill Anderson, it was the only family role they were sure of.

Career-Oriented Men

The other men who had mixed feelings about their wives' working were career oriented but unlike Martin Holling had reason to fear that their lives would not be the same after their wives went to work. Although most of them also felt strongly about their roles as providers, most were earning enough money so that this role was not easily threatened. What was threatened, however, was the well-ordered home life to which they had become accustomed. Thus, when I asked Ted Collins how he felt about Joan's decision to continue working after the family debt was repaid, he expressed his reservations:

> To be honest, I deep down thought that would happen. Joan, being the kind of person she is, I thought she would keep working. At times I wish it was different, but I think she's happy. She says she is.

Bob Dooley, an assistant professor married to a finance analyst, echoed these feelings:

B.D.: I think Anne's happier. . . . She's a very bright girl [sic]. And now she has something to do with her head. I'm basically a chauvinist, and I would prefer that she not [work] and just live a life of leisure. Kind of shows my status, I guess.

J.C.H.: That you could support a wife at home?

B.D.: Yes, yes. I'm more of a housewife today than I would prefer to be. On balance, I say, "All right, that's what she wants."

Furthermore, Anne Dooley had no illusions about Bob's feelings when she went back to work. She told me, "I knew that Bob didn't want me to go back, but he realized that I needed an outside outlet."

For career-oriented men such as Ted Collins and Bob Dooley, their wives' return to work at the wrong time could affect their own occupational success, especially if the wives were themselves ambitious and became as committed to their work as their husbands were to theirs. When Joan went back to work, Ted Collins was dissatisfied with his place in the company and realized that he could not go any further without moving his family from their home and Joan away from her job. The more involved Joan became in her work, the harder it would be to do this, however. Likewise, Bob Dooley worried that Anne's work would continue to cut into his work time as it had begun to when he used his summer vacation for child care rather than research.

In contrast to job-oriented husbands, these men could foresee conflicts between their own occupational goals and new family demands. As we will see in Chapters 4 and 5, some career-oriented men were better able to insulate themselves from these demands than were others, and some wives expected more than others did. However, career-oriented men whose wives did not make all of the adjustments felt increased conflict between work and family demands as a result of their wives' return to work. Superproviders, on the other hand, were freer to decide between keeping their second jobs and devoting more energy to family relationships, but they had to decide whether or not they could get back into their families. Could they reestablish themselves as parents now that their children were in high school? Could they develop a companionship with their wives after 10 to 20 years of going separate ways? Although both career-oriented men and superproviders were in danger of having their work/family priorities challenged by their wives' return to work, job-oriented husbands were not. For men to whom work had always been simply a means of supporting a family, having a working wife usually meant that they could now afford the time to enjoy their families more. Perhaps this is why they usually forgot about the misgivings they had had when their wives first went back to work, whereas career-oriented men not only did not forget their objections but also continued to have them.

In describing the 16 families as they were when the wives returned to work, I have outlined four major variables: (1) family bond type, (2) wife's reasons for returning to work, (3) husband's work/family priorities, and (4) husband's orientation to his work. The last two variables overlap considerably in that career-oriented and superprovider men are most likely to give their work roles priority over family roles, whereas job-oriented men do the reverse. However, since within each of these categories, men vary in the relative importance they attach to work as opposed to family, it is, therefore, important to separate the two concepts analytically. I have not talked much about wives' work/family priorities other than to say that initially some wives went back to work primarily for their families and therefore can be assumed to place family before work. What about those who went back to work for themselves? They and their husbands had to decide what emphasis the wives would place on their new work roles. When wives of work-committed men became increasingly involved in their own work, the couple then had to decide whose work was to come first. Men who had always given family first place, however, were happy as long as their wives could arrange to be home at least some of the time that they were. The weight that the wives assigned to their new jobs, then, was up for negotiation and was not independent of the husband's own work/family priorities.

In the remainder of this chapter, I will describe how two different families adjusted to the wife's full-time work outside the home. In the first family, Jane Devore, the wife of a career-oriented man for whom work has always come first, decides to begin building more of a life of her own. Work is just part of this process. Because the Devores have a large income and because their children are almost all on their own, Jane Devore does not need a great deal of help from her husband John, but she does begin to resent having all the responsibility for the home while John continues to devote nearly all of his energy to his work. They struggle, therefore, over how much of the responsibility John should be expected to take on now that Jane is trying to free more space for pursuit of her own interests.

Cynthia and Mike Davis are very different from the Devores in a number of ways. As a job-oriented factory worker to whom family has always come first, Mike Davis was relieved when Cynthia went back to work to help out. Now they could make it financially without his having to work two jobs. Mike did not object to assuming more responsibility in the house but would now like Cynthia to take even more responsibility for providing than she does. She, however, is content to remain at her present job with little prospect of making more money. She feels comfortable having Mike as the main provider.

In these two examples, we see two couples with different family bond types, different reasons for working, and different combinations of work/family priorities, each trying to make a new bargain.

TWO FAMILIES

The Devores

I interviewed Jane Devore in her hospital office on a summer afternoon. Jane was working as a claims analyst and was explaining something about health insurance to a client as I entered. She was wearing an attractive purple and white dress and her curled brown hair and soft brown eyes somehow did not prepare me for the story of personal struggle and hardship that began to wind onto the tape recorder.

Jane was born the seventh in a farm family of 11 children. Since five of the children were born with a congenital defect that caused retardation, Jane's parents had to work very hard both with the children and on the farm. Jane remembers her father doing all household tasks from diapers to dishes. Because her family could not afford to pay the bus fare to Catholic school, Jane went to work in a restaurant at age 12 instead of going to high school.

John Devore's family bought the restaurant, and he and Jane started dating when he got out of high school. John then worked in the restaurant for five years, during which time he and Jane married and had two children. Then John decided to enroll in a university premedical program. Shortly after they moved to University Town, Jane gave birth to a third child. The family then had an infant, and a 1- and a 2-year-old.

When the children were ages 2 to 5, Jane began full-time work at a women's hospital while her husband was both working and finishing college. Jane worked for five years until she was seven months pregnant with twins. Shortly after the twins were born, John finished medical school, and the family moved to another state where he began his internship. After he finished the internship, the family then moved once more, this time back to their home state where John practiced medicine for six years.

The Devores spent the first years of John's practice in much the same way that other middle-class families of seven might. Although Jane had not finished high school, she taught herself to read John's medical journals so that she could discuss his work with him. The couple socialized with other couples they met in church and the neighborhood, and they took their children on trips all around the country.

Jane remembers the first years of her marriage as ones in which she and her husband were of roughly equal status even though his family owned the restaurant in which she worked. However, as John worked toward becoming a doctor, their statuses became more and more discrepant and she found herself deferring to him and beginning to assume that he would always be right. Thus, while Jane was working to help her husband through medical school and raising five children, she was also doing all the housework and waiting on her husband, who would sit down and wait to be served. Having come from a family with only two children, John did not have a "helping father" as Jane had had. His father, a paint decorator, had owned a hardware store when John was young and John's mother did all the child care and housework. In Jane's words, her mother-in-law "became a martyr."

When the twins were a little over 3 and the other children 11, 12, and 13, Jane gave birth to her sixth and last child. Jane trained the older children to help with the younger ones and with the house so that they would not be "like their father" in that regard, but she still remembers doing 60 to 80 hours a week of child care and household work in the five-bedroom house they lived in during the child-rearing years.

Meanwhile, while John was working long hours at the hospital, he was also developing a drinking problem. After three years of problem drinking, he decided to fall back on the California license he had gotten after finishing medical school and move to California. Maybe a change in environment would help. Jane stayed behind, unconvinced that "running away" would do anything. After a year and a half of separation, Jane took the youngest child, Robert, then 10, and the teenaged twins and joined John in California to see if they could make their marriage work again.

These were difficult years in the Devores' marriage, and Jane handled them by working on herself so that she could withstand her husband's "fits" as she called them. She went to high school in California, studied accounting, obtained her graduate equivalency diploma, and then began taking college courses. She also began talking to the social worker who was treating her youngest son for his stuttering problems and got further support for going in her own direction.

Shortly after Jane moved to California, John developed a heart condition complicated by alcoholism and began to show signs of mental illness as well. Jane then took over his bookkeeping and when it appeared that John might not live much longer, she move him and the rest of the family back to their home state so that they could be closer to the older children.

While John was incapacitated, Jane became the head of the family, and it was during this period that she "decided that she was a person," as she put it. As John's physical health defied predictions and grew better, Jane learned to wait out his regular temper tantrums and then go ahead and do whatever it was that had set him off.

Her decision to return to work after moving occurred in this context. John was still ill and was terribly upset when she told him she wanted to return to work. Attributing his reaction to his illness, Jane went ahead and got a job. One morning she got up early and dressed to go to work. John came out and asked where she was going. She told him. He asked why she had not let him know before. That morning was a good morning. When Jane explained that John had not let her share it with him, he did not have another tantrum but instead apologized.

The Devores in 1976

A year after I first interviewed Jane, I arranged to interview John and to talk with Jane again, this time at their home. When I called to make the arrangements, I was told that John was at a meeting and would be home at about 10:00 pm. I called later and got an appointment for the following Sunday afternoon.

On Sunday, as I walked toward the door of the large white house, I noticed that the yard had a slightly unkempt appearance that made it stand out in a neighborhood where every blade of grass seemed kept in place. I found John waiting for me. He was a man in his fifties, balding, with straight grey hair combed over the top of his head. He was overweight and had the soft look of a person who avoids physical activity. Dressed in a blue-grey polyester suit, white shoes, and dark tie, he ushered me into his "home office," motioning me to the "patient's chair." Clearly, John practiced his professional role in interviews as well as on his job.

It was in my interview with John that the story of his alcoholism, emerged. Jane had kept it from me during the previous year's interview and brought it up only after I had talked to John that Sunday:

Jane D.: I'm not sure whether I told you about the alcoholism or not.

J.C.H.: I don't think you did.

Jane D.: That might stem from the fact that it took awhile before I really felt that it [the cure] was really going to hold.

I also learned that although their companionship is now less husband centered, due largely to Jane's insistence that she do her own thing, John still does nothing in the house or that rather unkempt yard. John recalled his disagreement with Jane about the yard work. As he tells it, she thought he should take an interest in the yard, but he has neither the time nor the interest. Jane had hired a housekeeper but decided to do the yard herself. Then one day after working in the yard all day, she refused to go out with John that evening because she was tired from doing what she called "his work in the yard." He then called someone to do "his work." (This solution lasted only temporarily, however, because the next time the yard needed attention, John did not hire the help.)

John had quit his previous job that he had held while recovering from alcoholism and the heart trouble and was now working at two full-time clinic jobs. When I commented that it seemed that he had increased his work rather than his leisure since becoming sober, he replied

> Exactly. I'm well aware that I am doing that. When my wife got upset when
> I refused to do the lawn, I said, "I'm not going to do that and I don't
> intend to do that."

In summing up his major contribution to the household, he saw himself as a provider above all. He said that he had not gotten as involved with the children as he "could or should be" but thought his involvement had been adequate. Because he didn't enjoy taking the boys to sports, he took them to plays or on trips to Europe instead and saw his role as having been educational and recreational. He wanted his children to have an appreciation of cultural things and of social proprieties.

Although his household roles have not changed since Jane returned to work, it is clear that his relationship with her has changed. He has been noticing that Jane is less apt to let things interfere with her own activities:

> I resented this for awhile. She's got a lot of interest in politics now.

And he has been expecting less service:

> If I came home from work and she hadn't fixed my dinner for me . . . or if
> she didn't get up to serve me, I would be irritated. Now it doesn't bother
> me one way or the other.

However, he was irritated when she refused to take time off from her class to go with him to his high school reunion. Then Jane's class schedule changed, so that she was able to go, and she gave in and went with him. This disagreement was for John "the biggest thing that's happened in the last few months" and "the only thing that's really meant anything."

Jane agreed with John's portrayal of himself as a man involved primarily in his work but saw some major changes in him:

> Well, since he stopped drinking, I think that he has become a very loveable companion. Before that, and when he first got out of school, he had the preconceived notion that money was all there was to life, and I don't think he feels that way anymore. I think that he realizes that enjoying life is much more important than all that. And because he feels that way, he's just a lot more fun to have around.

She thought that "most of the time he has felt that he didn't know how to relate to his children" but attributed a lot of that to his drinking in the later years.

Would she have been happier if John were more interested in household affairs?

Jane D.: No. I don't care whether he does the work or not, but I sort of resent the responsibility of having to oversee *everything*: the inside, the outside, the kids, whatever. Sometimes I do resent that. I don't mind that we have a gardener do it instead of him, except that I have to pick the gardener and I have to leave the gardener messages that I want this done and this done and this done.

J.C.H.: So he's not taking the responsibility?

Jane D.: None of it [emphatic].

J.C.H.: But he will about redecorating?

Jane D.: Yeah, he likes that. And he will spend hours going through Hudson's looking for just the right thing or whatever. He enjoys that and he'll do it.

The yard issue was particularly upsetting to Jane because she thought she had negotiated an agreement with John when they took the house:

Jane D.: And one of the things that I sort of resented was that before we took this house (it had a big yard) and I said to him, "Since I'm working, I don't want the responsibility of this yard, and if we take this house, then I would assume that it means that you're going to accept the responsibility of the yard." So we took the house, and never once has he accepted the responsibility of the yard.

J.C.H.: What did he say when you told him that you assumed that he would?

Jane D.: He just agreed.

J.C.H.: He just went along with it?

Jane D.: Yeah [self righteous tone]! "If I agree, it keeps her quiet" [imitating his attitude]. And so sometimes I do resent that, and other times I think life is too short to face resentments on some dumb thing like that.

Other than the move towards a more companionate marriage and an increase in Jane's personal power there has been one more change Jane reported that is worth noting. This is illustrated by an incident that happened during the second interview.

Jane and I had finished our talk, when Robert, then 15, knocked on the door. He wanted to know where the shoelaces were. There were none in the drawer. Why hadn't Jane bought any? "Nothing gets bought that is not on the shopping list," said Jane, shifting the responsibility back to Robert. He could have noticed before that he needed shoelaces and put them on the list.

Jane explained the change in the following way:

If you just let these kids alone, they're going to grow up to be decent people. If you quit nagging, they're going to grow up and be more contented with themselves.

It took her the first three children to learn that. Now, she does not nag Robert about paying attention to things like the shopping list but simply lets him learn the consequences of not doing so for himself. More importantly, she does not let herself be talked into taking responsibility for seeing that *he* has what he needs at age 15.

Commentary

The Devores' example is complicated by John's alcoholism. Many of the changes we see in both of them and in their marriage can be attributed to his alcoholism, their separation of a year and a half, and his subsequent recovery. However, Jane's work is an important factor in her recovery of herself. It is a source of self-esteem that helps her stand up to her husband, pushing their companionship from a husband-centered arrangement to a more symmetrical couple-centered one.

I have selected the Devores' story for special attention to illustrate that a wife returning to work is often part of a complex set of events in family history and must be seen in its full context before we can begin to separate the effects of her working from other concomitant events.

Some of the important things to recognize about this example are

1. The development of a husband-centered marriage in which life revolves around the husband's needs and his work while the wife takes care of him, the house, and the children.
2. The devotion of the husband to his work and his pattern of working two jobs or going to school and working full-time.
3. The inability of the husband to remain integrated in the family during the child-rearing years. (We cannot tell whether he began drinking because of this or lost his family because of his drinking, of course.)
4. Jane's returning to work as part of a process of self-recovery that had begun several years before.
5. Jane's new self-esteem lead her to insist on her own rights and assert her personhood separate from her husband and the relationship of her work to this.
6. The outcome of a more companionate marriage, and Jane's allowing the last three children more space while insisting on more responsibility from them.
7. Older children and a high enough income to hire outside help, making it easier for John to avoid household work.
8. John's attitude toward Jane's return to work and his insistance upon insulating himself from household responsibilities.

In considering the impact of Jane's return to work on the change observed in the Devores' marriage, we must keep in mind both her years as substitute head of household and her growth as a person and as a mother over an extended period of child rearing. As we will see in the other example presented here, a woman's return to work does not occur in a vacuum. It is part of a longer chain of events in a couple's marital history and is the result of what has gone before as well as a cause of some of the changes that take place afterward.

Cynthia and Mike Davis

It was a cold snowy day when I first interviewed the Davises. I drove carefully down the icy street and parked at the end of an almost treeless block of pastel-colored houses decorated with icicles. As I approached the door, I noticed a small homemade ice skating rink in the lot between the Davises' house and the freeway. When I entered the small two-bedroom house, I was greeted by a large, friendly German shepherd with Cynthia Davis close behind. "Down, Clodo! Down, Clodo!" Cynthia shouted, trying to control the dog to make room for me. With Clodo under control, I was able to move further into the room where I saw a Siamese cat curled up on an overstuffed chair and a full bookcase lining one wall of the living room. The overall impression was one of a neat and comfortable, but not spacious, house.

While Clodo kept a watchful eye over the tape recorder on the couch, I began the interview with Cynthia. She was a small thin woman with dark hair done in a pouf reminiscent of the 1960s. A soft, full-sleeved maroon blouse complemented her dark eyes and softened the sharpness in her face. Her voice was tired, making me wonder why she was contributing her time and energy to my study. Surely this frail and tired working mother of two young children must have had more important things to do on a Saturday afternoon than to talk with me. The five dollars I would pay her could not have been much of an incentive.

Cynthia Davis

After explaining that Mike had gone to bring Mary Ann, aged 9, back from her dancing lessons, Cynthia began to describe her family background and the circumstances that had led to her return to work seven years ago. She had been born in 1943 in a small town in southern Illinois and lived there with her mother and two sisters until she was 10. Her father, a shopkeeper, had divorced her mother and moved north when Cynthia was 7. The mother and children moved north themselves three years later, eventually settling in Michigan. Cynthia's mother took a job as a housekeeper in a state hospital. Now everyone but Cynthia and her father have moved back to southern Illinois and Tennessee.

Mike, Cynthia told me, was born in Kentucky in 1939 but was brought to Michigan when he was a baby, making him a "northerner." His father worked in a factory, and his mother was a housewife. At the time of the interview, Mike's mother was still living in the area and would sometimes help with the children as had Cynthia's mother until last year when she returned to Illinois.

Cynthia told me that she had left high school just two credits from graduation and had begun working full-time.

> I was short about two credits, which I should have went back and finished, but I didn't. I just didn't care at the time, but now, if I had to do it over again, I probably would have finished up. I could have gone to summer school to finish those two credits. . . . I started working when I was about nineteen years old, in different small jobs. I started babysitting, then small factory jobs, and then I worked at a small discount place for about two years before I got married.

She and Mike had met through Mike's sister when Cynthia was in junior high. Nothing came of this then, but later when Cynthia and Mike were both working and Mike was attending a community college, they met again. Mike didn't remember having met her earlier, but this time something did come of it. They got married when Cynthia was almost 22.

Mike then stopped going to college and continued his job at Ford, where he has been for 15 years. When I interviewed them, Mike was working as a general stores clerk.

After marrying Mike, Cynthia quit her job and stayed home for a few years. Within two years she was pregnant with her first child, Mary Ann, and then a year later became pregnant again with Mikey. At the time they were still living in a rented apartment; but when the children were about 1 and 2, Cynthia and Mike began to talk about getting a house of their own. Mike was working a second job at a department store to support them, but there was still not enough money and not enough space for their growing family.

It was at this point that the Davises began talking about Cynthia's going back to work. Although Mike had high blood pressure and Cynthia suffered from fatigue, they decided that Mike would keep both his jobs and that Cynthia would begin a full-time job as well. Cynthia's mother would help with the children when neither parent was home and Mike would help with cooking and other household work. Cynthia would have been glad to stay at home with the children for a few more years, but, as she said,

> I just knew that I needed to work to have more income . . . and when you feel you have to do something, you just do it.

Given Mike's willingness to help at home, she would not object to working outside the home.

The Davises were a three-job family for only a short while before Mike caught pneumonia and had to go into the hospital. After this, he decided to quit his second job:

> What happened was that eventually my health got so bad . . . my resistance . . . that I caught pneumonia and went in the hospital. Sometime after this, I decided that it wasn't worth it to burn both ends of the candle.

In spite of this, because Cynthia's full-time job paid more than Mike's part-time job at the department store, the Davises were able to buy their present home two years after Cynthia's return to work. Now, they even have some land in the country where they plan to build a larger house when they can afford it.

Had it not been for Cynthia's job, the Davises might not have their present home, let alone own land in the country, but the first seven years of being a two-job family have not been easy years for them. Cynthia remembered the first job she took, working the midnight shift at a convalescent home:

> It just didn't work out because the kids were little and when I got home, I would be tired and the kids would be ready to get up and be fed. The pay rate was outrageous. It was terrible. . . . So my husband said, "Just quit." . . . It wasn't worth the pay.

Cynthia quit that job but then got another one at the hospital where her mother was still working as a matron. For two years, she worked the swing shift while Mike worked days and both grandmothers and a variety of baby sitters cared for the children when both parents were working at the same time. The swing shift, however, was not much better than working nights:

> I worked one day, two afternoons, and two midnights or something like that, or maybe straight midnights, if the lady happened to be off. . . . I was just like relief. It wasn't good at all. It was really hectic and would seem like I was running back and forth all the time, and the children were really little, and it was hard to get any rest, but I managed.

Cynthia managed, and after two years, the hospital eliminated her job classification and moved her to her present job as a ward housekeeper. The job includes a lot of mopping and sweeping, but working on the same ward allows her to get to know some of the patients. She likes that:

> There are a few patients that I might sit down and have a cup of coffee with them. I enjoy that . . . a few pets that I have [she chuckles].

However, after doing housecleaning on her job all day, Cynthia does not feel like doing more of it when she gets home at 7:30 pm. She told me:

> I really don't feel like coming home and doing too much, but my husband helps me as much as he can. He might vacuum. He cooks. He cooks supper, and when I come home, I have a hot meal.

Not only does Mike cook every night, but he also will do grocery shopping and spends a lot of time with the children. Cynthia told me:

> He goes to the grocery store. Like last night before I got in from work, he had gone to the grocery store and shopped, and that helps me today. I don't have to go out and do heavy shopping. I might go out and pick up a few items. He is good with Mikey and Mary Ann. He takes them places and spends a lot of time with them.

Sometimes he will also do laundry, but (in 1976 at the time of the second interview), the Davises had a baby sitter who did laundry, some housecleaning, and baking five mornings a week for $20.

Given their present partially alternating shifts and the availability of good low-cost help, the Davises are able to keep their household running fairly smoothly. Their main problem is that Cynthia and Mike have very little time together during the week. Mike leaves for work at 5:30 am and gets home at 3:30 pm. He picks the children up from school and later makes dinner for them and himself. Cynthia gets home at 7:30 pm, eats dinner in front of the television, and visits with Mike and the children for a short while before all three of them must go to bed. At 9:00 pm everyone but Cynthia is in bed. Needing extra sleep because of a heart condition (the cause of the fatigue mentioned earlier), she goes to bed by 11:00 pm even though she does not have to be up until 8:00 am in order to get to work by 9:30 am. If Cynthia had her choice, she would return to her previous 7:00 am to 3:30 pm shift, which allowed her to do errands and visit with people in the afternoons and gave the whole family more time together in the evening. That way she would not have to take time off from work to keep dentist appointments and could go out to dinner at Mike's lodge during the week. She also would get to know more of the neighbors if she were home in the afternoons. Thus, although alternating shifts make child care easier, the Davises' work schedules also make it difficult for them to spend time alone together or to socialize with others during the week.

Mike Davis

Having heard so much about Cynthia's helpful husband, I was looking forward to talking with Mike when he came back with Mary Ann. After Cynthia had brought me up to date on her work history, Mike and Mary Ann came home and Mike joined the interview. I also talked to Mike alone a year later. The following information is drawn from both interviews.

Mike Davis is a man of medium height and somewhat overweight. His smiling blue-grey eyes look out from under brown hair that seems to form fringes around his face. He is easy to talk with and both more expressive and less tense than his wife. Although I had had to work to make Cynthia comfortable, Mike seemed to be trying to make me comfortable. He wanted to know about me and my life and how this study fit into it. With the Siamese cat purring in Mike's lap, Mike and Cynthia continued the interview. It was then that Cynthia said that sometime she might like to work in a factory because Mike had told her that there are more opportunities in industry now and that she could get paid twice as much as she is earning now without working as hard.

Later in the interview, after Mike had left the room, Cynthia seemed to reverse herself:

C.D.:   My husband wants me to go to work for Fords, and he has wanted me to go to work for Fords for a few years, and I said,

"No," that I was content where I was. But he is thinking of more money and an easier job and you know. . . .

J.C.H.: You could get an easier job there?

C.D.: Sure.

J.C.H.: Why don't you want to do that?

C.D.: Well, I don't think that I would really like factory work. I have worked in a small factory before, but not a big factory . . . I don't know. Just too much noise and too much confusion all the time. There are people bickering back and forth, and if you have to work a line, you have dozens of people all over, fighting. People are unhappy. And the job I'm in, I'm by myself, and when I want to get off by myself, then I can do it.

Cynthia is not the sort of person who enjoys interactions with many strangers, and she would rather work in a low-pressure job than earn more money.

In my second interview with Mike, however, I learned that he had been trying to encourage Cynthia to be more outgoing and independent of him. He would like her not only to make more money but also to have some social life of her own as he does at his lodge and club. He also thinks that he is taking on too much responsibility around the house. It was in the following conversation that Mike expressed both of these feelings:

J.C.H.: You say you'd like to see her [Cynthia] more independent. In what ways is she not?

M.D.: She's too much oriented to me.

J.C.H.: How?

M.D.: I just always did things, and I seem to be biting off more all the time.

J.C.H.: What kinds of things?

M.D.: Everything [laughs for no apparent reason].

J.C.H.: You mean stuff around the house, or what?

M.D.: Yeah. Shopping. It's not good for anyone to become dependent upon a man too much. For anyone to become dependent. I try to tell her, "I may not always be around."

J.C.H.: People are dependent in different ways. Some women depend on their husbands financially but not emotionally. What area would you say she was most dependent in?

M.D.: A little of all of them.

J.C.H.: Are you dependent on her in certain ways?

M.D.: I don't like to think I am. I'm sure I must be. If I ask her to do something, I expect it to be done.

Mike finds himself being more responsible than he wants to be and yet has a difficult time letting himself be dependent upon anyone. He is afraid that he will keep "biting off" more and more and that Cynthia will stand by and let him.

As he discussed his fear, he described himself as the kind of person to whom people tell their problems, the sort of person who is always the center of things. Somehow all the children in the neighborhood end up in his yard and he finds himself fixing their bikes. He said

Well, I'm kind of the unofficial babysitter, I think, and if people want to dump their kids. . . . If I get underneath the car, I usually have five or six kids underneath with me. One kid's father took their pool down and sold it because this kid was always in our pool. . . . I have kids that sometimes I even wonder where they all come from. . . .

Mike Davis, then, is the kind of person who seems to invite responsibility and attract dependents, even if, as he says, he really does not want to.

The conflict over responsibility and who should be dependent upon whom seems to be an underlying theme in the Davises' marriage. This theme is played out in series of paradoxes. On the one hand, each told me in separate interviews that Mike is the "man of the house."

C.D.: Mike is the man of the house and that's the way I want it to be.

M.D.: I think there can be only one head to any household. Someone's got to be the one to take the initiative.

On the other hand, Mike would like less responsibility for the family and the household than he now has, but Cynthia has no objections to things the way they are now. Mike earns $12,000 a year and Cynthia, $8000. Mike does the cooking during the week, child care in the afternoons, some shopping and cleaning, and all the yard and car work. Cynthia takes most of the responsibility for keeping the house clean and seeing that the laundry is done and she is the one who arranges for baby sitters and household help.

Cynthia is appreciative of the "help" she gets from Mike, but Mike feels that somehow he is doing more than he has bargained for.

Given this tension about the division of responsibilities, I was interested in how the Davises dealt with conflict and asked them about this during their joint interview. Mike started by saying that he will blow up at anybody: "her, the kids, the dog." Cynthia then stays out of his way until he cools down. Given this description, I wondered what Cynthia did with her own feelings and the following conversation ensued:

C.D.: I kind of let them out when I . . .

M.D.: [Interrupting] She doesn't let things bother her that much.

C.D.: When I feel that it is necessary to say something that I've got out of my . . .

M.D.: [Interrupting again] The fact is that when we first got married, I hate to use this word, but she would pout. She would be perturbed about us and she wouldn't talk about it or say what it was, being that something was wrong. It got so that I would set her down in a chair, and if I had to push her down, and I would say, "I am going to sit here until it comes out." And if we sat there for two hours, we sat there for two hours, and we would play with our fingers and look at each other. I would physically keep her in that chair until whatever was bothering her was here. . . . Let's really get it out in the open and kick it around. Is it really a problem, or is it something that has been blown out of shape?

They then agreed with each other that now she will say when something bothers her, yet Mike also told me in his separate interview that "she's not a whiner or a crier. When she says it hurts, you can bet it hurts."

Thus we are presented with a somewhat confusing picture:

1. Mike wants Cynthia to get out and make more money and be more independent of him, yet he agrees with her that only one of them can be the head of the household and that should be he.
2. Mike and Cynthia agree that she will now speak up when something bothers her, but she goes along with Mike's idea of her working in a factory in his presence and then contradicts this privately.
3. Mike wants Cynthia to speak her mind, but in the interview when she is trying to explain how she handles feelings, he interrupts twice and answers for her.
4. Cynthia has a heart condition that fatigues her and makes her need extra sleep, yet she has remained at a physically exhausting job for eight years, enduring irregular shifts, while raising two young children.

5. Cynthia praises Mike for the help he gives her, putting it in such a way that it seems to have been part of the original bargain. Yet Mike now feels that too much of the household responsibility falls on his shoulders.

Cynthia and Mike Davis are sharing much more household responsibility now than they were before Cynthia returned to work, but they have not reached an agreement about exactly how much more Mike should take on in the house given Cynthia's work outside of the house. Although reaching such an agreement would be difficult in any circumstances, the Davises' changing work schedules make it even more difficult for them to arrive at a new division of labor satisfactory to them both. Nonetheless, they have become a role sharing couple in spite of themselves because that is the only way that they can each work full-time, remain in good health, and manage their household.

Discussion

If neither Mike Davis nor John Devore really wanted more household responsibilities, how has it happened that Mike has assumed more additional responsibility than he wants to, whereas John has managed to avoid doing anything but make one call to a gardener? There are several differences between the two families that I think help to explain why Mike Davis has become a role sharing husband and John Devore has not. To begin with, John Devore is a physician making over $50,000 a year (in 1976), whereas Mike Davis is a factory general stores clerk earning up to $12,000 a year with overtime pay. Jane Devore went back to work after the children were grown primarily to get her mind off the family crisis created by her husband's illness and alcoholism. Her income, although an important supplement to the family income while her husband was ill, was not the main reason for her return to work and is certainly not the reason that she continues to work. Jane is working for self-fulfillment.

Although Cynthia Davis enjoys some aspects of her job as a ward housekeeper, she is not working for self reasons. She went back to work with two toddlers at home because her family needed the money. Unlike Jane, who enjoys her work and looks forward to moving up to the next job classification, Cynthia is concerned mostly with the scheduling of her work and the ways in which it interferes with her family life. She is not looking for a more challenging job, but rather one that will conflict as little as possible with the rest of her life and one that she will not find emotionally taxing. Thus, as a *self*-motivated woman, Jane Devore is trying to find some relief from family responsibilities, whereas as a *family*-motivated woman, Cynthia is looking for a way to fulfill as many of her family responsibilities as possible while working full-time. In other words, Cynthia and Jane have different *role attachments*.

If the wives have different role attachments, so do the husbands. John Devore is career oriented almost to the exclusion of anything else in his life. He buys his way out of additional family responsibilities and makes it clear that he does not intend to take care of more things at home just because Jane is working. He will not expect her to do as much for him, but that is as far as he will go. Mike Davis, however, goes a lot further. He is a job-oriented man who has always put his family first. Therefore, although he may grumble about the amount of responsibility he now has, he nonetheless prepares dinner, chauffeurs the children to their activities, cares for them in the afternoons, and does food shopping as well as some housecleaning.

In the Davises' couple/child-oriented marriage, the main issue is who should be most dependent upon whom, whereas in the Devores' more husband-centered relationship, the conflict stems from each partner's attempts to gain or protect independence from the other and the family. This means that the two couples are making very different kinds of bargains. If we listen to the bargaining going on underneath Jane and John Devore's squabbles, we can hear John saying to Jane, "OK, work if that's what you want to do, but don't let it change my life and don't complain about what you have to do around the house as long as I am making more than enough money to hire help." Jane's position is, "You have your work and before this, you had your alcohol. Now I have my work and my outside activities. If you want to have a big house and work two jobs, then don't expect me to take the responsibility for managing it all, now that I have a life of my own." This is where John and Jane reach an impasse. Jane would like John both to give her more personal space and to accept more household responsibility. John would like more of her attention than he gets and uses his heavy work schedule as an insulation from household demands. However, he has relinquished the right to be the center of attention all the time and does expect less service from Jane than he used to. He is also paying more attention to her emotional needs, making the marriage less husband centered than it once was. But this is probably as much as Jane can expect from John, and as she said about his not taking care of the garden, "Life is too short to face resentments on some dumb thing like that."

The Davises have not given up dealing with resentment, and they are still reallocating family responsibilities. Their bargaining began with Mike's need for Cynthia to go to work. His position was, "I can't make the money we need to have a new house and the things we want for this family without endangering my health. If you take more of the responsibility for providing, I'm willing to do more in the house, but I want to make sure that you are holding up your end and I want to know that I can depend upon you." Cynthia's reply is, "I'm willing to work if you do more with the children and in the house, but don't push me too far. You are still the man of the house and that's the way I want it. I have no desire to be a superwoman." The result is that Cynthia works but does not try to find a job that will bring in more money, and Mike Davis shares more household responsibility but keeps trying to limit how much more he will assume. Meanwhile, Mike resents going shopping whereas Cynthia appreciates his shopping but resents being pushed to work in a factory. The Davises are sharing roles in ways that the Devores never have and never will, but they have not yet worked out the terms of a new contract that each of them can endorse.

CONCLUSION

Although the Davises differ from the Devores in almost all the ways that a role sharing couple can differ from a role-segregated one, the contrasts between couples who role share and those who do not cannot always be drawn in such bold lines. Having described the 16 families as they were prior to the wife's return to work and having told the reader what happened next for the Devores and the Davises, I will describe in the next chapter the changes that took place in all 16 families.

4
WHAT CHANGED?

In Chapter 3, I described the 16 families as they probably were before the women returned to work. In this chapter, I will describe the changes that took place in four marital roles as a result of the wife's return to work. These are provider roles, marital companionship, parenting, and housekeeping. In considering the changes reported, the reader should remember that these data were gathered through open-ended retrospective interviews rather than through a series of time-budget studies. Thus, I know that James Mooney now considers it his responsibility to keep track of his children's progress in school, but I do not know in hours and minutes how much more time he spends with his children now than he used to before Jill went back to work.

Of the four role changes under consideration, the clearest shift is, of course, in definition of responsibility for providing. Because none of the wives were earning money before their return to work and all were doing so afterward, all couples had to renegotiate the responsibility to provide. By the time of the second interview, six couples saw themselves as coproviders without any qualifications, four others were somewhat more ambivalent about the wife's providing role but were sufficiently dependent on her income to be considered coproviders, and the remaining six had become main/secondary providers with the wife in the "junior partner" position (Scanzoni, 1972:35; 1978).

Twelve of the sixteen families experienced some reallocation of either custodial child care or more extensive parenting responsibilities, and the same number, although not always the same couples, moved toward more companionate marriages with more equal sharing between husband and wife. Changes in housekeeping tended to involve a reorganization of the whole family so that the children and/or husband were assigned regular tasks while the wife retained responsibility for seeing that things got done. Only 2 of the 16 husbands took on sufficient added responsibility for housekeeping that they could be considered to be sharing that role. Thus, of the four areas considered, I observed the most dramatic changes in parenting and the symmetry of marital companionship, and the least in reallocation of housekeeping responsibilities. At the end of this chapter, then, the reader should have an overview of the role changes experienced by the 16 couples and should be prepared to move on in Chapter 5 to a consideration of how these changes came about and why some changes that perhaps would have been expected never happened.

REDEFINING THE PROVIDER ROLE

By analyzing both the uses of the wife's income and each spouse's statements about the division of financial responsibility, I have been able to arrange the families according to how much the family depends upon the wife's income and the extent to which the wife is defined by both herself and her husband as a coprovider. The couples range from the Devores who now rely hardly at all on Jane's income due to John's two clinic jobs to the Mooneys who pool their incomes and have created a two-job life-style that they cannot foresee changing in the near future. In between these two extremes are five couples who see themselves as main/secondary providers, four who express ambivalent and inconsistent attitudes toward the division of providing responsibilities but who have nonetheless become dependent on the wife's money, and five in addition to the Mooneys who agree that they need the wife's income and have adjusted to mutually agreed upon coprovider roles. The outcomes are represented in Table 4.1.

Much more will be said about the renegotiation of provider roles in Chapter 5. Here I simply want to acquaint the reader with the basis for the categories used, report the outcomes observed, and comment briefly on a few obvious patterns that distinguish main/secondary, ambivalent, and coprovider couples.

Secondary Providers

Although it is possible that Jane Devore should not be defined as a provider at all, I have included the Devores in the "secondary" provider category because, even though John said that they did not need Jane's income at all, Jane told me that she does use it to get things for the children and herself. Furthermore, there was a time during John's illness in which they were dependent on Jane's income, establishing Jane as a potential provider during crises. The five other couples who see themselves as main

TABLE 4.1 Provider Role Definition by Husband's Work Orientation, Occupation, and Proportion of Family Income Earned by Wife

Husband's Work Orientation	Husband's Occupation	Wife's Occupation	Wage Ratio %	Provider Roles[a]
Professional				
Devore	M.D.	Staff benefits clerk	15	S
Correlli	Engineer/businessman	Secretary	14	S
Holling	Engineer	Secretary	25	S
Reade	Engineer	Secretary	30	S
Collins	Engineer	Title editor	42	A
Dooley	Professor	Finance analyst	44	A
Marx	Family franchise business run jointly		50	C
Superproviders				
King	Fire person	Clerk	22	S
Williams	Foreman	Switchboard operator	30	A
Anderson	Factory worker/electrician	Data analyst	44	C
Job				
James	Skilled worker	Secretary	30	S
Hutchins	Foreman	Clerk	33	C
Schultz	Machinist	Secretary	33	C
Mooney	Machinist	Clerk	30	C
Meyers	Administrator	Secretary	33	C
Davis	General stores clerk (factory)	Hospital maintenance work	40	A

[a] S, Main/secondary providers; C, coproviders; A, ambivalent coproviders.

61

and secondary providers do not have the Devores' current financial resources. Unlike Jane and John, they would have to cut back their expenses if the wife stopped working. Although they all told me that they could "get along" without a second income, they did not look forward to the sacrifices it would entail.

Bess Holling, a college-educated secretary, and wife of a well-paid engineer, is working to finance her three children's college educations. She is the wife quoted in the introduction who said

> It isn't as if we were going to starve, we're not dependent upon my salary for living expenses. With two in college in the fall semester, we would have had to take out a loan. . . . It would have been more of a strain if I weren't working.

For couples like the Hollings, it is important that the wife's money not be used for groceries, utilities, or other day-to-day expenses, although it may be used for health insurance, mortgage payments, children's educational expenses, or to get "a little something extra for the kids." Thus, because Theo James' income is used "only for house payments," she too is a secondary provider even if she does earn 30% of the family income. As her husband, Richard, a machinist, told me,

> Like now, we just use her paycheck to pay the house payments. So, that's about all we do with hers — just pay the house payments. So that's a whole lot of money I don't have to worry about.

From the rest of the interview, however, we learn that because they no longer have to pay house payments from his check, they eat out more, buy more expensive clothes, have a second car, and take more elaborate vacations. Nonetheless, both are comfortable with the idea that Theo's income is "just used for house payments." Limiting the uses of the wife's paycheck to capital improvements and temporary expenses helps to maintain the definition of the wife as a secondary provider who can "quit anytime she wants." Husbands of secondary providers often described their wives' incomes in words similar to those used by Maria Correlli's husband,

> Of course, he tells me I can quit any time I want . . . and, then he'll turn around and say, "Gee, I don't know what we'd do if you didn't work. What you make is like the frosting on the cake, a little extra as we might have."

Couples who define themselves as main/secondary providers rely on the increased income for improvements in the quality of their lives but earmark the wife's check for specific expenses. They keep open the possibility that the wife may "quit whenever she wants" and in some cases actually expect her to stop working when the need for additional income ends. Except for Theo James, who was making 30% of the total income at the time of the second interview, wives in this category contributed 25% of the family income or less (see Table 4.1).

Coproviders

In contrast to the secondary providers, coproviders pooled their incomes and/or failed to distinguish between types of expenses payable by each spouse. They had become dependent on the wife's income and agreed that she would probably continue to work indefinitely. Husbands defined as coproviders appreciated their wives' contributions and felt sorry for men who had to provide for their families unaided. As Mike Schultz, a machinist married to a secretary, told me

> I could probably swing Cathy staying home, but it's so expensive. Cathy's income helps. It takes a little worry off my mind. . . . Like I say, it helps. . . . I'm glad she goes to work. We can afford things. . . . I could work seven days, twelve hours a day if I wanted to. That's what I'd have to do if Cathy wasn't working.

James Mooney, also a machinist, felt the same way about the money that his wife, Jill, was earning at her clerical job. Even though she was contributing just 30% of the family income, when I asked him to describe their roles as they are now, he said

J.M.: I think it's more of a fifty/fifty deal. We're both providers and we're both homemakers and we're both parents.

J.C.H.: Although you're making quite a bit more money than she does, you still think of her as a provider?

J.M.: Ya, I think she's helping quite a bit. I think we're sharing our responsibilities. I feel very good about that part of it. . . . I've seen some situations where the wife doesn't work, and they really have to watch their money [he sighs], and she doesn't *want* to work. . . . Maybe it's because she feels homemaker is her position and that's the way it should be, but in our situation, I think we share responsibilities pretty evenly.

J.C.H.: It feels good to you then?

J.M.: It does, ya. It takes a load off my neck. . . . I've seen a lot of wives nagging their husbands because they don't have enough money. I figure, well, they could get out and help. It's very easy to sit back and say, "You gotta go to work every day, can't take a day off because we need money" and be sitting home themselves . . . maybe I'm a male chauvinist, I don't know. . . . I believe the responsibility should be evenly divided.

Coproviding husbands were relieved to have their burdens shared and typically spoke of a "load off my neck" or a "worry off my mind." However, as the reader will remember from Chapter 3, they did not always feel this way. Even now[1], Bill Anderson is "not crazy about" Mary's working, and James Mooney who is so enthusiastic about sharing responsibilities still wistfully dreams of coming home to a hot meal:

I kinda missed that, I guess even now . . . all my life, I dreamt of that, you know, working day shift and coming home to a hot meal, and it really doesn't work out like that. I guess you get a vision of what life is supposed to be like, when you're younger, and when you start working, you find out that it's not quite like that.

But James knows it would be hard to support the family alone:

You kinda wonder, you know, if she actually could [quit]. I imagine we could survive on my check. I've seen guys do it, but they really have to watch the money.

As husbands got used to sharing the provider role they forgot not only their earlier objections to their wives' working but also any fears they might have had about what would happen if their wives became financially independent of them. Mary Anderson, for example, remembered that when she first went back to work, her husband Bill thought that women who worked got too independent and were apt to leave their husbands. Years later, when I asked him what he thought of that idea, he said

No, I don't feel this way. I don't believe I feel this way. The way I feel . . . that if I have to keep her because of financial responsibility and because I have to support her and everything, then it's really not all that great anyway.

In fact Bill Anderson is now considering quitting his second job doing maintenance at a factory, which would mean that Mary, a trained data analyst, would be earning more money than he would at his remaining job as a machinist.

Coproviding couples were not only less concerned about the relative amount of money each spouse earned but also felt no need to earmark the wife's paycheck for specific and temporary expenses. If it is assumed that a wife will always work, then the couple can as easily rely upon her money for ongoing expenses as they can upon his. This is reflected in Mary Anderson's description of the way they pay their bills:

> He pays some of the bills and I pay some of the bills. Whatever we have left is ours. The credit union takes some of the bills out of his check, and I pay the light, phone, and things like that.

Coproviding couples had, over the years, achieved a comfortable mutual definition of their shared responsibilities and saw the arrangement as permanent.

Ambivalent Coproviders

Although it is true that coproviding wives on average earned a larger proportion of the family income than did secondary-provider wives (36% vs. 22%), wage ratio alone did not determine the definition of provider roles. After all, both Theo James and Jill Mooney were earning 30% of the total income and yet James Mooney thinks of his wife as a coprovider and describes their role relationship as "a fifty/fifty deal" whereas Richard James emphasizes that "all they do" with Theo's check is make house payments. The relationship between wage ratio and provider role definition becomes still more confounded when we consider wives earning 40% or more of the family income. Two of the four wives in this category are what I have termed *ambivalent coproviders*. Although their families are dependent on the wives' incomes, ambivalent coproviders cannot agree about whether or not the wife is actually sharing the provider role.

Among the 16 couples, ambivalence about coproviding took somewhat different forms depending upon each spouse's role attachments. Whereas Joan Collins and Anne Dooley were fighting with their professional husbands to have their own work taken seriously without wounding their husbands' egos, Cynthia Davis and Nancy Williams, wives of factory workers, were doing their best to hold onto their right to be provided for. However, all four couples described the wife's income in contradictory terms.

Bob Dooley, an assistant professor of business administration, is worried about becoming too dependent upon the salary his wife Anne is earning as a finance analyst for Datan. When I asked Bob about his and Anne's relative contributions, he said uncomfortably, "I'm about two thousand dollars ahead of her." Since some professional husbands of "secondary workers" had dismissed their wives' incomes by telling me that "after taxes, there's nothing left," I asked Bob, "After taxes, are you still ahead with her working?" He replied

Oh, yeah. Since she started working, we put in all new furniture and about three or four thousand dollars in the bank. But what scares me is what would happen if she weren't working. I think maybe I better do more consulting, maybe leave teaching, because we couldn't survive as we live today on just my salary.

Anne, however, insisted that her husband was the breadwinner and that his job had priority over hers even though, from the rest of the interview, it was clear that they moved to their present location, so that Anne could work and that Bob was left with the major household responsibility last summer because of Anne's desire for a job and the demands of the job she took on.

Ted Collins also worries about their dependence on Joan's salary and, according to Joan, he has changed from saying "poor Joan you work so hard and you bring such a little amount of money" to "making snotty remarks about big companies overpaying their employees." To me, he said of Joan's salary:

Yes, we are dependent on it right now. When your salary goes up, your standard of living goes up, and it's almost impossible to keep it down.

Joan, however, like Anne, sees her husband as "the provider":

My feeling is, I'm not working so we can save money. I'm working so we can belong to the swim club and take trips and drive a new car and do things that would be difficult to do with the kids at this point. And I'm saving money, I mean. I'm having money taken out of my salary and he's providing the basics. And I love working thinking we can do fun things with my money.

In spite of Joan's recent promotion from an hourly to a salaried worker, she confidently insists that she will never catch up to her husband's salary. He seems to be not as sure since, according to her, he drops comments about how as soon as she makes as much as he does, he'll quit work and let her support the family. (These remarks always have a little edge to them and are often snuck into dinner conversations at his mother's house.) Another indication of Ted's discomfort with Joan's career mobility was his reaction to a high rating Joan got on a job evaluation. According to Joan, Ted said, "Too bad they don't give a rating for 'bitch' because you'd get a six on that one too."

Whereas these professional husbands of newly professionalized wives seem uncomfortable with their wives' competition, the factory workers married to clerical and service workers try to rationalize the violation of their own expectations that the husband should be the sole provider for his family. This is apparent from the following dialogue I had with Don

Williams, a factory foreman who had to quit his second job after a heart attack:

D.W.: I don't think that a wife should support the family. . . . I don't believe in that. I couldn't tell her that . . . she'd argue with me, but . . .

J.C.H.: Is she supporting the family now?

D.W.: No. No. She's not. She's helping.

J.C.H.: Some men I've talked to feel that as long as they are paying for the rent and the food that they are supporting the family, even if their wives make more money than they do. What do you think about this?

D.W.: I don't feel that way. I know it was that the man is the head of the household, but whenever you get married, you go in as one. . . . I mean you're supposed to be together, you're supposed to work together. This is how I feel. Maybe I'm wrong in feeling this way. Now it takes her money to pay the bills, it don't bother me. Why should it? The bills have got to be paid. She belongs to me. There's times in life when the man is going to be set back a bit and the wife has to come in and take over . . . whether he likes it or not.

In spite of all this, however, Don still feels that it would be better if Nancy could stay at home.

Furthermore, from his reports, Nancy appears as ambivalent about her financial responsibilities as Don is. Although he told me that she would argue with him about whether or not a woman should support the family, he also said that she is upset when he is laid off and threatens to quit her job as a goad to get him to look for something else. When she does the family bookkeeping, as she normally does, he quotes her as teasing him with, "That's your job. Ain't you man enough to do it?" And Nancy herself had told me that she thought about quitting work now and then since she had many things she wanted to do around the house. From all of this, I conclude that, given Don's heart condition, it is probably necessary for Nancy to work, but that neither Don nor Nancy is really comfortable with Nancy's role as a coprovider. Therefore, both of them do things to reduce the discrepancy between their values and their behavior. Don insists that Nancy is not providing but only "helping" and that this is all right because she is, after all, an extension of him. Nancy, for her part, tries to push Don into the male breadwinner role by urging him to take charge of the family accounts and threatening to quit her own job after he has been laid off from his. Using this combination of rationalizations and putdowns, the Williamses continue to function as coproviders even though neither is willing to accept this definition of the situation.

Mike and Cynthia Davis, whose story appeared in the previous chapter, are a second example of a working-class couple who are ambivalent about their coprovider roles. Cynthia went to work because Mike's health forced him to quit a second job. Mike would like her to take a higher-paying job, but she is not anxious to move from her present one. Cynthia told me that she is working because she has to. However, when I asked her husband if he thought Cynthia would be happy at home full-time, he said at first:

> I'm sure she'd be. Right now she understands that it can't be done. Right now in our society, it's becoming more and more difficult for a woman to stay home.

Later in the interview, I asked him if he had noticed any changes in Cynthia after she had started working:

J.C.H.: Did you see any changes in your wife after she went back to work?

M.D.: Yeah, I think she felt better.

J.C.H.: In what way?

M.D.: Two babies hanging on her were getting on her nerves. I know that it was better for her.

J.C.H.: How did that show up?

M.D.: Just in general. Laughing more.

J.C.H.: Now that the kids are older, would it be different for her if she were home full-time?

M.D.: She probably would like more time at home. I don't know if she would really like to quit. She might think that she'd like to quit altogether, but I don't think she would. I think that if she worked five or six hours a day, it would be ideal for her.

Although Mike and Cynthia agree that it is necessary for Cynthia to work, they are inconsistent about whether or not Cynthia really likes working. It seems that Mike would like to think that working is the best thing for Cynthia since it is best for him that she work, whereas Cynthia, especially with her history of heart trouble, might very well benefit by a less exhausting schedule. Cynthia will not say that she wishes Mike would make more money so that she *could* stay at home. She will, however, resist pressure to take a factory job in order to earn a still larger proportion of the family income than she already does.

The ambivalent coproviders are couples who do in fact depend on the wife's salary but feel uncomfortable with this arrangement. The professional husbands are uncomfortable with their wives' ambitions for advancement and the pressure they feel to make up for the family time lost to their wives' work. They fear becoming dependent on their wives' salaries because they have not accepted the idea that their wives will always work, and they wonder how their families would manage on one income.

The two blue-collar husbands are not as worried about what would happen if their wives quit, because they know that realistically it is not possible for them to manage without a second income and that, whatever they may say, their wives do not really have this option. However, they make sure that the interviewer undestands that this arrangement is not ideal, and their wives second this opinion by expressing their own hesitancies about accepting as much financial responsibility as they have. In all four cases, the responsibility of providing is acknowledged as "really the man's job," but, for one reason or another, the wife is now doing a substantial part of it.

Summary

In Tables 4.2 to 4.4, I have summarized the relationships between husband's occupation, wage ratio, and provider role definition. From Table 4.2 it is clear that secondary-provider wives make a smaller proportion of the family income, whereas coprovider wives make more and that some ambivalent co-providers make a larger share of the family income than do some wives in either of the other two categories. Wage ratio, therefore, affects but does not solely determine provider role definitions.

In Table 4.3 the reader can see that there is some association between husband's occupational prestige and the wife's provider role. Of eight professional, managerial, or sales workers, only two have clearly defined their wives as coproviders, whereas two others are ambivalent. Yet, of the eight factory or service workers, four agree that their wives are coproviders and two are ambivalent. Factory workers were somewhat more likely than were professionals to recognize their wives as co-providers. This relationship becomes clearer when we substitute the husband's orientation to work for occupational prestige. In Table 4.4, we see that with one exception, all job-oriented husbands become co-providers, ambivalent or otherwise.

Not all co-providing husbands, though, were job oriented at the time their wives returned to work. Peter Marx was a career-oriented clerical

TABLE 4.2 Provider Role Definition by Proportion of Family Income Earned by Wife

Wage Ratio	Wife's Provider Role			
	Secondary	Ambivalent	Coprovider	Total
Under 33%	6	1	1	8
33% +	0	3	5	8
Total	6	4	6	16

TABLE 4.3 Provider Role Definition by Husband's Occupational Prestige

Husband's Occupation	Wife's Provider Role			
	Secondary	Ambivalent	Coprovider	Total
Professional, managerial, or sales	4	2	2	8
Factory worker, service	2	2	4	8
Total	6	4	6	16

TABLE 4.4 Provider Role Definition by Husband's Orientation to Work

Husband's Occupation	Wife's Provider Role			
	Secondary	Ambivalent	Coprovider	Total
Professional/ career	4	2	1	7
Superprovider	1	1	1	3
Job	1	1	4	6
Total	6	4	6	16

worker working 60 hours a week at an entry-level job when his wife Gisela decided to return to work. When Gisela Marx found that she and Peter saw even less of each other after she began selling cosmetics door to door, she convinced him that they should both quit their jobs and open a family franchise business together. They then became a work-sharing couple and began to create a life-style in which there were very few boundaries between work and family for either of them. Both Peter and Gisela Marx have "career" orientations to their work, but together they have found a kind of work into which they can integrate both each other and the children. On school-day afternoons and Saturday mornings, the whole family is "at the shop."

Bill Anderson is a different kind of exception. When Mary Anderson went back to work, Bill was a superprovider working at two full-time jobs. After Mary had been working for several years, Bill became comfortable enough with their shared provider roles to consider quitting his second job. For Bill Anderson, sharing the coprovider role was inconsistent with being a superprovider. Both Bill Anderson and Peter Marx, then, are exceptions that prove the rule.

Finally it should be noted that the work orientation of the husband does not correlate perfectly with his occupational prestige. David Meyers had a job orientation to a middle-management position, whereas Peter Marx was just as absorbed by his family business as John Devore was by his two clinic jobs. These relationships raise the following questions which will be discussed in more detail in Chapter 7: what is the relationship between social class and role sharing, and to the extent that there is a relationship, what is it about social class that creates the differences observed?

TOWARD A MORE COMPANIONATE MARRIAGE

Although 16 couples experienced at least some shift in the allocation of financial responsibility, other role relationships did not always follow suit. However, if any changes took place at all, a move toward a more companionate marriage was likely to be one of them. Twelve of the sixteen couples experienced at least some increase in the symmetry of their relationships. The types of changes discussed here come under three headings: (1) an increase in two-way communication about events in each other's lives, (2) a decrease in the wife's emotional dependence upon her husband, and (3) the withdrawal of hostess-wives from their husbands' work-related social networks. In addition, since husband-, couple-, and child-centered couples each had different kinds of marital relationships before the wives' return to work, family bond type is used as an intervening variable in the following analysis of changes in marital companionship.

Two-Way Communication

Changes in the symmetry of communication took place on two levels. On the most superficial level, couples found that they had more common ground. Husbands found their wives' conversations about their work places more interesting than the complaints about leaky faucets and plans to buy school clothes for the children that had formerly been part of the dinnertime conversation. Wives commented that they could now listen to their husbands' complaints about work more easily and were more understanding of their spouses' postwork fatigue or the need to go back to the office to finish a project. On a deeper level, couples that had been primarily husband centered prior to the wife's return to work renegotiated old understandings about "who listens to whom about what and when." Wives needed, demanded, and often got more listening time from their husbands, and in some cases husbands who had kept their work lives to themselves began, in exchange, to share more as well.

As we shall see in the following discussion, the extent of change in each couple is conditioned by the strength and symmetry of the bond existing between the husband and wife before the wife's return to work. Couple-centered spouses placed a high emphasis on couple communication and had already established a more or less symmetrical pattern of exchange. Child-centered couples attached little importance to the couple relationship and tended to operate as a "joint management company" whose purpose was to provide for and rear children either with the husband doing the former and the wife the latter or with husband and wife each relating to the children independently and to each other primarily about household matters. Husband-centered marriages are a middle-class phenomenon and are often the result of what has come to be known as the two-person career (Mortimer, et al., 1978; Papanek, 1973). The wife of a man engaged in a two-person career must organize her life around her husband's needs, keeping things running smoothly so that her spouse can devote most of his energy to his work. All husband-centered marriages were, therefore, asymmetrical by definition.

Common Ground

Cathy and Mike Schultz (a secretary and a factory worker) have a child-centered marriage and maintain separate friendship networks, but Cathy's return to work means that, as Cathy says, "we have more to talk about, now, than just children." Theo James and her husband Richard, a machinist, had a more couple-centered relationship than did the Schultzes and shared recreation and friends even before Theo took a job as a secretary for an auto sales company. Nevertheless, Theo also described a change toward a more balanced companionship in her marriage. Before Theo went back to work, she had had difficulty listening to Richard talk about his workday. She remembered:

Before, there was nothing else in my life except those kids. I would be crabby towards him. He would say something that happened to him at work . . . and I didn't care. I didn't want to listen to how his day had gone. And now we usually sit and usually talk over what had happened.

However, now that the Jameses can listen to each other better, Theo thinks of Richard differently:

> Sometimes I think of Richard as not only being my husband, [but] as being a helper and a friend, someone to talk to, where a lot of my friends don't feel that way about their husbands. That's just their husband. . . . But, I can talk to Richard about anything. I guess I'm lucky . . . I don't think I used to be able to . . . maybe I couldn't communicate with him, because he got tired of me nagging. Undoubtedly he did too. When I was home I would just complain and gripe about every little thing.

Regardless of how close the couple had been before the wife returned to work, when wives as well as husbands began to leave home every day, each couple gained some additional common ground. For most of them, this meant not only *more* but also *better* things to talk about at the dinner table.

Joan Collins also had more to talk about with her husband (an engineer) after she began working with computers in her job as a title editor. However, unlike other wives of professionals whom I will describe shortly, Joan was not a hostess for her husband's co-workers. In fact, she refused to socialize with Ted's engineer friends because, according to Ted, she found them "dull." Their marriage resembled the husband-centered relationships of other professional men only in that Joan was expected to prevent the family from interfering with Ted's work and leisure. Otherwise, Joan and Ted talked with each other primarily about household details and the children. However, now that Joan is also working in a large organization, she is more understanding of Ted when he does not want to talk about his work and also more likely to demand listening time from him when she wants to talk about her problems with supervising or co-workers. Joan told me:

> I used to gripe about the job when I didn't like my old boss. I'm really not complaining as much as asking for consolation. Sometimes, I don't even want to talk about work. Ted used to be that way. Now, I understand his not wanting to talk about work.

From Ted's point of view, their conversation is less one-sided than it used to be:

> Joan works with people a lot. With computers. So we talk a lot about that. She's more knowledgeable and the talk is not as one-sided as it used to be. I don't talk about people at work, but Joan likes to do that.

However, although talk is less one-sided and Joan seems happier, Ted sees his wife as being more "on edge." When I asked him what living with her had been like since she took on additional responsibilities in her job as a title editor, he said

> It's different. It tends to be difficult with two people coming home and releasing moods in the environment. Before, the house was really kept up. Things were more relaxed in the home environment, although she wasn't as happy before. It's a fine line. . . . It's hard to compare the two.

Then he added

> It's tough on her too. I help out. I help with cleaning up in the kitchen and help clean house on Saturdays.

Thus, Ted and Joan Collins have a more symmetrical relationship than they once did. This is more satisfying for Joan but not noticeably so for Ted. Even though Joan feels that she is more understanding of him than she once was, her increased demands on him for listening time and help with running the house coupled with a decrease in the time and energy she has available to him do not add up to a plus.

Sharing the Stage: Bob and Anne Dooley

Although child- and couple-centered spouses emphasized their new common ground, husband-centered couples more often described a new balance in the share of attention each spouse demanded from and gave to the other. Before Anne Dooley began her career as a finance analyst for Datan, she had played a major part in her husband's career plans. First she helped him with his CPA practice. Then she worked with him on his dissertation, and, the year before she returned to work, she served as the treasurer for the faculty wives club at his new university. However, when Anne began her own highly demanding job, her focus shifted, and Bob lost his "faculty wife" but gained a colleague. As Bob described it:

> In a positive sense, Anne is meeting new people, developing new relationships, confronting new problems. . . . People she works with are bright and think about other things than the job. She's become a lot more interesting. . . . I suppose that sounds awfully chauvinistic.

Things did not go very well, however, during the summer when Bob was home from the university and doing full-time child care while Anne was working up to 60 hours a week helping her company establish a new data management system. At that point Bob found it difficult to give Anne the extra support she needed while he himself was feeling starved for adult companionship:

During the period that she was working all this overtime, I was feeling very neglected, very neglected, very unloved and I thought that working was one of the shittiest things that people could do . . . and yet at times I would say . . . "that's the way I am, a very goal oriented, very ambitious person, and she's very much the way I am." So at times I would say, "Yeah, you're doing the right thing, this is what you're supposed to be doing," but I wasn't as supportive during that period of overtime as I could have been.

Although Bob Dooley valued his wife's companionship and wanted to be supportive of her, he had trouble giving her more attention when she was giving him less.

Paula and Harold Reade

Whereas Anne Dooley and Joan Collins have each worked themselves into highly demanding managerial positions that do intrude upon their family time and energy, Paula Reade was more careful to limit her work as a secretary to 40 hours a week. She told me, "If I'm in a meeting and it gets to five o'clock, I walk out." Her husband, Harold, in contrast, puts in 50 to 70 hours a week as an engineer doing classified research. He often comes home with a locked briefcase full of work and is never able to completely divorce himself from the laboratory: "There is no way that I've discovered where you can turn a switch," he said.

Furthermore, because Harold's work is classified, he cannot get it off his chest in the same way that some of the other husbands do. However, now that Paula is coming home with stories about her work situation, he thinks that perhaps he is finding more about his own work that he can share:

I have a problem in that most of the work I've been doing in the last nineteen years is classified. You get in the habit of not talking about it at all . . . even the things you could talk about. Now that Paula's coming home from work, this is really the first time that we've talked about work at all. I can talk about people at work, but I can't talk about the problems that really frustrate me . . . but certainly some things I talk about more than I used to.

Although the basis for the Reade's communication has widened, the atmosphere for both conversation and Harold's evening of work is less calm:

People are tired more. She's tired more, but not just her; others are tired. There's more confusion. Evenings are more hectic. . . . There's more confusion, misunderstandings, quarrels between kids. "Oh, I didn't think it was my turn to cook" [mimicking his 11-year-old son], and "If I'm cooking in here, you stay out of the kitchen." There's more friction with people moving around. More room for disagreements.

Even though Paula works at a less demanding job than does Joan Collins or Anne Dooley, she still has found it necessary to change the organization of their family so that, from Harold's point of view, "there is more confusion." Like Ted Collins, Harold Reade finds that his wife's working deprives him of his quiet organized home.

Thus, although the professional men enjoyed expanding the range of topics covered in conversations with their wives and, in general, found their working wives more interesting, they also were subjected to new demands for listening and support from their wives at the same time that they felt themselves losing their own relaxed, ordered home lives. In sum, the symmetry of their relationship increased as the "wife's marriage" improved and the "husband's marriage" became in some ways less satisfying than it once was (cf. Bernard, 1972:15).

Dependency Balance and Social Networks

The very self-enrichment that made wives more interesting also shifted the dependency balance in the wife's favor in at least ten of the sixteen couples. This relationship was most pronounced in those husband- and couple-centered relationships that had placed a high emphasis on companionship and least prominent in child-centered relationships in which husband and wife were already accustomed to going their separate ways.

Bob and Anne Dooley

Bob Dooley, for example, found that not only did he feel neglected when Anne worked overtime but he also began to be jealous of the male attention Anne was getting from her colleagues. At first, as he explained, he felt more dependent on her:

> What happened in our relationship was that when she started to work, I became very dependent on her. But it evolved into me becoming less dependent on her. . . . in a positive way.

Bob went on to explain how he had begun to take care of his own needs better. Now when a button comes off his shirt, he either throws it away or fixes it himself. (He didn't tell me whether it was the button or the shirt he threw away!)

Now that Anne has new male colleagues as well as a peer group of other professional women, she no longer has time for the faculty wives club. She said

A.D.: I'd joined the group before I went back to work. When I was home, I really didn't have anything to talk to them about. Bob's co-workers' wives have small children . . . they talk about that. I also get the feeling that they don't approve of me working. . . . Faculty wives are conscious of the status of being a faculty wife . . . giving teas, being available for your husband socially.

J.C.H.: You're not doing that?

A.D.: No, I like to entertain, but we don't very much.

J.C.H.: So you don't fit the role of faculty wife? Are you still seeing these people occasionally?

A.D.: Yes, occasionally. At parties, we gravitate toward couples whose wives work.

Meanwhile, Bob has gotten to know the men that Anne works with, including one who would rib him by asking "How do you get your socks clean?" (This ended when the man's own wife went back to work.) Bob has lost his "faculty wife," but gained a new social network to support his two-job life-style.

Mike and Cathy Schultz

Mike Schultz, a German-born machinist and in a child-centered marriage, neither had nor wanted a hostess-wife. Before Cathy began her job as a secretary at Datan, Mike's social life consisted of a few men he would drink or play pool with after work. Cathy knew none of their wives and would spend her time talking with neighbors or her mother who lives down the street. She didn't meet other people because her husband didn't want to go out anywhere. When she brought female friends home, he would get angry. Now, however, she demands a lot more from Mike and she does more on her own:

> I was always scared to do something on my own. If he didn't approve, I didn't do it. Now, I'm more aggressive.

Part of being more aggressive for Cathy means that she insists that he take her out:

> Now I say, you take me out or else . . . I worked all day. I want to get out.

She also goes out more with her own friends after work.

Since their relationship was not based on emotional dependence from the start, it was not Cathy's withdrawal that shifted the balance but rather

her new support system outside the marriage and her confidence that she could make it on her own if she had to:

> Before if he said "no," that was it, but now, I guess the assurance I've found is that I can make some money, in case he leaves me. I'm braver.

Tom and Roberta Hutchins

Tom Hutchins, a factory foreman, has always enjoyed a much closer relationship with his wife Roberta than Mike Schultz has with Cathy, but he had been more used to talking than listening and was not very good at putting his feelings into words. Like Cathy Schultz, Roberta, a receiving clerk at Datan, will occasionally use her paycheck as a lever for getting what she wants by suggesting, according to Tom, that she doesn't need him "for financial support or much of anything really." But, because Tom is so deeply attached to his wife, this kind of remark cuts deep. It hurts just as much when she uses the reverse tactic and complains that he doesn't need her and doesn't appreciate her. Either way, Tom is forced into motion. In the following pieces of dialogue, Tom describes two scenes in this battle over the reallocation of attention and recognition:

J.C.H.: Do you talk about your jobs with each other much?

T.H.: Yeah. This has been a slight bone of contention with Roberta because she would like to reiterate the day, "so and so this, and this happened," and I can't relate. I have a tendency to ignore her then. . . . I heard about that one loud and clear, so I decided I better quit ignoring her. . . . The terrible thing is that I want to do the same thing. If she listens to me, great. So I find that I'm not in the right by ignoring her!

Later in the interview as we were talking about his and Roberta's feelings for each other, Tom was not sure that his wife knew how much he cared for and respected her:

> She was having a real down and finally she said something about it. She said, "I feel that you have no real feeling of my worth . . . you don't need me." I hope I didn't come on too strong, but I was sincere, and just let the feelings roll. I told her, "Baby, I love you. I don't want anybody else, I do need you. You're the greatest wife and mother that can be."

It seems to me that Roberta has become sufficiently independent of Tom so that she can make more demands on him, and he, a man who has always put his relationship with his wife above everything else, has responded by doing everything he can to overcome the things in himself that make it hard for him to listen to her after work and hard for him to verbalize his feelings for her.

What was true for Tom and Roberta tended to be true for other couples who also had a strong emphasis on the couple relationship prior to the wife's return to work. They worked at finding time to be together and had a high investment in resolving the differences that emerged with the added strain of a second job. Some tried to smooth over the differences without ever confronting each other, and some had regular battles until the differences became more clear and could be negotiated. However, all couples to whom the marital relationship was central worked to keep it that way in the face of reduced time together and increased stress on them both. Because, in almost all cases, it was the wife who was now giving less emotionally than she had been and demanding more, husbands felt loss, frustration, and challenge in varying amounts.

Summary

Twelve of the sixteen couples developed a more symmetrical companionship as a result of the wife's return to work. Child-centered couples to whom marital companionship had been relatively unimportant before the wife returned to work reported some increased commmunication as a result of having more in common with their spouses. Husband- and couple-centered spouses who had placed greater emphasis on companionship prior to the wife's return generally reported more extensive changes (see Figure 4.1). Husbands in formerly husband-centered marriages described feelings of loss and confusion as their wives gave them less attention while demanding more. Husbands and wives in couple-centered relationships, however, more often described themselves as feeling closer to each other and having better friendships as the result of the wives' return to work. In these cases, husbands who had been unable to listen to wives tried harder to do so, and wives who had difficulty hearing their husbands talk about their work now found it easier to pay attention.

Couples Who Did Not Change

Because the shift toward a more companionate marriage was observed in so many of the couples, it is worth taking a special look at the couples for whom no change was reported or observed. They are the Kings, the Hollings, the Williamses, and the Davises.

Billie and Forrest King

Billie and Forrest King are a child-centered couple who believe strongly that home and family are the wife's primary responsibilities. Billie is working

FIGURE 4.1   Bond Type and Shift toward Companionate Marriage

Bond Type		Extent of Change Reported or Observed	
Child Centered			
King	None		
Anderson		Some	
Schultz		Some	
Collins		Some	
Correlli		Some	
Husband Centered			
Holling	None		
Reade		Some	
Devore			Extensive
Dooley			Extensive
Couple Centered			
Williams	None		
Davis	None		
Mooney		Some	
Hutchins			Extensive
James			Extensive
Marx			Extensive
Meyers			Extensive

only because her family needs her to. In the early years of their marriage, Forrest (a firefighter) was an outsider who spent most of his time with male friends outside the home after he brought home the paycheck. However, according to Billie, since Forrest's religious conversion, he has taken more interest in his family and spends more time at home. Nonetheless, he and Billie do not do things without the children, and they have trouble dealing with conflict. Said Forrest:

> Billie's as hard to communicate with as I am. She's the type person who will keep things bottled inside her and so am I. . . . Number one, her and I are a lot different in our thoughts. She can remember things that I said to her ten years ago or fifteen years ago. I can't. But I don't remember stuff. . . . She's a grudger. It's awful hard for her to say "I'm sorry."

Given the Kings' low emphasis on marital companionship and their inability to resolve conflicts combined with Billie's relatively low work commitment, it is not surprising that they are one of the couples who changed least.

Martin and Bess Holling

In addition to the Kings, the Hollings also had a strong commitment to what Martin described as a traditional division of labor:

The one word that comes to mind is traditionalist. I grew up in a house where my mother didn't work. She played the wife-mother role and figure. For most part of my married life, Bess didn't work and we had a somewhat similar environment. This carried me through the first forty-two years of life. I don't anticipate too much fundamental change at this point.

Furthermore, whatever changes took place happened in Bess's life and not in Martin's. When I asked him to evaluate the effect of Bess's working on his life, he said that it was "minimal." This was, he explained:

Probably because I haven't given her the support she deserves. . . . Basically I think that we've [sic] adjusted to it fairly well. She's made a greater adjustment than I have and I respect her for it.

Martin also hopes that in two years it won't be necessary for Bess to work. What would happen if she didn't quit but continued to move up in her career as she already has done in the past year (having changed from a clerical to supervisory position)? Well, Martin wants her to do what she wants to do and doesn't expect that it will change his life drastically in any case . . . *even if she did become very much career involved.* In that case, they might move to a smaller house, maybe a condominium, now that the kids are gone, and that way Bess could keep up with the housework and still devote herself to her new career. Bess also stressed tradition in explaining their situation, saying that when they were married, the wife was expected to take on all the household responsibilities and so she did. She didn't resent it at all. Perhaps if she had had young children when she returned to work, she might have wanted more help.

I got a slightly different impression, however, when I ran into Bess at the supermarket one day and asked how she was doing with her new job. She replied that it had been hectic. She had been working through lunch hours and until 6:00 pm at night to have time for family emergencies. For example, she had had to be home for the furnace man the other day (her husband works 10 minutes away from the house) and for the last four weeks they had had guests:

B.H.: Oh, Martin loves to have company. Just loves it, but I barely get through cleaning up after one batch before another batch would come, you know.

J.C.H.: He doesn't have to do any of the work?

B.H.: No, he doesn't. He just enjoys them.

It then looked as if Bess was beginning to resent the pressure of her dual role, whether or not she was saying anything to Martin.

Another observation I made is that during the second interview, when it was Bess' turn, Martin wanted to listen. I told him that he had to go away "just like Christie," the dog (indeed, he did seem to be tagging along like a puppy). Later he interrupted the interview to take money from Bess' purse to buy a six-pack, saying he wanted to play Flo and Andy Capp. Martin was used to having Bess' attention when he was home and clearly he did not like being excluded.

The Hollings are a couple committed to a traditional marriage and to making as little change as possible. Given that only one child was still at home when she returned to full-time work, Bess was able to adjust to working without making many additional demands on Martin. However, as she seeks more and more challenging work, she has begun to feel the strain and, although she may not be saying anything to Martin, she is also feeling resentful. It is difficult to tell whether or not this resentment will explode into the kinds of demands other wives learned to make upon their husbands. However, if it does, the Hollings will either have a less husband-centered marriage or no marriage at all.

Don and Nancy Williams

Don (a factory foreman) and Nancy Williams (a switchboard operator) stress companionship and family life in their marriage. They do most things together as a couple or as a family. Much of their social life is centered around the church, neighborhood, and extended family. Nancy's mother lives just down the road, and there are a lot of exchanges between the two households.

Don told me his view of marriage:

> It's got its ups and it's got its downs; got its good points and its bad points. This is something I could never see . . . why women and men never need to get married sometime in their life. If they didn't like it, they could always call it quits. Why wouldn't they want a companion to share their life with them?

Don also describes their marriage as one in which they tease each other a lot, blow up at each other from time to time, but never really iron out differences. Nancy said that when they fight she usually gives in because she doesn't see any point in arguing.

In addition to this teasing companionship, they also seem to have a fair amount of emotional interdependence. When Nancy and Don worked different shifts so that they never saw each other, Don didn't like it at all. While Don was laid off from work, Nancy called him three to four times a day. Don says that she is concerned about his heart condition, which prompted Nancy to work full-time in the first place. However, it also seems that they simply enjoy talking to each other. Thus, Nancy and Don have a high emphasis on companionship and are also emotionally interdependent but do not resolve conflict through confrontation. Furthermore, Don's heart condition complicates the negotiation of demands between them. For example, Don told me that Nancy would like to get things done when she wants them done, but that he has had to take a more relaxed attitude since his illness:

D.W.: There's a lot of times that Nancy . . . I've got problems . . . lot of times when it bothers me . . . my health. I won't let her know anything about it. I just keep it to myself. She bugs me a lot because maybe she thinks maybe I should be doing this and I should be doing that. But she doesn't know how I feel.

J.C.H.: She bugs you to do more things?

D.W.: Yes. Around the house and things like this. But there's times when I'm not up to it, but I don't tell her. I just let her go ahead, because I can take it.

Nancy would also like Don to conform better to the image of male provider. Even though the family did quite well on the combination of his unemployment insurance and her paycheck, she was not comfortable with his being laid off for most of the summer. As the reader may remember, she teases him for not wanting to do the family accounts by prodding: "Ain't you man enough to do it?"

Given the Williams' strong emphasis on companionship throughout their marriage, the reluctance to see conflicts through to the end, Nancy's desire to conform to traditional sex-role expectations, and Don's partial invalid status in the family, there are several possible reasons why there is little evidence of change in their companionship. I think, however, that the two major reasons are: an already high level of companionship prior to Nancy's return and the difficulty of going beyond a certain point in improving the terms of exchange due to their avoidance of conflict and Don's need for special attention as an invalid. Furthermore, Nancy seems to be looking more for support in her wife and mother roles than in her work role and she generally gets this support from Don without making special demands for it.

Cynthia and Mike Davis

Cynthia Davis, discussed at the end of Chapter 3, is similar to Nancy Williams in her desire to protect her dependent status. She is also working primarily because her family needs her to and at least partly because her husband's health does not allow him to work overtime. If they had their choice, both Cynthia Davis and Nancy Williams would be at home more than they are.

Mike Davis, however, did not try as Don Williams did to protect his "provider" image. Instead, he would like to dispense with even more of it than he has. He wants Cynthia to be more independent and complains that she lives vicariously off of him rather than developing more of a social life of her own. Furthermore, although the Davises claim that they have developed the art of confrontation, they also said that they had not had a fight in six years. Certainly, if the resentment Mike expressed about household responsibilities (Chapter 3) is any clue, the Davises do not readily settle differences.

Given these observations, I think that both the Williamses and the Davises are in stalemate situations. In both cases, the wife is forced by circumstances to work outside the home but wants to retain her "protected" status. Nancy Williams pushes her husband to be the bill-payer, hunt for a new job when laid off, and do "masculine" things around the house to help her out, even though he has a heart condition. Cynthia Davis retreats behind the four walls of her house and stays in a low-paying job. Unlike the other women in the study, neither of these women embraced the independence that working can bring, and therefore neither initiated the exchange that would have increased the flow of communication between themselves and their husbands. In addition, both are acting to protect the health of their husbands on whom both are emotionally dependent, and this further complicates things. The men's health problems make the men more dependent on the women, and the women reject this new imbalance by trying to retain other kinds of dependencies.

Conclusion

Of the four couples who made no noticeable change toward a more companionate marriage, two had what could be described as "traditional" role attachment, and all could be described as conflict avoiders. Furthermore, in two couples, dependent wives were trying to preserve their dependence while also protecting their husbands' health and are therefore in a double-bind situation. If any of the couples do change in the future, I predict that it will be the Hollings because theirs is the marriage in which the dependency balance is most likely to be upset, and as we have seen in the other examples discussed in this section, a change in dependency balance was one of the major impetuses toward a more symmetrical companionship.

BECOMING COPARENTS

After the wives returned to work, it was almost as common for husbands to become more involved with their children as it was for them to develop a more balanced companionship with their wives. Although increased parenting by the father was usually matched by some decrease in parenting given by the mother, this discussion focuses on responsibilities added by the father. Whereas mothers changed their behavior simply by not being around when the children were getting ready for school or when they needed to be chauffeured to the YMCA, some fathers changed from occasional playmates and irregular babysitters to coparents who shared the daily responsibility for their childrens' overall well-being. Other fathers became regular babysitters who gave daily custodial care during specified hours while their wives worked but returned to the playmate role as soon as their wives came home. In this analysis, I have divided the fathers into three categories: (1) those who showed no evidence of change, (2) those who helped more with child care but did not assume much additional responsibility for parenting in general, and (3) those who had begun to share responsibility for meeting a wide range of their childrens' needs.

No Change

The four husbands who made no changes in relationships with their children after their wives returned to work were all fathers of teenagers at the time. When asked about child rearing, they spoke of feeling "left out," and expressed regrets that they had not spent more time with their children and/or anger that they now had so little control over their adolescent offspring. Bill Anderson, John Devore, Joe Correlli, and Martin Holling each expressed feelings of this sort.

Although Mary Anderson said that her husband Bill "spends more time with the kids than most men do," when I asked him about his relationship with his children, he sighed, shook his head, and said quietly, "That's a bad one. I have done what is me. No sense in saying I would do this and that." When asked if he was satisfied with the time he was spending at home, he said

No, I should be spending twice as much time as I do. Three times. But working two jobs, it's awful hard. It seems like we should spend more time just being a family. You can't work two jobs and sleep and be with people.

Since Bill had told me that he was thinking of leaving his second job, I asked him what he planned to do in the time he would then have free. His first answer was "hobbies."

My first interpretation of Bill's answer was that he was a man who escaped from his family into his hobbies. I was, therefore, very grateful to Mary Anderson for her comments on an earlier version of this manuscript. In December 1982, nearly two years had passed since Bill's sudden death[2] and Mary found it difficult to remember things as they had been in 1976. However, she wrote

> In your book, I was surprised to find that you felt that these were only Bill's hobbies. We all worked and restored engines [and] the truck. I refinished furniture after Bill repaired it. Bill never gave up his second job because he was able to take the boys to work with him and he felt that it was good training. But he did come to a time where the only worked five days a week.

Bill's hobbies were, therefore, a way of relating to his family rather than escaping from it. He, however, thought of himself as an absent father nonetheless.

Like Bill Anderson, John Devore was also an absent father during much of his six children's upbringing. Jane Devore will tell you that she raised the children by herself, but the reader may remember that John did act as an educator and "distant overseer" of the childrens' development. He took them places and showed them things but did not get close enough to talk with them about how they were feeling. This is reflected in Jane's description of John at their son Peter's college graduation:

> When he went to Peter's graduation, tears were rolling down his face, he was so proud. But he cannot *show* them that he's proud of them.

John also lost some of his authority over his children due to his alcoholism and will now complain that the twins do not clean their rooms or that his youngest son does not mow the lawn and that he feels powerless to induce his children to do what is left undone.

Joe Correlli also complained to me that his teenage children did not accept his authority. When they were younger he would take them to plays and to the aquarium. He even used to have a blackboard in the kitchen where he would instruct them in arithmetic and spelling. Now he would like his teenage daughter to stay at home more rather than frequent all of the local beer places with her friends. When he asked her why she couldn't stay home and read a book once in awhile, why she had to go out every night, he said that she "got angry and said, 'I go out to get away from you. That's why!'

Although fathers of teenagers often expressed concern about whether they had been strict enough with their children and whether the children would be all right on their own, concern about loss of authority was concentrated among men like John Devore and Joe Correlli, who had restricted their parenting roles to being authority figures and who had not developed a daily pattern of communication with their children. They often regretted this but felt that by the time the children were teenagers it might be too late.

For Martin Holling, the situation was different. In spite of his career as an engineer in industry, Martin had been actively involved with his two boys when they were young. However, when the boys became teenagers, they drifted away from him. As Martin said (also quoted in Chapter 1)

> It was always a joint venture, although Bess was with them more. I always thought that the children had a close relationship with Bess and, until they became teenagers, with me. It's probably a natural phenomenon that teenaged boys develop a communication gap. We can talk about cars and sports, but we don't sit down with each other every night and talk about what we've done during the day. I'm sure you must see that with other father-children relationships. *The mother probably retains the day-to-day communication* . . . [Emphasis mine.] When the kids were growing up, I was active in the PTA, Cub Scouts, and Boy Scouts.

Bess' return to part-time work when the youngest son was 14 did not change the situation, and by the time that Bess was working full-time, the Hollings' older son and daughter were in college and the youngest was finishing high school.

It is difficult to know what would have happened with the Hollings had the children been a few years younger when Bess began full-time work. If the experiences of Richard James, Mike Schultz, Peter Marx, Tom Hutchins, Harold Reade, and Don Williams are any indication, it is likely that Martin Holling might then have continued his involvement with his children through their adolescence.

Secondary Fathers Who "Helped"

All of the men I have just mentioned spent more time with their children after their wives returned to work than they had before, and all had at least one child under 12 years of age at the time. In addition, with the exception of Harold Reade, all of these men worked different shifts than did their wives so that they could be with the children during all or part of the time that their wives were at work. However, although spending more time with the children often led to the fathers' taking a more active interest in their childrens' lives, these fathers still considered themselves to be "secondary" parents. Their wives were still the ones who *really knew* what to do when the children had problems, and their wives were still the ones with the primary responsibility for the children if anything went wrong.

Richard James

When I asked Richard James, a machinist, how he would rank his family roles in order of importance, he said:

> I suppose I would put provider first, companion, and then father. Is that odd?

I then asked him whether or not his involvement with his two boys, ages 6 and 8, had changed since Theo had gone back to work two years before. He told me about how, when he was laid off, he had gone to the parent-teacher conference in Theo's place:

R.J.:   I know when I was laid off, I went to conferences. I wouldn't ever think of going to conference before while I was working. I had the time, so she (Theo) didn't have to arrange anything special, because . . . whatever time that they wanted, I was planning on going.

J.C.H.:   Did you like going?

R.J.:   Yeah. I enjoyed it. I'd say that probably ninety percent of the times it's always the mother that goes to conference. So it was a new experience and something that the teacher doesn't always get. I don't know if I . . . I suppose I'd consider it again. I think maybe she [Theo] would relate more if she went to conference. I don't know if she would grasp more. . . .

J.C.H.:   You don't think you do it as well?

R.J.:   No. I don't think I pay enough attention or something, maybe [a bit sadly] I don't know. Maybe she would get what needs to be done faster.

J.C.H.:   It sounds like you're saying that you think she's better at being a parent than you are?

R.J.:   Yeah. I think she is [no hesitancy at all].

J.C.H.:   Why is that?

R.J.:   I don't know. I just don't think I'm the greatest parent. I don't know why.

Richard James does spend more time with his children as a result of Theo's work. In fact, when he works day shift, he picks them up from school and stays with them every day until Theo gets home from work. But Richard James does not feel more adequate as a parent as a result of his increased contact with his children. He does not play with them much because they are too little to do the kinds of things he enjoys doing. As he said;

> They're still too little. I'm just kind of waiting for them to grow up, so we can do things together. Go hunting with them, play sports.

Like many fathers of small children, Richard James isn't sure that he could do things right and, therefore, defers to his wife on child-rearing matters. When his boys get older, however, he expects to become more involved with them.

Don Williams

When Don Williams' children were young, Don was rarely home because he worked two jobs to support his family of seven. When his children were in school, he was working the second shift and saw little of them during the school year. When I interviewed Don, he had been laid off for part of the spring and most of the summer. This had given him more opportunity to be with his two youngest boys aged 14 and 17:

> Now, whenever you've worked second shift, and I've worked plenty of that, the kids wuld be in school and when I'd get to see my kids would be on Saturday and Sunday. Now my oldest daughter, she was cheerleading and I didn't get a chance to see her cheerleading. I just didn't get a chance to be with my family, and when I got laid off . . . [that's when] I got a chance to be with my boy and to watch him . . . that's done me more good than anything else. I'd rather done that than someone walk up and give me a thousand dollar bill. I need it. I need the money, but to me, being with my two boys this summer and during basketball games and things like that, it's been worth it to me. . . . Myself, I'd rather have been with my kids. Because, like as far as I can see, you have kids, they grow up and they're gone. One time. You can work all your life.

Nancy described the family as close and said that the children will come to both of them with problems but that the boys go to Don with money problems whereas the girls are closer to her. It seems that it was not Nancy's job so much as Don's being laid off that provided the opportunity for Don to attend his son's basketball game. However, if Nancy were not working, Don would not have been as free as he was to remain unemployed all summer and spend time with his children.

In addition to the extra time Don had with his children that summer, he had also been home days for the past year because he had finally gotten enough seniority on his present job to switch to the third shift.[3] He did this so that he could be home while Nancy was working. Even if he was sleeping much of the time, he would be there when the children came home from school and would be around during vacations. If they needed him, they could always wake him up.

Although Nancy describes Don as close to his children and Don himself stresses the importance of being with his children, when asked to rank his family roles, Don put companion first and then had trouble separating "provider" from "father":

> These have got to all work together to do what you've set out to do. And that's to provide for your family, take care of your family.

Thus, for most of the child-rearing years, Don has been more of a provider than a parent. When Nancy went back to work, his children ranged in age from 10 to 17. However, he did not really find more time to spend with them until he was laid off four years later. Although he cares about his children and values his time with them, he has not changed his parenting role as a result of Nancy's work.

Mike Schultz

Whereas Richard James is waiting for his children to get older so that he can play with them and Don Williams had trouble finding time to spend with his adolescent children until the summer he was laid off, Mike Schultz has been spending weekdays alone with his two children ever since his wife Cathy returned to work five years ago. His children were ages 3 and 5 at the time, and Mike worked afternoon and midnight shifts. Then he cared for the youngest child all day long. Now, during the school year, he gets the children up in the morning, feeds them breakfast, and takes them to school. His wife Cathy said that he is good at child care and that he has gotten to know the children better since he has been taking care of them. However, when I asked her how he relates to the children, she said

> He's good. He doesn't spend as much time with them as some other fathers. He doesn't go play baseball. But he cares for them. Gets them dressed, feeds them, . . . watches them.

This seemed somewhat paradoxical. Mike after all was spending whole days with his children while Cathy was working, but Cathy said that he "did not spend as much time with the children as other fathers did." When Mike joined the second interview I had with Cathy, I understood a little better.

Mike told me then that he liked working nights in the summer because it gave him a whole day to go to the beach with the kids. He'd take a nap in the sun while they played. And when he works afternoons, he does projects around the house before he goes to work. If the children are home, they play by themselves and come to him when they need anything. In fact, 7-year-old Terri had told me in the first interview that she would rather be with her mother because her mother played with her, whereas her father was always too busy doing things around the house. "I like you better," she had said to her mother.

Mike Schultz, then, does spend more time with his children as a result of Cathy's return to work, but he spends this time primarily in custodial care. He has also become closer to his children and probably thinks about them more as a result of his increased custodial role. However, Cathy is still the one who thinks about the childrens' overall well-being and development, and until Mike begins to share more of this, he will be more a secondary than a coparent.

Peter Marx

Peter Marx also spends more time with his children than he did previously, but not all of the change can be attributed to Gisela's return to work. Only after Peter and Gisela opened up a family franchise business did Peter begin to have the time and energy to play with his children after dinner and do things with them on weekends. Peter told me that he is more "high strung" when around the children. However, Gisela said that since he changed jobs he has been spending more time with the children and is less nervous and edgy. Because the Marxes now do almost everything as a family, Peter is with his children almost as much of the time as is Gisela. During the workday when both parents are at the shop, Tasha, age 3, goes to a licensed home in the neighborhood and Sheldon, age 8, goes there for lunch and stays there after school. Sometimes on Saturdays, Peter will take the children into the shop with him so that Gisela can get caught up on the housework.

However, even though Peter has been paying his children more attention, Gisela is still the main parent. Gisela spoke of the child-care arrangements in the first person:

> When I first started, I had Tasha in a nursery school and I had a high school girl come here after school and Sheldon would stay with her too, and then she would pick Tasha up from the school, but that turned out to be too much of a hassle, and Tasha hated going to that school. . . . I took her out and put her over there [a licensed home] and she seems to like that a lot better.

In addition, I observed that, although Peter was putting the children to bed while I was interviewing Gisela, this was not usual for him. Every once in awhile Peter would interrupt the interview with a question shouted (in German) from the bathroom or the childrens' bedroom, and once Gisela looked at her watch and announced that it was time that Tasha was in bed. Had the Marxes been sharing child rearing responsibilities as coparents, both would have arranged child care and Peter would probably have put the children to bed without any input from Gisela.

In addition to the secondary fathers discussed in this section, Harold Reade, Tom Hutchins, and Forrest King also said that they were spending more time with their children now that their wives were working. Tom Hutchins, like Don Williams, worked the afternoon shift and so was home during the day when his wife Roberta was at work, and Harold Reade was now picking his 12- and 15-year-old boys up from school and had time to visit with them on the way home. Forrest King is home alone with the children more in the winter when he doesn't work at his second job. However, these men did not change their parenting roles to the extent of becoming coparents. They were not thinking about the children from day to day and making provisions for their activities or listening to feelings. With the possible exception of Don Williams who was making up for lost time, these men were "filling in" for their wives more than they were sharing the responsibility for parenting.

Coparenting

Ted Collins

Of the five men who had begun to share parenting responsibility with their wives, Ted Collins was the father most ambivalent about this. The change had been recent. At the time of the first interview, Joan told me about how she had planned the children's summer schedules so that child-care problems would be at a minimum and each child would have interesting things to do. By the second interview, Joan reported that Ted had planned the summer schedule:

J.C.: I would say our child-care responsibilities are pretty evenly divided. In fact I would give Ted fifty-five percent and me forty-five percent. He really does the hard part as far as planning their free time. Like who's at the "Y" which day.

J.C.H.: Did that come about as a by-product of his being with them in the morning?

J.C.: No . . . just logistically. For example, he goes by the "Y" on the way to work, so it was easy for him to stop by and sign them up and pick up the schedule. . . . But this summer he really did an incredible job. Last year, I really nagged to get it done. I made him sit with me . . . you know, "when are we taking our vacation, etc. How will we plan our summer, because we can't leave the kids unsupervised, etc." *And this year, I sort of woke up one day and he had done it!*

J.C.H.: That's a big change.

J.C.: It was wonderful. I sensed a little resentment, but when it was done, I think he felt really good about it.

J.C.H.: But you didn't tell him to do it or anything?

J.C.: Oh, as a matter of fact, I was subconsciously sort of hoping that it would go away, and I ignored it to the point where it got done. And, you know, he did an *incredible* job.

The process Joan decribed of relinquishing responsibility and waiting until Ted assumed it is probably the major way in which roles are changed without direct negotiation. Ted did not decide that he wanted more responsibility, and Joan did not ask him to take it. However, Ted was very concerned about the children, and he was afraid that the children would not get enough attention. He told me:

T.C.: I try to spend as much time at home as possible. I try not to let work rule my life.

J.C.H.: Do you think you'd be as conscious of spending time at home as you are if Joan were home full-time with the kids?

T.C.: I would not be as conscious. I feel that the kids get somewhat neglected.

J.C.H.: Do you see signs of that?

T.C.: Not now. They are having to act more adult and do things for themselves. Raising kids is the most difficult job to do. You're not trained for it. It's an important job.

J.C.H.: So you think quite a bit about it?

T.C.: Yeah.

Because Ted is so concerned about his children and takes his and Joan's responsibility seriously, he finds himself compelled to pick up what Joan drops, even if he wishes that he did not have to.

Ted does not like having to juggle his work responsibilities on days when the kids are sick and worries about what would happen if there was an overload at work for him at the same time that there was a crisis at home. At such times, he finds himself wishing that Joan would quit her job which is now a salaried managerial position involving weekend business trips.

At the end of the second interview, Joan and Ted talked to me jointly for a few minutes:

> T.C.: [To Joan] We haven't experienced yet what would happen if something critical happened to one of the kids and neither of us could get off work.

> J.C.: My boss, who is vice-president, opted for a career when it was not popular for women to work. She took a lot of criticism from her family. My boss's husband has been very sick. Her kids have had crises, and she takes time off. Other people handle it.

> J.C.H.: So, Joan, you don't have any fear that it will get to the point that you can't handle it?

> J.C.: If I saw that my family needed me and that my marriage was suffering, I would probably quit. I don't perceive that happening.

I suspect that every 1 of the 16 women in the study would say that were there a family crisis, she would quit her job. Joan Collins is no exception. However, given her optimism about the family's ability to cope and her commitment to her career, there is very little that will keep Joan at home. Her statement, then, is more lip service to a value than a prediction of what she would actually do in such a situation. Just as both husband and wife needed to acknowledge the husband as main provider, both also acknowledge the ultimate maternal responsibilities of the woman. They do this in spite of the manner in which they actually live their lives.

David Meyers

In contrast to Ted Collins, David Meyers has *always* put his family before his job as a hospital administrator. He is not sure why and thinks that it might be because of "guilt feelings," but compared to his own father he describes himself as being "probably more concerned with my kids, who they are, where they are, what they are doing." In fact, after Linda went to work, the children would call David at work if they needed something as often as they would call Linda. David's work schedule is more flexible, and he is more likely than Linda to be able to come home early or take time off if he is needed at home.

It is difficult to say how much more David Meyers is doing with his children as a result of Linda's working because he always did a lot even before she returned to work. There was, however, a noticeable change in David's parenting responsibilities from the first to the second interview. During that time, David had to have a back operation and was home convalescing for three months. He had hoped that his extended stay at home would mean more time with Linda. Instead, a month after he got back from the hospital, Linda was asked to work overtime at Datan and began working 60 hours a week. Even though he was supposed to be convalescing, David found himself taking over all of the chauffeuring for the children, aged 11 to 15, and was responsible for all the day-to-day discipline as well. As he told Linda and me during the second interview;

> D.M.: [To Linda] Now [end of May] you're working fifty hours, and I had a back operation in November. I was convalescing for about three months. And that didn't work out the way we had anticipated it would work out. We, or I, anticipated that she would go to a four-day workweek, and we'd have a lot of time together, Friday, Saturday and Sunday. I was mobile, could still drive, but had a thirty-pound cast on. . . . My expectations were that it would be good to get away from work. Be good to spend time with the kids. But I was stuck with all the free time and Linda's time vanished. . . . The overtime started about Christmas time. I had to pick up all the discipline, the driving. There was no way she could have done that. I don't like to cook a lot either. Do grocery shopping. I was supposed to be convalescing, but I was stuck with all these tasks.

Picking up all the discipline for David meant that he had to be the "hatchet man":

> I had to be the hatchet man because when Linda was around, the kids cherished her time.

This meant that David found himself playing the role that most women play. He was nagging the children to get their chores done and making sure they told him where they were going when they left the house. He was always available, and, therefore, he was "no one special." Linda, on the other hand, was someone special because she was rarely home. Perhaps, if I had interviewed the Meyers before Linda began working, I would have found the roles reversed.

David Meyers had always been involved with his children, but he was not used to being the primary care giver or household manager every day. They had shared the driving and discipline while Linda was working, but before Linda went back to work, she was primary care giver. Each of her three children has had household chores since the age of 4, and it was she who trained them. David was not used to seeing that the children get their tasks done precisely because Linda had always done this. Keeping after teenagers until they do their jobs is not much fun, but David was still doing that in May when I interviewed him, even though Linda had cut back her overtime and he had returned to work.

I would say that a major change in the Meyers' parental roles came as a result of Linda's working overtime while David was home. However, David's predisposition to accept parental responsibility (his guilt, as he put it) and the gradual increase in sharing that followed Linda's return to work prepared the ground for David's new role as household supervisor. Since David doesn't like being the hatchet man, I suspect that he and Linda may work out a more equal sharing of that role after awhile, but nonetheless David will still have added more responsibility than he previously had.

James Mooney

Whereas David Meyers is unhappy about being responsible for all the daily discipline and Ted Collins is worried about possible conflicts between his and Joan's work and the children's needs, James Mooney has also become a coparent but would have it no other way. Jill and James Mooney, a clerk and diemaker, respectively, have worked out what is probably the most equal sharing of child-rearing responsibilities that exists in any of the 16 families. This arrangement evolved gradually and is an example of how a father doing custodial care may eventually develop a parent role that is qualitatively different from the one he had before his wife returned to work.

Jill Mooney returned to work when her two boys were 2 and 4. Her oldest son Chuck was hyperactive, and the combination of the two small children made her so nervous that she developed eczema:

> A nervous reaction. . . . Me and children we get along when they're older, but babies?

She, therefore, returned to work on doctor's orders. Since James was working afternoon shift, she saw no problem in leaving the children with him while she worked from 7:00 am to 3:30 pm at a telephone company. They could get a baby sitter for the hour between the time James went to work at 3:00 pm and the time she returned at 4:00 pm.

Jill remembered the first months of this arrangement as difficult ones. James was even less used to small children than she and had been in the habit of retreating to the basement to his model trains when at home. When Jill started work, he was with the boys from the time they got up in the morning until the time he left for work five days a week. He was with them for more of their waking hours than their mother who took over at 4:00 pm until bedtime. Jill told me that at first her husband would call her at work several times a day to complain that the children had gotten into his trains, spilled milk on the couch, had fallen and banged their knees, etc.

> I finally said, "If you're going to complain about them, why don't I just quit work and stay home. I can't concentrate on my work and have you call me and bother me at work." And we used to have quite a few arguments about that. . . . I'd say, "If you want me to work, then don't complain to me."

When I interviewed James five years later, he had just gotten back from a picnic lunch with Jill and the boys at her job and had an appointment to take Chuck to the doctor at 2:00 pm so that he could be back by 3:00 pm to let the baby sitter in before he left for work. During the interview, he dealt with the children's interruptions calmly, giving them enough attention to satisfy them but still letting them know that he was not available for extended periods of time. I felt that of the two parents, he was more at ease with the children. When I asked him if he could imagine how it would have been if Jill had not returned to work when she did, he is the husband who said

> Yeah, I see situations like that, where the wife doesn't work. It seems like the wife is "the parent." The father is always working. Whereas the situation we have . . . I never really thought . . . it might just be the way the situation was out of necessity. . . . I was brought closer to my kids.

In other words, although neither Jill nor James had planned it that way, James had become a coparent because he happened to be working afternoon shifts and was available to do child care when Jill returned to work.

Now James is giving his children much more than custodial care. As he described it:

> Some days you feel like knocking their heads together. I think it's good, though. I'm thinking that later in life, when I get older, they'll be closer with me. And I like to be close to my kids. I think there's too many kids that are on their own nowadays. And when they get older, they get in trouble and the parents can't figure out why . . . and I figure it's because the parents weren't there when the kids needed them. Now, when they're young and everything, you should be developing their life. . . .

And "developing their life" is a responsibility that James takes very seriously to the point that in the past year he has been going to PTA conferences by himself, allowing *Jill* to remain at work. This, he explains, is very different from his own childhood:

When I was coming up, the only time there was shown interest was when I brought my report card home. I figure that is kind of late to show interest. . . . It should be right then, when he's doing it.

Through the force of circumstances, James Mooney has stepped out of the "distant father" role he learned from his own upbringing and has learned to be there for his two boys whenever they need him.

In addition to the families just discussed, I also considered the Dooleys and the Davises to be sharing child-rearing responsibilities as a result of the wife's return to work. Because the Dooleys' experiences are somewhat similar to the Collinses' and because I have already discussed the Davises in detail in Chapter 3, I have not included their stories in this chapter. However, Bob Dooley has been getting the children up, dressed, and off to school each morning since Anne began working. In addition, the Dooleys' reluctance to use baby sitters meant that Bob had virtually all the responsibility for the children and the house while Anne was working overtime in the summer. The Davises did use baby sitters and help from grandmothers, but nonetheless Mike Davis has become a coparent not only for his own children, but also, if we are to believe his accounts, for many of the children in the neighborhood as well (see Chapter 3).

Summary

What is it about James Mooney, Ted Collins, and David Meyers or about their situations that led to their sharing parental responsibilities more equally with their wives than either Mike Schultz or Martin Holling? Comparing the three categories of men, a few patterns emerge:

1. Those who share roles all had wives return to work when children were still young. Those who experienced no change at all had some teenage children at home whereas those having some change varied (see Table 4.5). Therefore, having young children at home at the time of the wife's return to work may be a necessary but not sufficient condition for changing the father's parental involvement.
2. In all cases in which the couple ended up sharing parental roles, the father's taking on responsibility was preceded by the mother's relinquishing it, as seen in the Collins, Meyers, and Mooney families. Therefore, it may be that the relinquishment of maternal responsibility is both a necessary and sufficient condition for the taking on of paternal responsibility. To test this we need to know whether mothers relinquished responsibility in other families without fathers assuming it.
3. Husbands who began to share parenting responsibilities were able to arrange their work or curtail their work responsibilities to allow themselves more time with their children. Therefore, the organization and scheduling of the husband's work may be a constraint on how much he can participate in child care.[4]

4. Husbands who shared child care placed their family responsibilities in a high priority compared to work, so that given a conflict between the two, family might be chosen. Husbands who did not share at all were superproviders who saw their paternal role as that of provider and "life planner." Therefore, a man's orientation to his work and work/family priorities may affect the probability that he will become a coparent after his wife returns to work.

TABLE 4.5 Change in Husband's Parenting Role by Age of Children at Time Wife Returned to Work

Age of Children	Change in Husband's Parenting Role			
	No Change	Helps More	Shares	Total
All under 12	0	3	5	8
One or more over 12	4	4	0	8
Total	4	7	5	16

These relationships raise several questions that will be explored further in Chapters 5 and 7. How does the age of the children at the time a wife returns to work affect the probability of parental sharing? Is role relinquishment a necessary concomitant of role sharing? How do standards of parenting affect work/family priorities and the eventual division of parenting responsibilities? Are upper-middle-class men more or less likely than are lower-middle-class men to become coparents?

For the moment, let me simply note that when describing changes in any of the three roles discussed so far (providing, companionship, and parenting), I have distinguished among (1) couples who made little or no change, (2) couples who made some changes but were not sharing roles by the time of the second interview, and (3) couples who were sharing a wide range of the responsibilities associated with a given role. Now, having described the areas in which most change took place, I turn to the one least affected by a wife's return to work: housework.

WHOSE HOUSE IS IT?

Of all areas, housekeeping was the one least likely to change. In only 2 families did husband and wife work out shared responsibilities, whereas in

11 families the wife either organized her whole family to help with the housework, with the husband helping less and the children more, or got help from her husband in specific areas. In three families, there was little or no change. The wife retained all responsibility for the management of the house.

No Change

The Hollings, Correllis, and Devores showed little or no change in the division of household labor. The reader may remember that none of these families had changes in parental roles either. Furthermore, whereas the Correllis and Devores reported changes in the symmetry of their relationship, the Hollings did not, and all three of these wives were considered secondary providers. In addition, all three wives returned to work late in their lives (ages 43–46) when their youngest children were 12 or older. All three husbands are professionals with high work commitment and a belief that household work is primarily their wife's responsibility.

In Chapter 3, I discussed Jane Devore's struggle with her husband John to get him to take responsibility for the yard. She thought that he had agreed to assume this responsibility if they moved to a larger house. When he did nothing, Jane resented it. John feels that the children should do more in the house than they do but steadfastly refuses to do anything himself. About the lawn, he remembered telling Jane, "I'm not going to do that and I don't intend to do that."

John told me that he never did housework as a child, not even the lawn, but that he had bought a popcorn stand at age 11 and "worked all day and into the night." His own children, in contrast, can cook and prepare their own breakfasts. His son washes the car and cuts the lawn, but the teenage daughters "can't even keep their rooms clean." He thinks that Jane should get after them more. Jane, however, has worked hard at training her children to do things for themselves, precisely because she does not want them to be like their father in this regard. She has developed her own way of relinquishing responsibility for their things and environments. Meanwhile, the Devores hire help, or rather Jane does, as it remains her responsibility to find the housekeepers and the gardeners.

Whereas Jane Devore resents her unequal share of responsibility, Bess Holling and Maria Correlli have never thought of asking their husbands to do more. Martin Holling does the yard work and will help with the dishes, grocery shopping, and cleaning once in awhile. When I asked him if there were any kinds of things he now did around the house that he didn't used to do, he said

> Yeah, but it hasn't made a fundamental difference. I'll help with some cleaning. The dishwasher and fixing dinner have always been ladies' work and that's continued to be.

When I asked Bess whether or not she *wanted* more help, she said that she really wouldn't feel too comfortable with Martin in the kitchen:

> If he ever took a notion to cook, it might be kind of a nuisnace. Now when my older son is here, he does cook, and I try to get completely out of the kitchen. If Martin was at all interested in cooking, that's the way I'd have to do it too. . . . It's hard for two people to cook in the kitchen at the same time. It works out better. Either this is your meal, or this is my meal. Doing it together does get kind of sticky.

As the following dialogue suggests, she has done everything so long that it just seems too hard to change:

J.C.H.: Have any things changed in terms of division of labor?

B.H.: No, not really.

J.C.H.: You are still basically doing it all?

B.H.: Yeah. Yes. Basically.

J.C.H.: Do you have any feelings about that?

B.H.: It's pretty hard at this point since I didn't work for so long, and I did do everything, and I really never felt that those things were for him to do. After you have done things like that for many years, it's pretty hard to say, "Look, you've got to do this or that."

When Bess compares herself and Martin to young couples who share household work more, she admires them but feels that when she married it was accepted that the wife should do everything and so she did. However, she thought that if she had had young children when she went to work things might have been different:

> It was accepted that the wife did these things. So I've come to accept them, and [now] I don't have the responsibility of the children. If I was working and had small children at home, then there might be more pressure brought to bear on Martin. Most of the time, there's just the two of us. Once in a while I would like a little more help. I don't resent doing these things.

Although Bess would sometimes like more help, most of the time the pressure is not so great that she demands it. However, as I mentioned earlier, when she has guests and a lot of pressure at work, she does begin to express, at least to other people, some of that resentment that she denied in the interview.

Maria Correlli echoes Bess on this topic. Her husband does the garage, lawn, and garden and "when I tell him to, he'll vacuum or mop or dust and he has his job in the kitchen too, on his week." However, she wouldn't think of asking him to do any more than this:

> I don't know. I just wouldn't feel it was right. Maybe if the kids were younger, I'd feel differently. . . . Well, *if they were younger, I wouldn't be working.*

I asked her to imagine circumstances in which she would expect Joe to do more, and she said that if he were alone in the house (for example, if she were in the hospital and the children weren't home) or if he were not doing anything outside of the family: "Then I'd feel it was his place. It would be his place to help." She remembers that when they were both working before they had children they shared housework more equally, but after the children came she didn't expect it: "I thought it was pretty nice when he did do it, though."

Whereas John Devore won't do anything inside or outside the house other than plan interior decorating, Martin Holling and Joe Correlli will help when asked and are responsible for some of the traditional "male" outdoor tasks. The children do more than the husbands in all cases and may be doing more now that their mothers are working (cf. Hoffman, 1958; Model, 1982). Maria Correlli mentioned that the children are expected to clean their rooms, and the girls now do their own laundry. Since she started working, she has insisted on it:

> I told them. I'm not going to touch a thing of yours. I found a big carton. . . . I was so proud of myself. I put the carton in the basement, put all their dirty clothes in the carton and then said, "if you want some clean clothes, you know what to do.

Before, she used to back down and wash things for them. However, she does do her son's wash, along with her husband's. One day she stayed home from work just to get caught up on the housework.

A case could be made for including Jane Devore and Maria Correlli along with the women who reorganized their families to do more of the work, because both did do this to some extent. However, I see these changes as minimal compared to the others we will discuss and consider the help they get from their husbands as token. Furthermore, it is not clear how much of their urging children to do things is something they were doing all along (Jane Devore trained her children from the start) and how much additional pressure they put on the children when they started to work (as in the example of Maria Correlli and her daughter's laundry). In addition, all three women either have husbands who are strongly opposed to doing household work or are themselves opposed to having their husbands do it, or both. Neither Bess Holling or Maria Correlli can "let go" of their household responsibilities enough to test their husbands' willingness to change. As with parenting, the relinquishment of responsibility is a necessary precondition to getting someone else to take it on.

Reorganizing the Family

Both Billie King and Mary Anderson have organized their families of four and six children, aged 6 to 20, into a household work corps with the major responsibility for overseeing younger siblings, cooking, and housecleaning falling on the eldest daughter.

The Kings

Forrest King described the system in his house:

J.C.H.: How is your life changed when she's working?

F.K.: I don't think it's really changed that . . . well, it has changed some. I think we all pitch in and help a little more. In the wintertime, there's a couple of months right up until Christmas when I don't do too much work, and when I'm home, I try to keep the laundry up, and I try to keep the dishes done, I try to have supper on the table when she gets home from work. When she was working over there [her former job ten miles from home], supper was ready when she came home. A lot of men don't do it.

J.C.H.: Who sees to it that the kids get things done?

F.K.: Either one of us. If her and I are working, notes are left, "You've got this and this and this to do today."

J.C.H.: Who leaves the notes usually?

F.K.: Billie does because she can write better than I can and it's more legible. In fact, she generally delegates what has to be done around the house because she knows more of what should be done in the house. . . . We've kind of separated. . . . For a long time we separated; my area was outside. I made sure that the lawn was kept and the garage was clean. I work in the garage. That's my place. If I have something that I want the boys to do outside, I say, "This is what's got to be done today. While you're writing, write this down. Tell the boys they have to clean out the garage, or whatever." I told them the other day the boat had to be washed out, and they did that.

Thus, although Forrest does help, his major contribution is limited to periods when he is not working at either his full-time job as a firefighter or his part-time jobs, repairing machines. He is not opposed to doing work inside the house, but he and Billie have established the inside/outside distinction that many couples follow; the boys help with outside work and the girls do inside work. Both Billie and Forrest are strongly committed to the idea of children doing household work, and Billie will make them clean a bathroom several times until it is good enough, especially if she thinks they have not put enough effort into their jobs.

Although all of Billie's children (with the exception of the 6-year-old) are expected to work, the oldest, a 16-year-old daughter, carried most of the burden. Billie describes Mary's responsibilities:

> She's responsible for the whole upstairs: to keep the upstairs clean, keep kitchen, have supper ready when I get home, keep the bathrooms clean, all this sort of thing.

Mary also usually does the laundry, whereas her younger brothers take dried clothes off the lines and fold them. Billie began training her children to do all this when they moved to their new house, figuring "I might as well prepare them for when I might have to go to work."

The Andersons

Relying on teenage children to do housework was most likely when these children were either female or under 16 or both. Male teenagers were quite often working outside the home. In Mary Anderson's family all the boys including the 11-year-old had summer jobs:

J.C.H.: What are the kids doing in the summer?

M.A.: The boys [aged 16 to 21] all work. They all have jobs. Mark [11] works for my mother and my uncle and that keeps him busy. Marianne [13] and Linda [16, a twin] keep the house cleaned up. Linda would kind of like to get a job, but I told her no big rush. . . . She'll have time to work when she gets out [of school]. She isn't that keen about working anyway.

At this point Mary is really dependent on Linda to keep the house going. Mary's husband, Bill, will cook occasionally but until recently has been working two jobs. He has never gotten in the habit of sharing housework other than repairs, and Mary often ends up doing even these. I got the impression, as Mary was telling me about discouraging Linda from getting a job, that Mary needed Linda at home more than she was willing to admit.

The Collinses

The Collins family has evolved a slightly different system than either the Kings or the Andersons. Joan, like Billie and Mary, is still the organizer of household maintenance, but now the whole family works from 9:00 am until noon on Saturdays until everything is done. This system came about after the Collinses had decided to let their housekeeper go because it wasn't working out for them. Then, during Christmas vacation when both Ted and the three children, aged 9 to 11, were home for two weeks while Joan was working, the house got out of control. Joan described the following scene:

> And during that time when they were all sort of mumbling around the house together, things got pretty rotten. So, when I came home from work I was really a beast. I just did one of my "Nothing-makes-me-happy — Grr — I'm-really-crabby-and-mean-and-ugly-and-what-are-we-going-to-do [routines]." And they all ran around and scurried like crazy and in about two hours, they had everything spotless. And so, at dinner time, we were able to laugh a little. . . . I didn't laugh very much . . . about how easy it was when everybody worked, so we gradually started assigning specific things.

Joan still does the meal planning and grocery shopping whereas Ted takes care of the cars and the garden. However, by the second interview, Joan was bragging that she had had a flat tire fixed and had done some of the spring planting.[5] Because it has become Joan's job to clean the floor, neither Ted nor the children will clean floors on their own initiative. Nonetheless, Joan thinks that Ted is a better housekeeper than she is because "if he finds something in his hand he will think, 'Now where does this go?' and he will put it there." Somehow, even though each person is doing what she/he does best, Joan has ended up with the responsibility for the floors, whereas Ted, "a better housekeeper," waits to be told what to do.

Whereas Joan was ambivalent about how equally responsibilities were divided, Ted was very clear:

> I think I do my share. I still feel that she has certain responsibilities to the home. I don't feel for instance, that I should have to cook the meals. But there are a lot of things I'll help her with. When it comes down to whose responsibility it is for some of those things, I feel that it's hers. . . . This equality thing goes only so far. Everybody has to have responsibilities that are theirs.

I think that the difference between Ted and Joan's responses is in part due to Joan's commitment to a vague principle of equality that Ted does not share and in part the result of a certain amount of "residual territoriality" on Joan's part. Just as Bess Holling finds it difficult to yield her kitchen to her oldest son, Joan Collins has trouble giving up her house. For example, Joan got rid of a housekeeper because the woman did not do things according to Joan's standards; and in Joan's words, "what she didn't break, she ate." Joan prefers to have her family assist because, at least that way, the process remains under her control.

Thus, the Collins family's division of responsibilities is still sex typed to a large extent, but more work is delegated than was previously the case. However, Joan does not perceive it in those terms. She told me

> It has worked out not so much that this is my job and this is his job, but it has worked out mainly [to] what he does best and what I do best. He doesn't like to grocery shop. He hates it, and I don't mind it. It's sort of a time when I'm off by myself and I can mumble to myself and I don't mind it. . . . So some things have just gotten to be his job and [some things] my job.

This pattern of the wife delegating more work to other family members was the most common but varied as to the relative contributions of husbands, children, and/or outside help.

Sharing the Housework

Very few couples actually shared household responsibilities equally. It was much more common for husbands to assume one or two additional responsibilities such as doing the shopping, the laundry, or the cooking than it was for the couple to have joint responsibility for all household work. In only 2 of the 16 families could I really say that the house was no longer "the wife's." These two families, the Meyers and the Dooleys, have wrestled with the problem for awhile.

I have already described how David Meyers has come to be the one in charge of getting the children to do their share. Before Linda went to work, however, David did many of the outside errands, including grocery shopping. Now Linda is taking over more of that and David is doing more in the house. Linda still does most of the cooking, including special breakfasts for her children in the morning (she does this, she says, because she feels guilty). David describes himself as compulsively responsible:

> I have a great compulsion to do everything. I can't give activities up.

Thus, when Linda went to work, she began to force him to give up some of the control he had over their lives. For Linda, this involved taking on more, rather than less, responsibility for household management.

The Dooleys started with Anne doing everything and then finally hiring a housekeeper. But the housekeeper didn't work out and then Bob and Anne began taking turns doing the housework. They don't have an agreement about this but seemed to take turns leaving it for the other to do. Both Bob and Anne agreed that they have no explicit agreement but they differed in their description of what happens. Although Anne stressed that they now split the shopping and both clean on weekends, Bob described his doing all the housework for a while, then shopping until Anne picked it up. Anne also said that the burden of housecleaning shifted back and forth depending upon each person's work pressures. During Bob's end-of-the-term rush, Anne did more of the housecleaning. While Anne was working overtime, Bob was doing almost all the household chores and child care. Now they are once more looking for a housekeeper, as neither likes to do housework and both would rather spend their weekends enjoying each other and the children.

Summary

In general, the families in this study observed a "double standard" when it came to housework. Although all of the women were working full-time, most husbands took on added *responsibility* in the home only when they themselves were laid off or unemployed. Furthermore, wives generally expressed the opinion that their husbands helped them enough and thought that husbands should be expected to do more than they already did only if the husbands were not working at all. Husbands who "helped" with housework were extolled by their wives for doing more than most men do around the house. Thus, it was by no means a norm in these two-job families that the responsibility for housework should be equally shared. Furthermore, in most families household work was divided into inside work done by women and girls, and outside work done by men and boys. When increased role sharing happened, it was usually in the direction of men taking on inside work rather than women doing outside work.

The single most important factor in determining whether or not a husband will take on additional inside work is the age and sex of the oldest children at the time the wife returns to work. The three women who do most of the work themselves went back to work late in their life cycle and had teenagers at home at the time. None had children under 12. Although the children were old enough to help, if they had not been trained to help by the time their mother started working, it was too late. Of the three, only Jane Devore reported training her children as they grew up, but the three children living at home when she returned to work were not a major source of household help.

The two families who received major help from children had children ranging in age from 3 to 15 at the time the wife returned to work and each was able to rely on a teenage daughter to take over household management. Both of these women reported that they had trained their children to help during their at-home years. Families in which the husband as well as the children helped did not have a teenage girl available to take over, whereas those that relied on the husband instead of the children had children too young to be depended upon.

Furthermore, because the amount of inside household work done by husbands has traditionally been minimal, the smallest increase is often gratefully acknowledged by wives as a major gift. As my colleague, Bill Mayrl, puts it "He gets more bargaining chips for what he does than she would get for doing the same thing." Due to this double standard in which expectations of wives' contributions to household work remain higher than those for husbands, it is difficult to judge how equally the work and responsibility is actually being shared without observing the family in action over a period of time and having them keep time-budget diaries. The reader will, therefore, have to judge the accuracy of my categorizations based on the data given to defend them.

SUMMARY AND CONCLUSIONS

In this chapter, I have described changes in provider, companion, parent, and housekeeping roles that were experienced by the 16 couples after the wife began full-time work outside the home. With the exception of Cynthia Davis who returned to work at her husband's urging, wives initiated the changes by their decision to return to work for either family or personal reasons. After the return, the couples struggled with the process of role renegotiation. Was the husband still the main provider or were they coproviders? Who should listen to whom at the end of a day's work? Was the wife still "the parent" or were they coparents or something in between? Was the wife still home-manager in charge of cooking, cleaning, laundry, and shopping? Did the husband still do outside work and repairs, helping with inside tasks only when asked, or had he taken on additional inside responsibilities, making household duties more equal?

Up to this point, I have described the ways in which marital roles changed but have not said much about why the changes happened as they did. In this section, I will summarize in tabular form the relationship between life cycle status at the time the wife returned to work and the sharing of household roles afterward, the relationship between provider role definition and role sharing, and the relationship between changes in companionship and changes in parenting and housekeeping.

The changes described in this chapter are summarized in Figure 4.2. With the exception of the Williamses, Davises, and Kings who change in

FIGURE 4.2 Changes in Marital Roles after Wife's Return to Work

Family		Cumulative Changes			
Holling	No change				
Anderson Correlli Devore		More symmetrical companionship			
King[a] Hutchins James Marx Reade Shultz Williams[a]		Companionship	Husband helps more with children and/or indoor housework		
Collins Davis[a] Mooney		Companionship	Helping	Couple shares parenting	
Dooley Meyers		Companionship	Helping	Parenting	Couple shares housework

[a] No change in companionship observed or reported.

other areas but not in companionship, changes in the symmetry of marital companionship and the division of parenting and housekeeping duties and responsibilities form a Guttman scale with the following steps:

1. No changes
2. Increased symmetry in companionship
3. Husband helps more with children and/or indoor housework
4. Couple shares daily parenting responsibilities
5. Couple shares indoor housework

Thus, if only one change took place, it was an increase on the symmetry of marital companionship, whereas if a couple shared indoor housework, it then followed that they also shared parenting, helped each other more in areas not yet shared, and had a more symmetrical relationship with each other.

In the discussion up to this point, the life cycle stage at which the wife returns to work has been mentioned as one of the most important determinants of role sharing. In Table 4.6, the families have been divided into

TABLE 4.6   Role Sharing by Life Cycle Status

	Number of Cases in Which Husband Helped More with or Began to Share More Responsibility for Parenting and/or Housework after Wife Returned to Work			
Age of Children at Time of Wife's Return to Work	*Husband Did Neither*	*Helped in One or Both*	*Shared One or Both*	*Total*
All children under 12	0	3	5	8
One or more children over 12	4	4	0	8
Total	4	7	5	16

those having all children under 12 at the time of the wife's return to work and those having any children aged 12 or more. Role sharing categories are divided into (1) husband neither helps nor shares additional parental or housekeeping responsibilities (categories 1 and 2), (2) husband helps in one or both (category 3), and (3) husband shares one or both (categories 4 and 5). Here we see that if the children were under 12, all husbands either helped more or shared one or both roles. In families where any children were 12 and over, five husbands did neither, three helped, and none shared.

Earlier in this chapter, I discussed the couples' definitions of provider roles and how these definitions relate to the husband's original orientation to his work. Provider role definition is also related to division of household duties and responsibilities as summarized in Table 4.7. If the wife was defined as a secondary provider, the couple did not share either parenting or housework responsibilities although in two of six cases, the husband helped more with one or both. If the wife was defined as a coprovider (even in an ambivalent fashion), six couples shared housekeeping and/or parenting, and of the four that did not, the husband helped more in three. In only one coproviding couple did the husband not add any more household duties or responsibilities.

Since, as the reader may suspect, life cycle status and provider role definition are related to each other, Table 4.8 shows their separate and combined effects on role sharing. Here we see that seven of eight couples with all children under 12 at the time the wife returned to work became

TABLE 4.7 Role Sharing by Wife's Provider Role Definition

Provider Role Definition	Number of Cases in Which Husband Helped More with or Began to Share More Responsibility for Parenting and/or Housework after Wife Returned to Work			
	Husband Did Neither	Helped in One or Both	Shared One or Both	Total
Wife seen as secondary provider	3	3	0	6
Wife seen as coprovider	1	4	5	10
Total	4	7	5	16

TABLE 4.8 Role Sharing by Wife's Provider Role Definition and Life Cycle Status

	Number of Cases in Which Husband Helped More with or Began to Share More Responsibility for Parenting and/or Housework after Wife Returned to Work			
	Husband Did Neither	Helps More	Shared One or Both	Total
All children under 12				
Coprovider	0	2	5	7
Secondary provider	0	1	0	1
Subtotal	0	3	5	8
Any 12 and over				
Coprovider	1	2	0	3
Secondary provider	3	2	0	5
Subtotal	4	4	0	8
Total	4	7	5	16

coproviders, whereas only three of eight with children over 12 did. This is to be expected because of the confounding of social class, age at which wife returns to work, and husband's orientation to work. In general, wives of blue collar workers returned to work earlier and had husbands with job as opposed to career orientations. However, as we have seen in the Dooley and Collins families, when the wife of a professional man went to work while the children were still young, the couple became ambivalent coproviders, and the husband was forced into role sharing due to a combination of his wife's letting go of responsibilities and the husband's own high standards for parenting and housekeeping. The husband then experienced conflict between his work and family roles that made it difficult for him or his wife to acknowledge the coprovider relationship, which was at the bottom of this conflict. If somehow they could manage on just the husband's salary, and the wife could again become a full-time housewife, then the husband's conflict would be resolved. However, this was not the reality, and as their wives continued to climb the organizational ladder, the husbands took on more and more responsibilities at home in spite of themselves.

In this chapter, I have described how both the proportion of the family income earned by the wife and each spouse's role attachments affect the redefinition of the provider role. Then, after describing the changes that took place in companionship, parenting, and housekeeping roles, I have discussed the interrelationships among all four kinds of role changes and demonstrated that both provider-role definition and the age of the children at the time the wife returned to work help to explain the extent to which husbands will take on additional household responsibilities after the wives return to work. Now, having described *what happened*, I will explain in more detail *how it happened* by reconstructing the bargaining process that led to the outcomes discussed in this chapter.

NOTES

1. The ethnographic present is used throughout. "Now" refers to the time of the second interview. More up-to-date information on the 16 families is included in Chapter 6.

2. He died in February 1981 from malaria contracted in Nigeria while doing work on his second job.

3. Workers are assigned to the second shift first, then to the third and first according to seniority.

4. Robert Clark's (1977) survey of 390 Seattle couples found that fathers' work time did decrease their sharing of child care but had no effect on their wives' perception of their competence as fathers. Pleck and Staines (1982:83) report that husbands who work shifts other than daytime do increase their household work and Presser and Cain (1983) in an analysis of Current Population Survey data report that when wives work in occupations such as nursing and waitressing between 30 and 43% of the fathers are primary caretakers for their children.

5. Joan Collins was the only woman in the study (with the possible exception of Linda Meyers) who made a conscious effort to take over tasks that had formerly been her husband's. In this sense, she is similar to the women in Linda Haas' (1982) of egalitarian marriages who have an ideological commitment to role sharing.

5
THE BARGAIN

When wives return to full-time market work, they and their husbands begin to renegotiate work/family priorities, rights, and duties. How is the wife's income to be defined? If her income is necessary for the family's well-being, should her husband and children do anything to make it possible for her to continue to work? What if her income is not used for family expenses at all? If the wife's work schedule and demands of her work role make it impossible for her to do all of the things she formerly did for the household, which of these things will no longer be done, which will be done by other family members, and which hired out? If a wife becomes so work involved that she relinquishes a lot of her household and parenting responsibilities, what determines whether her husband will assume them himself or demand that she withdraw from her work role so that she can take better care of the family and the house? This chapter draws on material presented in Chapters 1, 3, and 4 to explain how husbands and wives make these decisions.

As we have seen in the previous chapters, the process is a complex one. The definition of provider roles described in Chapter 4 is central to the bargaining process. This definition is influenced by:

1. The nature of the marital relationship.

2. The wife's motivation to work.

3. The wife's work/family priorities.

4. The husband's orientation to his work.

5. The husband's work/family priorities.

6. The husband/wife wage ratio.

By earning the definition of coprovider, a wife gains in status relative to her husband and has more reason to expect him to share household and parenting responsibilities. However, not all husbands are equally likely to relinquish part of their responsibility to provide and not all wives are equally willing to give up their control over the household or their right to be provided for. In addition, couples vary in the extent to which the wife must give up some of her household responsibility due to role overload, as well as in the wife's reasons for working and the proportion of the family income she earns. The more the wife relinquishes household responsibility, the more pressure the husband will feel to take on those parts of it that cannot be overlooked or delegated to other family members or outside help. However, if the wife's income is thought of as extra money on which the family does not really depend, the husband may respond to this pressure by saying, "If you can't take care of the children and the house, then why don't you either quit working or find a less demanding job?" The more the wife's money is seen as essential to the family and the more her self-esteem increases as a result of her work experience, the greater her bargaining power and the more likely she is to be defined as a coprovider rather than a secondary one (cf. Scanzoni, 1978:78)

However, husbands do not have to recognize their wives as coproviders and, in addition, vary in the extent to which they are motivated to accommodate to their wives' desire to work. Some, after all, adopt the position that no matter how much money their wives make, the money is not really necessary and the wife must, therefore, continue to accept the responsibility of housework and child care. The more career oriented the husband, the less he will be willing to relinquish providing responsibilities, because, in doing so, he opens himself to more household demands. However, this need for insulation is tempered by the husband's emotional dependence on his wife and his need to win back some of the attention she has shifted from him and his needs to her new job. Based on the work of Willard Waller (1938) many family sociologists would attribute such a husband's predicament to his being in the "position of most interest." According to Waller, the partner who has *most* need of the other's affections is in the *least powerful* position. Conversely, the partner who can best withstand the other's anger and withdrawal, "waiting out" difficult periods, is in the *most powerful* position. Now in the position of "most interest," some husbands try to become more aware of their wives' needs in an attempt to regain this lost attention. However, at the same time that the husband's social support system is contracting, the wife's is expanding with the addition of new workmates and, in some cases, approving supervisors. To the extent that their work experience contributes to their self-esteem, wives improve their bargaining positions relative to those of their newly deprived husbands.

How wives use their improved bargaining positions depends upon what they want and need from their husbands, i.e., their goals. Some wives do not really want to be coproviders or to become more powerful relative to their husbands. They would prefer that their husbands earn more money and they work mostly because they know that their husbands' health would suffer from any added pressure. These wives do not use their new bargaining power in the same ways as do women who have become committed to their work roles and now want to "buy out" of some of their family responsibilities. Whereas the former allow their husbands to help them, they remain ambivalent about working outside the home and hold onto symbols of the housewife role. The latter use their bargaining power to gain recognition as coproviders and to relieve themselves of the sole responsibility for the home and the children.

Although it is important to remember that not all husbands and wives use their bargaining power in the same ways, in this study most wives did in fact use their new power to try to get more recognition and help from their husbands. Women like Jane Devore, whose families were grown, needed less help and tended to get less, especially if their husbands were as career oriented as was John Devore. If, like Jane, they made only 15% of the family income, they had little hope of being defined as coproviders and had to rely entirely on their new self-confidence as they bargained for a more equal companionship with their husbands. If, like Joan Collins, they had young children, made 42% of the family income, and took weekend business trips, they were more likely both to need help from their husbands and to gain recognition as coproviders, however grudging that recognition might be. On the other hand, some wives such as Jill Mooney soon discovered that their husbands preferred being home with the children to working overtime. These wives found their husbands taking on more and more of the household responsibility, especially child rearing. Although this situation was ideal for a work-oriented woman, it was difficult for a family-oriented woman.

In this chapter, I will argue that the amount of additional household responsibility husbands assume in exchange for their wives' market work is largely determined by the way in which provider roles are redefined. As illustrated in Figure 5.1, the bargaining process proceeds in three stages. In Stage I, after the wife has been working for a while, each spouse begins to form *bargaining goals*. Depending upon her household *role attachments, reasons for working*, and role overload (determined by the age and number of children and amount of housework already done by the husband), the wife decides how much additional help she wants and/or needs. The husband, depending upon his *orientation to work* and his own *work/family priorities* will be either more or less willing to relinquish some of his provider role rights and responsibilities in exchange for assuming more responsibility for child care and housework. In addition, in husband- and couple-centered marriages, the *dependency balance* may swing in the wife's favor as the husband assumes the position of more interest. In Stage II, the bargaining goals (determined in Stage I) and the new balance of power (affected by wage ratio, changes in the wife's self-esteem and the dependency balance) govern the bargaining process which results in a new provider role definition. Then, in Stage III, the balance of power, further changed by the redefinition of provider roles may result in reallocation of parenting and housework responsibilities, depending upon each spouse's bargaining goals at that point.

The main task of this chapter, therefore, will be to trace the bargaining process from the couple's agreement at the time the wife decided to return to work through the renegotiation of the provider role to the reallocation of household responsibilities. However, since the couples' style of conflict resolution affects the bargaining process, the chapter ends with a discussion of marital conflict.

THE ROLE BARGAINING PROCESS DEFINED AND ILLUSTRATED

Definition

A student of mine recently interviewed a woman who had chosen to work throughout the early child-rearing years. However, despite the burden of two small children and a full-time job, she expected no additional help from her husband. "After all," she explained, "I don't *have* to work. I'm just working because I *want* to." Her husband spent quite a bit of time with the children because, as he put it, "With her job and all the housework to do, she doesn't have enough time to spend with them." This example illustrates three important components of role bargaining. First, there is an implied agreement between the husband and wife that unless the wife must work for the survival of the family she does not have the right to *expect help* with her housework. Second, although the housework is *her* work, the children are their joint responsibility. The agreement to rear children is similar to a joint agreement to take out a mortgage on a house. The partners are responsible *jointly and severally* so that if one cannot meet the terms of the agreement, the other is held responsible. This means that when the wife reduces the amount of attention she gives the children, her husband feels impelled to make up the difference. Third, the couple has standards about how much attention children ought to receive from their parents and will not let the total amount of parental attention given fall below a certain level.

I suspect, therefore, that one of the elements lacking in most applications of exchange theory to marital relationships is the recognition that we are dealing not only with *two actors*, a husband and a wife, but also with an entity called *a family* and with two adults who have a joint commitment to maintain it. Thus, although some exchanges are of the form, "If you do this, I will do that," others are of the form, "If you don't do this, then I know I will have to

Figure 5.1   The Role Bargaining Process

Stage I

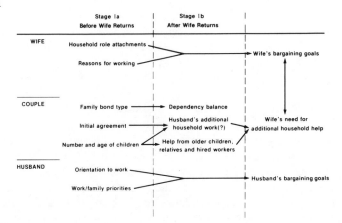

Stage II

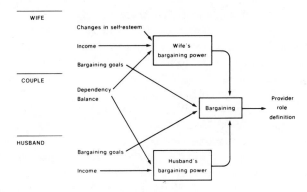

Stage III

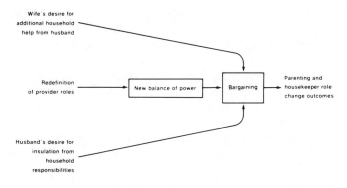

do it." The latter type of exchange begins with a relinquishment of responsibility by one partner and ends with the assumption of that responsibility by the other in order to fulfill a joint obligation.

In his discussion of exchanges between loved ones, Blau says:

> Contributions to the welfare of a loved one are not intended to elicit specific returns in the form of proper extrinsic benefits for each favor done. Instead they serve as expressive symbols of the individual's firm commitment to the relationship and as inducements for the other to make a corresponding commitment and continue the association. (Blau, 1964:35)

I would broaden this to include family welfare and symbols of commitment to the family as a whole. This does not mean that all exchanges within a family are of the altruistic nature described by Blau. In addition to making the more general contributions to each other's welfare, which Blau describes as "symbols of commitment," spouses also exchange goods and services on a *quid pro quo* basis. However, such exchanges are made within a framework of assumptions about how rights and responsibilities are allocated. I cannot bargain to exchange one of my responsibilities for one of yours unless we are both clear about who was responsible for what in the first place. Thus, a husband can offer to do the dishes one night in exchange for his wife's walking the dog only if it is normally his wife's responsibility to do the dishes and his to walk the dog. Whereas in the above example husband and wife would simply be exchanging duties, if they agreed to a permanent change making it the wife's responsibility to walk the dog and the husband's to wash the dishes, then they would have been engaged in role bargaining.

The more egalitarian a marriage is, the more bargaining will take place within it, for, as Blood (1972:425) notes, "Only in egalitarian marriages may concessions from one partner be expected to trigger similar concessions from the other." Sussman (1975:567) goes further to point out that given the present emphasis on equality in marriage, couples must engage in continuous negotiations and renegotiations over the life cycle as needs, interests, and capacities of each spouse change. Although a commitment to equality may force continuous renegotiation over the life cycle, even marriages without this commitment are subject to renegotiation as conditions change. In fact as Strauss (1978:16) and other interactionist theorists would argue, all social order may be viewed as the product of continuous negotiation. In marriages, however, in contrast to more formal negotiation contexts, the contract being renegotiated is often hidden. The more the marriage follows both partners' normative expectations of what marriage is supposed to involve, the less likely it is that the terms of the marital role bargain will have been made explicit. Thus, in the case of a woman who dropped out of college to marry an engineer and raise three children, it may simply be assumed that her job as a wife is to provide what Gowler and Legge (1978:50) call "back up services," while her husband advances in his career. It is only when such hidden contracts are challenged by abrogation that they become explicit. The following case history provides an excellent example of how contracts must be renegotiated when old assumptions are violated.

Ted and Joan Collins: An Illustration

As mentioned in Chapter 3, Ted and Joan Collins owed money to Ted's parents. Joan had been planning to return to the university in the fall, but Ted's parents convinced them that it would make more sense for Joan to earn money to repay the debt than to spend money on tuition. After the debt was repaid, she could quit work and return to school. Although it was clear that Joan was working for the family and not by choice, she and Ted made no agreement about what Ted would do in the house. Her work was, after all, only temporary. Then, as Ted explained in the first interview, what started out as a temporary job with a flexible schedule "kind of grew into this permanent type position." Joan got promotion after promotion and continued working after the family debt was repaid. Three years after starting, she was in an "exempt" managerial status and planning to take weekend business trips, leaving Ted alone with the children.

Ted did not take Joan's growing commitment to her work easily. He was the husband described in Chapter 4 who responded to his wife's high performance rating with "Too bad they don't have a rating for 'bitch,' because you'd get a six on that one, too." He recognizes that Joan is happier at work but does not think that her working makes her any easier to live with and feels that the order of his life has been upset now that "two people are coming home releasing moods in the environment." He is worried that the children are not getting enough attention and purposely cuts back on evening work so that he can given them more. He keeps telling Joan that he hopes they won't regret her working when the children are older, with the implication that if the children turn into juvenile delinquents, it will be because Joan worked when they were younger.

Joan fights back by leaving things undone. She is the wife who left the planning of the children's summer schedule until her husband did it himself, and she is the wife who fed her family sandwiches one night because she wanted to finish a project she had started in the garden. She also is not afraid of open confrontation. The Collins family housework issue came to a head as a result of a temper tantrum Joan had during one vacation.

Because Joan and Ted are both more oriented to the children than they are to each other, and because Joan was never a hostess-wife for Ted's co-workers, Ted did not suffer the loss of companionship that men in previously husband-centered marriages did. However, as she brings her new friends into the family to share with him, his is piqued at her continued opposition to social relationships with his co-workers. As he told me, "Joan says most people from my job are boring." Joan herself is more on edge during the week and blows up more often, making her more difficult for Ted to live with:

J.C.H.:   Can you think of times you've come home from work? What were things like?

T.C.:   Things are O.K. Joan tends to be more on edge. Her job takes up more time, and she doesn't feel like doing housework.

J.C.H.:   Does she get on edge about the house?

T.C.:   Yeah. She gets uptight during the week. Blows up.

J.C.H.   Are you a "blowing up" type person?

T.C.:   I take a long time to wind up. But it takes me quite a while to get to the point that I blow up. Joan's moods are more extreme.

Although Joan is happier now that she is working, she is more tense about housework so that, other than not having to worry about where the money is coming from, Ted doesn't feel that her work makes things any better for him. Since Joan started working, they have moved to a bigger house and have taken more expensive vacations. As Ted said,

> If she were to quit tomorrow, we'd still go on living. But we'd cut down. Right now, we live better... .

> When your salary goes up, your standard of living goes up and it's almost impossible to keep it down.

Ted, therefore, admits that they are now dependent on Joan's salary but wishes they were not. At the time of the second interview, Joan was earning 42% of the total family income ($16,000 to Ted's $22,000) and had opportunity for continuing to earn more. Ted had little prospect of promotion in his organization without moving to another city. When I asked him if Joan's job would prevent him from looking for positions in other cities, he said:

> I wouldn't say it's a prime factor, but it's a consideration. She tells me that she'd move. The company that Joan works for takes care of its employees. Joan works hard. She's a lot happier now that she's working.

Thus, it seems that Joan has gained considerable power in the relationship due to her working. She has earned the right to place demands

THE BARGAIN / 121

on her husband and children and is not afraid to make those demands. She says that when she was not working, she and Ted had a more difficult time resolving issues. There was a lot of anxious talk and rehashing of problems. Now they can zero in on a difficulty and identify nonproblems as nonproblems. I would attribute this to Joan's increased self-confidence and sense of her own power. She now expects to be taken into account and asks more directly for what she needs. This means that more things are negotiated explicitly than was the case before and that consequently more changes are possible in their allocation of responsibilities. Joan and Ted are still fighting over the housework, however. Ted's position (also quoted in Chapter 4) is:

> I still feel that she has certain responsibilities to the home. I don't feel, for instance, that I should have to cook the meals. But there are a lot of things I'll help her with. When it comes down to whose responsibility it is for some of those things, I feel that it's hers. This equality thing goes only so far. Everybody has to have responsibilities that are theirs.

Joan says that she chooses to do the meal planning and the laundry because she does it better than anyone else and that she also does most of the shopping and cleaning. However, when asked which of the two of them do most housework and child care, she thinks that Ted is now doing 55% of the total. Nonetheless, if we are to believe Ted, Joan still has more than half of the responsibility and seems to deal with this by blowing up periodically until Ted or the children relieve her of more of her burden.

Until Ted and Joan resolve the underlying issue of whose responsibility is whose, Ted will continue to feel put upon as he sometimes does and will continue to suggest that Joan is neglecting the children. And, until the Collinses agree on whose work will be sacrificed in the event of a family crisis and what each of them is willing to do to further the other's advancement at work, Ted will continue to feel threatened by Joan's promotions and increased work involvement and will continue to make well-placed comments about how as soon as Joan earns enough, she can support him.

Thus, Ted and Joan have begun the bargaining process and renegotiated some things such as how much help Joan can expect on Saturdays and that Joan will continue working because that is what she needs. They do not, however, have a new contract satisfactory to them both and are still engaged in a sort of subterranean "guerilla warfare" about the strength of Joan's work commitment, whose job comes first, and to whom the housework *really* belongs. Nevertheless, the bargaining process in which they are engaged has many things in common with the pattern of negotiations followed by the fifteen other couples in the study. This pattern will be described in more detail in the remainder of this chapter.

THE BARGAIN

The Prior Agreement

In Chapter 3, I described the context for the wives' decisions to return to work, their motivations for returning and their husbands' first reactions. All of these things helped to shape the first understanding each couple had of what would be expected of each spouse after the wife began full-time work. Women who returned to work because the family needed their incomes for an indefinite period of time, but who themselves might rather stay home, had more bargaining power than women who wanted to go to work and whose families did not really need their earnings at the time. Whereas the former could always threaten to quit when things were not going well, the latter were told by their husbands, "Well, if you can't handle your job and keep up with the house and the children, then why don't you quit?"

Wives who returned to work to help the family for a limited period of time had less bargaining power than those whose incomes were needed indefinitely and were less likely to be recognized as coproviders. Since they were expected to stop working at a predefined time, they were working only to "help out," and, although husbands might themselves be expected to "help out" a little more at home, husbands initially did not expect their lives to change very much as a result of their wives' working.

Although, in general, wives who went back to work only because they wanted to had the least bargaining power, their positions were affected by the nature of family bonds. The more couple centered the family was, the more accommodating the husband would be, regardless of whether or not he thought the wife's income was necessary. Here the husbands' attitudes were like Bob Dooley's:

> I think Anne's happier . . . she's a very bright girl, and has to do something with her head. So, in a way it's better for me if she works. But, I'm basically a chauvinist and would prefer that she not [work], and just live a life of leisure. Kind of shows my status I guess. [That you could support a wife at home?] Yes, yes. And I'm more of a housewife today than I would prefer to be. But, on balance, I say, "All right, that's what she wants."

In husband- and in child-centered families, however, it was more likely to be expected that if the wife wanted to work, that was her choice and it was up to her and her alone to figure out how to fulfill all her household responsibilities as well. As Bill Anderson said:

I'm not crazy about her working and I think that it's just that she would like to work and everything, and if that's what she wants, then O.K., because I know it's hard enough for her to work plus have to take care of the house too.

In families with young children, spouses had to negotiate child care *before* the wife returned to work. Thus, the fact that the wife was working at all was the result of the husband's agreement to take care of children during times that would not be covered by relatives or paid baby sitters. This agreement was made by fathers of young children regardless of the wife's reasons for returning and regardless of the nature of family bonds. This suggests that mothers of young children who are married to the least accommodating men were excluded from this study and that women such as Jane Devore or Maria Correlli might have returned to work earlier had they been able to get their husbands to take over child care for certain parts of the day as were Ann Dooley, Jill Mooney, and Cathy Schultz.

To summarize then, couples fall into four major categories defined by the wife's reasons for working and whether or not the husband is willing to accommodate to help meet the family's needs after her return. These are represented in Figure 5.2.

FIGURE 5.2 Husband's Response to Wife's Decision to Work by Wife's Reasons for Working and Family Bond Type

Wife's Reasons	Family Bond Type	
	Couple Centered	*Husband or Child Centered*
Family	Since we need her to work, I'll do the best I can to help out at home.	She's just helping out for a while, and I really don't expect things to change very much for me during this time.
Self	We don't really need the money, but if she wants to work, I'll do what I can to make it possible for her to continue … and maybe the money will help.	We don't need the money and I'd rather she stay at home, but if she can still handle all the household responsibilities, then I guess I can't object.

The Next Step: Renegotiating the Provider Role

The reader may recognize that these initial positions already go a long way toward defining the provider role eventually assigned to the wife. This is no accident, since, as I said in Chapter 4, one of the major factors in provider role definition is the manner in which the wife's income is viewed. Thus, couples who had agreed that the wife would work only temporarily or that her income was not really necessary to the family's welfare had defined the wife as a secondary provider as soon as she began work. Likewise, those who agreed that the wife's income was not only necessary but necessary indefinitely were coproviders as soon as the wife brought home her first paycheck. However, many couples began by thinking of the wife's income as "extra" only to become so dependent on it that, as Ted Collins explained, their family's standard of living would suffer considerably if Joan were to stop working. As second incomes turned dreams into realities, wants became needs, and it was more and more difficult to think of the wife's earnings as merely "icing on the cake." When icing on the cake became part of the cake itself, wives were no longer secondary providers but coproviders who, like their husbands, could demand concessions from their spouses and children.

The next step in the bargaining process, then, is becoming dependent on the wife's income. As was discussed in the previous chapter, several factors influence both this process and the clear recognition that the family is in fact dependent on what the wife brings home. I would like to suggest, however, that because husbands who admit dependence on the wife's income give up the prerogative to say "You can quit whenever you want," they do not admit this dependence unless they have become willing to give in to more demands at home or unless it is already clear that they will not lose any ground at home by giving up this bargaining power. Paula Reade, for example, makes about 30% of the family income but is not recognized as coprovider by her husband Harold an engineer.

When Paula took a job as a secretary for a real estate firm, she reorganized her household by giving her two boys and her husband each specific responsibilities. Her husband, who worked up to 60 hours a week, chose the bathroom "because it was the smallest" and complained to me that things were less relaxed at home now that all four of them get home at once and the boys quarrel over their new kitchen responsibilities. Harold does not consider Paula's income significant. He says that it is difficult to "sense any extra money." They eat out more, buy more clothes, and wouldn't be sending the boys to a private school if Paula were not working. They also would not have a second car. But then if Paula were home, they would not need to eat out as often or have a second car and would not have considered the private school. Thus, although Harold Reade is aware of some disadvantages of Paula's working, he feels that she couldn't just stop working as that would mean taking the boys out of their school and getting rid of the second car. Harold is, therefore, saying two somewhat contradictory things: (1) it is hard to sense any extra money, and (2) because of this extra money, several things in our lives have changed so that our current life-style is dependent on it.

If Harold saw Paula's contribution as essential, he might have to allow his life to be changed more than it has been. As it is, Paula was already an assertive, self-confident woman before she returned to work. She had had several important unpaid leadership and organizing jobs and was not timid about making demands on her family. Harold, however, works 50 to 70 hours a week, and Paula makes a point of stopping work exactly at 5:00 PM even if she is in the middle of a meeting at which she is responsible for taking notes. Even though she is a powerful and ambitious woman, she curtails any ambitions she might have for occupational advancement. For his part, Harold is willing to make some contributions to household maintenance and organization by taking the boys to school and cleaning and cooking on a rotating schedule with Paula and the children. However, there is an implicit understanding that this is as far as it will go, and the tone of Harold's remarks suggests it may already have gone too far. Paula's work will never become central or be as important to her as Harold's is to him and that is understood by both. Her income allows them to have certain luxuries that they otherwise wouldn't have. Nonetheless if she were not working, they might not really miss these luxuries. Paula is therefore a secondary provider rather than a coprovider. Although she gains bargaining power because her boys' schooling and dinners out would not be possible without her income, she is not in the same position as is Cathy Schultz whose husband would have to work overtime if she were not working.

Cathy Schultz makes only slightly more of the family income than does Paula Reade (33% vs. 30%) and yet her husband Mike sees her income as a major reason for her working and is grateful for it because it "takes a load off of his back." Unlike Harold Reade, Mike does not bring work home in a briefcase at night and would be happy not working at all. He does not like working overtime and feels that he would have to if Cathy were not working.

This means that if Cathy Schultz quits work, Mike's life will be considerably less pleasant. He likes taking the children to the lake on summer days before he goes to work in the late afternoon and he likes being around the home, doing projects. If he had to work two shifts, he wouldn't have this freedom. Even though he values order, he does not complain as much as he used to about the fact that housework is undone. He puts things away himself now rather than nag Cathy and does what he can to make it more possible for her to keep working. He sees few disadvantages to her working and has begun to count on her income as a permanent part of the family's finances. Cathy is, therefore, in a stronger position than is Paula Reade. Furthermore, although both women went back to work initially because they wanted to, Cathy's work has become less rewarding so that she is now working less for herself and more for the family, giving her an added edge. She uses this power mostly to get Mike to do other things.

> If I want him to do something, I'll say, "Listen, I work and why not?" It works . . . I say, "You can take me out, or else! I worked all day, I want to get out."

The more of their providing responsibilities husbands relinquish, the more they leave themselves open to new demands from their wives. However, this can be viewed as an exchange. Husbands such as Mike Schultz who are job rather than career oriented have less to lose and more to gain from sharing the responsibility to provide. They typically enjoy puttering around the house and/or being around their children more than they enjoy working, and regard overtime work as a grueling drain on their energy that they do only out of necessity. Husbands like Harold Reade who are already working long hours at salaried positions in absorptive occupations usually need insulation from family demands more than they need their wives' income. They are therefore less willing to unequivocally grant their wives coprovider status regardless of how much of the income their wives contribute. Professional and superprovider men are the most likely to be uncomfortable about sharing the provider role. Although wives who earned 25% or less of the family income were easily defined as secondary providers, wives, like Paula Reade, who earned 30% to 33% of the family income had to be *put* into that category. Wives earning 40% or more of the family income, however, could not be dismissed as secondary providers, and were therefore likely to become ambivalent coproviders whose income was considered necessary but whose role as provider was not entirely acceptable to either or both spouses.

Another kind of ambivalent coprovider is the woman who wants neither the responsibility of providing for her family nor the power it gives her. Both Nancy Williams and Cynthia Davis would rather be provided for, but neither have husbands who can provide sufficient income for the family by working 40-hour weeks and neither man can withstand the stress of overtime work. The women express their mixed feelings about helping to provide in different ways. When Don was laid off from work one summer, he did a lot of the housework but told me that Nancy redid it all on the weekends and was threatening to quit her job so that he would be forced to find work before his company called him back. Cynthia Davis expresses her ambivalence by continuing to work at a low-paid custodial job even though her husband encourages her to look for factory work which would be less exhausting and pay more money. In contrast to the work-committed women married to professional men, these women are struggling to retain their "provided for" status and would not want their job-oriented husbands to become too dependent on their wives' earning power.

Thus far, we have considered how the wife's bargaining power changes when her income is defined as necessary to the family's welfare and how her need to be provided for as well as her husband's need to retain his rights as main provider help to define each spouse's goals, i.e., what each wants from the bargain. How much bargaining husbands and wives must actually do depends of course on whether they have competing or complementary goals (cf. Chapter 1). As we saw in the beginning of this discussion, some couples were able to agree on changed definitions of the provider role and how this would affect household roles from the start, whereas others, like the Collinses, were still battling over whose job was to come first over two years after Joan's return to work. As Bailyn (1970) has found in her research on female British university graduates and their husbands, women seeking to combine work with family commitments fare best with family-oriented men, whereas women who place family first are better able to cope with career-oriented men. In this study, men who placed family first and defined their work as "just a job" put up little resistance to work-committed wives who wanted to be considered coproviders, and wives who preferred that their husbands retain the responsibility for providing gladly accepted the definition of temporary and secondary provider. However, when both spouses wanted to put work before family or when each would have preferred staying home with the children to working, there was much more to be negotiated. It was in these cases that the nature of the marital relationship was most important.

The Marital Relationship

Lest the reader begin to feel that husbands and wives in this study had little concern for each other's welfare, we must also consider how the closeness of the marital relationship affects the bargaining process. Earlier in this chapter, I pointed out that couple-centered husbands were more likely than were self-centered ones to accommodate to their wives' return to work regardless of how much the family needed the second income. For them, part of being a husband meant that they should support their wives in whatever their wives needed to do to grow and be happy even at a sacrifice to themselves (see Figure 5.2). Couple-centered marriages also tended to be closer than were either husband- or child-centered ones in that the spouses saw each other as favorite companions and best friends and often confided in each other. Self-centered husbands might have considered their wives as their best friends, but their wives would be less likely to see their husbands that way since most of the attention flowed in one direction (F. Rubin,

1983). These husbands were, however, dependent on their wives in a way that child-centered husbands were not. This means that whereas couple-centered husbands try to anticipate and accommodate their wives' needs, self-centered husbands experience a loss of their wives' attention and become painfully aware of their dependence on them. They then do whatever they can to win back the attention. This may include being more attentive to their wives as was John Devore or it may involve a series of childlike antics such as the one Martin Holling engaged in when excluded from the interview with his wife Bess. They are, however, now in the position of most interest since the dependency balance has swung in the wife's favor. By this I mean not so much that the husbands are more dependent on their wives than they were previously, but, as discussed in Chapter 4, the withdrawal of their wives' attention makes them aware of this dependence and causes a "panic" reaction.

Whereas husbands are experiencing a loss of companionship, wives are adding new sources of social approval and support on their jobs. For many women, positive feedback from their supervisors is the first direct appreciation they've had in years for work done. They are also making new friends outside of their family network. Thus, more of their social needs are being met at the same time that their husbands are experiencing a reduction in the total amount of social support. This is perhaps why surveys of the impact of wives' working on marital satisfaction sometimes find that, especially among professional men, the wife's marriage improves while the husband's gets a little worse (Burke and Weir, 1976; Scanzoni, 1970; Bird, 1979).[1]

As wives gain new self-confidence, they also become more direct in their bargaining strategies. In the illustration given at the beginning of this chapter, we saw how Joan Collins' new self-esteem affected her ability to resolve differences with her husband Ted. Rather than engage in "anxious talk" as they did previously, they now "zero in" on problems. Although such a change might have come about as a result of maturation of the relationship whether or not Joan had returned to work, I think that Joan's success at work has contributed to a recognition of her own power and made her bargaining strategies more direct.

This change was reported by many women in the study. For example, Jane Devore does not suppress her resentment as much as she used to. In my first interview with her, she described a conversation she had had with her husband John just two weeks earlier:

> I said to him, "I'm building up kind of a resentment against you." He said, "You can't do that, only alcoholics can build up resentments." Then he said, "What's it about?" and I said, "When you get home from work, about fifty times a day you take out the coffee, the cream and the sugar and

make yourself a cup of coffee and it ought to be just as easy to put it all back in the cupboard as my coming along behind you and putting it back in the cupboard." And he didn't say anything about it, but ever since then, he's been putting it back in the cupboard.

Again, as the reader knows from the discussion of the Devore family at the end of Chapter 3, some of the changes in Jane and John's relationship were the result of John's long struggle with alcoholism during which Jane had had to learn to become more independent. She had "decided she was a person" two years before she returned to work and had learned to wait out his temper tantrums and refuse to be bullied. However, her self-confidence grew still more when she found that she could work and earn money. As she explained her reasons for returning to work:

> It was a kind of feeling as to who I was . . . what I was capable of doing . . . I always felt that I wasn't capable of doing all these things.

Thus, although it is difficult to prove, I think that most women in the study did enjoy heightened self-esteem as a result of their work and that this did translate into increased directness and assertiveness in their dealings with their husbands and children (cf. Scanzoni and Szinovacz, 1980: 31–32).

So far I have said that a wife's bargaining power is determined by her reasons for working, the amount of self-esteem she gains following her return to work, and the proportion of the total family income she earns. Her success in enlisting her husband's support for her work also depends upon the nature of the marital bond and each spouse's work/family priorities. Whereas couple-centered husbands are apt to have altruistic responses, agreeing to do what they can to make it possible for their wives to continue to work, self-centered husbands make no such agreement but instead react strongly to the loss of their wives' attention and disruption of household order. Now in positions of most interest, they often make concessions to their wives in an attempt to win back lost attention. In either case, the wife's bargaining power is positively related to how close her husband feels to her and how highly he values the marital relationship. In addition, the amount of negotiating to be done varies depending on whether the couple's work and family priorities are complementary or competing. Thus, a woman like Joan Collins who is in a child-centered marriage and who is competing with her husband for the right to have her work taken seriously not only has more to bargain for but also is likely to have more difficulty bargaining than is a woman like Jill Mooney who is in a couple-centered relationship and whose husband has little desire to advance in his job. Whereas in the former case, redefining provider responsibilities is a major battle ground, in the latter there is little contest.

Role Overload and Role Relinquishment

Given a husband and wife whose work/family priorities are not complementary and given an increase in the wife's bargaining power, what determines whether or not a wife will use her advantage to get her husband to share more of the household responsibility than he previously did? I have already given examples of women who did not want to share either the responsibility to provide or the responsibility of running the household with their husbands. Even though it was necessary for them to work full-time outside the household, they were unwilling to relinquish either the role of housekeeper or that of financially dependant wife. Other wives, however, were willing to relinquish some of their responsibilities to their husbands but found it unnecessary either because they now had comparatively few household responsibilities or because help from older children, neighbors, or relatives was more readily available than help from a recalcitrant husband. Thus, the likelihood that a wife will put pressure on her husband to assume traditional household responsibilities is determined not only by how much power she has gained and whether or not she wants help but also by her role overload.

A simple concept of role overload assumes that there is a finite amount of time and energy available to any one person at any one time and that role responsibilities accumulate additively until all available time and energy are exhausted, making any additional role responsibilities an overload. Critics of this closed system, zero-sum approach argue that both time and energy are expandable resources and that the more committed a person is to a role, the less that role is experienced as a drain on his or her energy (Marks, 1977; Sieber, 1974). Although I find this argument intriguing, to take it fully into account would be beyond the scope of this book. Since the former definition of role overload is sufficient for the purposes of this research, I am using it with the understanding that it is oversimplified and that, indeed, working wives and husbands may get energy from their jobs and from the children as well as give energy to both (Hood and Golden, 1979:576).

Using this definition, role overload simply means having more demands on one's time and energy than one can manage. For the women in this study, the two factors most useful in predicting role overload were the ages of their children and their standards of work and family role performance. Thus, Anne Dooley who worked 60 hours a week in a highly responsible position during her 7- and 10-year old children's school vacation, who believed that there was no acceptable substitute for parental child care and who had high standards for both her home and her garden, had one of the highest overloads, whereas Roberta Hutchins, who worked 40 hours a week in a routine position, had children aged 10 and 16 who cared for themselves, and was relaxed about housekeeping, had a smaller overload.

Women can deal with overload in several ways: They may (1) delegate tasks to others while retaining the responsibility for them, (2) not be available when a given task or set of tasks needs doing or put things off until someone else does them, (3) bargain with other family members to induce them to accept more responsibility, (4) lower their standards or reduce in some way what is expected of them in one or more roles, or (5) by sleeping less and cutting down on their leisure time.[2] Although delegating work and lowering standards both help to solve the overload problem, only going "on strike" or bargaining will result in a new division of responsibility.

Going on Strike.   Joan Collins often goes "on strike." As the reader may remember, she went on strike when she put off arranging the children's summer schedules until Ted finally did it. This strategy works best when the things left undone are things that other family members feel *must* be done. If the wife is the only one in the house who cares about clean windows, then leaving them dirty will not prompt anyone else to clean them. However, if she stops baking chocolate chip cookies, it probably will not be long before her 12-year-old son will learn to make them himself. Likewise, a messy wife married to a neat husband is in the best position to induce her husband to do more of the housework. Cynthia Davis and Linda Meyers each find it easier to let things go than do their more compulsive husbands. Consequently, they let things go until their husbands take over. However, husbands who assume responsibilities in such circumstances do not always accept responsibility as their own from then on. They are more likely to complain about their wives' laxness. Thus, although going on strike may force the issue, it is unlikely to result in a permanent reallocation of responsibility unless schedules are such that the wife is never around when the task in question needs doing.

Husbands who are at home alone with young children during the day are often faced with situations for which they must accept the responsibility. When Jimmy Mooney broke his arm while trying to fly down the stairs, his father had to take him to the hospital. Because Anne Dooley was gone for long hours during the day while Bob was home on his summer break, Bob found himself doing many of the errands that Anne used to do before she went to work:

A.D.:   I used to do the running around, like to the bank, etc. He's doing a lot of the running around now.

J.C.H.:   [To Bob] Do you volunteer to do these things, or do they get delegated to you?

B.D.:   It's kind of a . . . they're not going to get done [loud nervous laughter] unless I do it, so . . .

Since Bob's work schedule as a university professor is more flexible than is Anne's as a business manager for Datan Corporation, Bob is more often the one who deals with things that must be done during the workday. Housework, however, can be done anytime, and as we learned in the previous chapter, the Dooleys are still trying to decide how housework should be done.

Although an explicit agreement to reallocate responsibilities might seem to be the easiest way of solving role overload, it was the least used method. Women delegated tasks as was illustrated in the discussion of housework in Chapter 4, but tended to keep the responsibility for overseeing the running of the household. Most women succeeded in giving up responsibility for, as well as the doing of, tasks only by not being available at the time the task needed doing. It is at this point that the wife's bargaining power becomes crucial. The less bargaining power a woman had, the harder it was to remain unavailable and the more likely it was that she would have to seek some other way of coping with her overload. One means of coping was to reduce one's work hours or to drop out of the labor force temporarily.

Cutting Back.   Theo James earns 30% of her family income, is enthusiastic about her work as a secretary and has two boys aged 6 and 8. Her husband, Richard, is more interested in leisure time pursuits with friends or with Theo than he is in his work or in spending time with the children. He complained that having to pick the children up from school cut into his free time. He couldn't just go off fishing with friends after work as he might otherwise have done. He considers himself the main provider and says that "all they do" with Theo's check is make house payments. He is willing to do some things to make it possible for Theo to work and does help around the house more than he used to, but Theo has not pressured him to do a great deal more. Instead she relies on her parents who not only baby sit but also often invite Theo and Richard to dinner, saving Theo the trouble of cooking. When I interviewed Theo a second time, she was looking for a job with the school system so that her work hours would coincide with her children's school hours. This way, Richard would not have to pick them up from school.

Richard James has been successful in preserving the idea that Theo's money is not essential and that she is working mostly because she wants to. They both know that her mental health depends on getting out of the house and that work is important to her self-esteem. The Jameses do not have a strongly couple-centered marriage and although she has come to think of Richard as a "close friend," Theo volunteered that the children were far more important to her than is her husband. Because Theo is working because she wanted to and because Richard places a higher value on being with his peer group in his free time than on being with his family, Theo finds it difficult to get him to assume more household responsibilities. She does, however, have an overload. Since she does not want to give up work, she relies instead on help from her parents and on the possibility of rearranging her work schedule so that she can both work and care for her family.

Theo James is not the only woman in the study who reduced her work commitment in between the two interviews. Maria Correlli was working part-time so that she could pay more attention to a teenaged daughter who was having problems, and Billie King took an easier job closer to home so that she could be more available to her children while at work. Joe Correlli is a professional, and Forrest King a superprovider. All three women were defined as secondary providers, were in child-centered marriages, earned 30% of the family income or less, and all retained the major responsibility for running their households. Did these three women reduce their work commitments because they were unsuccessful in getting more help from their husbands? If so, we might ask whether or not a husband's help is a necessary condition for some women to remain at full-time jobs. If it is, we could then predict that women most likely to either reduce their work hours or drop out of the labor force would be women with high overloads (young children and high standards), in child-centered marriages, defined as secondary providers, and likely to be married to either career-oriented or superprovider husbands. These are the women who are most likely to need help from their husbands but least likely to get it.

To summarize the argument made to this point, wives gain bargaining power when their families become dependent on a second income. At this point, some couples have little difficulty agreeing to share both the responsibility of providing and more of the responsibility for child care and housework. Such couples are likely to involve work-committed wives and job as opposed to career-oriented husbands. If husband and wife do not have such complementary goals, then the couple must renegotiate work/family priorities. It is in this instance that the nature of the marital bond becomes very important. Couple-centered husbands try very hard to be fair and to accommodate their wives' desire to work. Self-centered husbands, now in the position of most interest, try to regain their wives' attention by granting concessions, but men in child-centered marriages make little movement in any direction without a great deal of pressure. At this point, the amount of pressure exerted by wives depends upon the extent of their role overload. Women with the least overload and least bargaining power get little or no additional help from their husbands, whereas those with the most overload and most bargaining power get the most. Women like Theo James with an overload but little bargaining power are often forced to modify their work hours or type of work in order to reduce the double burden of home and work responsibilities.

The struggle to be taken seriously as a coprovider is the main battle to be fought by wives seeking to share more household responsibility with their husbands (cf. Scanzoni, 1978:78). However, the nature and difficulty of the battle depend upon each spouse's work/family priorities, family bond type, and the extent of the wife's overload. Because the women in this study were all still in the labor force at the time of the second interview, they are by definition more successful bargainers than women who unwillingly dropped out of the labor force and were, therefore, excluded from my sample.

How hard did they fight? Some couples fought long and hard, hammering out new marriage contracts in the process and others avoided conflict whenever possible, preferring either to give in without a battle or to avoid any confrontation. Although I suspect that I did not learn as much about conflict and its resolution as I wanted to, what I did learn is discussed in the following section.

CONFLICT AND CONFLICT RESOLUTION

Linda and David Meyers have worked hard on their marriage and have sometimes thought of getting a divorce. It is usually David who will talk about splitting up. He did this when Linda was working 60 hours a week, and this is his way of saying that he is really upset. Then he and Linda will sit down and talk. In this particular conflict, David described the outcome:

> Finally when I understood that work was a goal for Linda, I could be more sympathetic.

The Dooleys and the Devores have also approached the breaking point, and they became closer as a result. Probably many of the 16 couples have had open confrontations that almost resulted in divorce, but conflict was one of the hardest things to learn about. David Meyers wasn't sure that he and Linda wanted to tell me about the times they had approached the brink but then went ahead after Linda volunteered. Jane Devore did not tell me until the second interview that she had once been separated from John for a year and a half. I, therefore, suspect that some couples who appear to have little open conflict have much more than they will admit.

I asked them to give me examples of issues on which they and their spouses disagreed and to describe a recent conflict and then probed to find each spouse's characteristic way of handling conflict. In that way, I found out that Nancy and Don Williams do not settle differences directly:

J.C.H.: How do you settle differences?

D.W.: Tell you the truth, I don't. She gets so mad at me, I get so mad at her. I'll turn around and walk off. Go outside, for maybe ten, fifteen minutes. Later [I] come back to the house, do something . . . . Then it's "Honey, did you do this," or "Honey, what about that?" It's . . . that's it. It happens. It's gone.

J.C.H.: And you never talk it out? It just evaporates?

D.W.: She threatens me . . . . "You do that again, and I'm leaving you." I say, "Help you pack your clothes. Don't let the door hit you in the rear end when you go out."

When I asked Nancy how they solved problems, she said that they very seldom had any big problems but that when they do she gives in easily. She told me "I figure, if there's nothing serious, what's the point in arguing?" For Nancy, the major problem is not getting enough help with the housework, and since Don's heart attack, she says she doesn't ask for much help from him. However, from his point of view, she bugs him about the house:

D.W.: There's a lot of times that Nancy . . . I've got problems . . . lots of times when it bothers me, my health. I won't let her know anything about it. I just keep it to myself. She bugs me a lot because maybe she thinks maybe I should be doing this and I should be doing that. But she doesn't know how I feel.

J.C.H.: She bugs you to do more things?

D.W.: Yes, around the house and things like this. But there's times when I'm not up to it, but I don't tell her. I just let her go ahead, because I can take it. But I don't use an excuse not to be doing anything. She'll start off, and I'll get off on something else and that's the way I'll get her out of it.

Half of the couples in this study used this conflict dodging strategy most or some of the time. One of these couples, the Correllis, communicated so little about what they really felt that Maria wanted me to tell her what her husband had said after I talked with him. Maybe he would tell me things that he would not tell her, she thought.

I suspect that women have more difficulty discussing marital conflict than do men and that several more interviews would have been necessary before I could have established the kind of rapport necessary for me to learn from each spouse how disagreements are handled. The information I do have suggests that the likelihood that conflict will end in a clear resolution is influenced by both the degree to which conflict is open and the investment one or both partners have in the marital relationship. Open conflict similar to that reported by the Meyers is characterized by direct confrontation of each other and free expression of angry feelings. Spouses who engage in open conflict generally know how their mates feel about things and can predict what will make them angry. However, some couples have repetitive conflict such as the Collins' daily tension over housework, whereas others more often see conflict through to resolution by talking things out and reaching understandings such as David Meyers' new appreciation for Linda's work goals. Staying with a fight until the issue is resolved requires a strong commitment of both time and energy from each spouse as well as a high level of confidence that the relationship can withstand the strain. The Mooneys, for example, are extremely dependent on each other and have few social outlets or supports outside of the family. If it is really true that they have little open conflict, this could be because they both fear dissolution of the relationship so much that they are not willing to risk it. The Meyers and Dooleys, however, to whom the marital relationship is equally important, do have enough other resources that they can risk disaster in an attempt to resolve underlying problems. (They are also the two couples who divorced between 1976 and 1982.) Although a complete model of marital conflict resolution would be far more complicated than this, I would like to propose the fourfold classification shown in Figure 5.3 as a start. Couples who have open conflict and a high commitment to the relationship will spend the time and energy necessary to work through the conflict to the end (I), whereas those who avoid open conflict but are strongly committed to the relationship will try to smooth things over by accommodating to each other (II). Other couples have short outbursts but then withdraw from the fight before the battle is over because neither trust the other or the relationship enough to believe that a permanent solution is possible (III), whereas those who avoid conflict and have little investment in the relationship have superficial interactions and each go their own ways (IV).[3]

Using my best guess to fit each of the 16 couples into one of these four categories, I find no clear relationship between a couple's style of fighting and role sharing. The Mooneys, who accommodate each other and share parenting equally, see themselves as coproviders and share some housework. On the other hand, the Devores have had more open confrontation but have reallocated hardly any responsibilities, although they are enjoying a more equal companionship.

Since, as I have said previously, some couples had less to fight about than did others, perhaps were able to renegotiate roles with less open confrontation than were others. Since the Mooneys are each doing what they want to do, they have little to fight about, but when Linda Meyers was working overtime while David was home alone recovering from surgery, there was a battle brewing. The Collinses always have a great deal to fight about but because they do not stay with their conflicts to the end they, therefore, have difficulty resolving underlying issues. The result is that

FIGURE 5.3   Modes of Dealing with Conflict

	Commitment to and Investment in Relationship	
Openness of Conflict	High	Low
High (open)	I. Conflicts worked through to final resolutions.	III. Outburst followed by short-term resolutions and withdrawal. Underlying problems remain.
Low (closed)	II. Accommodation without clear negotiation of terms; resentment may linger.	IV. Avoidance of conflicts and most interaction at superficial level. Spouses are "roommates."

although Ted has taken more responsibility for the children than he did before Joan returned to work, he resents this and wonders out loud if Joan's working will turn their children into delinquents. It would seem, therefore, that the frequency and the skill with which a couple fights are better predictors of how happy they will be with the changes they make than of how much they will change.

CONCLUSIONS AND PREDICTIONS

In this chapter, I have developed a theoretical framework for understanding the bargaining process that takes place when a wife begins full-time work. I have argued that wives who succeed in being taken seriously as providers are also more successful in getting their husbands to assume more responsibility for parenting and housework. Although the family's dependence on the wife's income, each spouse's work/family priorities, and the nature of the marital bond help to determine whether or not the wife will be recognized as a coprovider, the extent of the wife's overload determines how much responsibility she must relinquish. Because some couples had more complementary goals than others, couples varied with regard to how much confrontation was necessary before changes could be made. Given a large area to be negotiated, couples who could openly confront each other and stay with a conflict to its conclusion were likely to be more satisfied with the changes made than were those who withdrew before the battle was over. However, couples could and did reallocate responsibilities without these conflict resolution skills.

Based upon the theory presented in this chapter, one could make several predictions both about the futures of the 16 families in this study and about families who share some of their characteristics. Will two work–oriented spouses be more or less likely to stay married to each other than will a work-oriented husband married to a family-oriented wife? Which kinds of wives will be most likely to stay in the labor force and, of these, which ones will increase their commitment to work and perhaps increase their share of the family income? If a wife increases her wage ratio, under what conditions will she also increase her bargaining power? For which kinds of husbands will a wife's increased work commitment and/or income pose the most problems? What categories of husbands are most likely to increase their share of household responsibilities in response to their wives' increased work commitment?

The material presented in Chapters 3 to 5 suggests answers to these and other questions that I will state in the form of testable hypotheses:

1. Wives working for "self" as opposed to "family" reasons will be more likely to remain in the labor force after the need for their incomes has diminished.
2. Couples with competing goals will experience more strain than those with complementary goals.
3. Increased work commitment on the part of a wife (accompanied by a decrease in the amount of companionship she is able to offer her husband) will cause most problems in husband- and couple-centered marriages and least in child-centered marriages.
4. Wives working for self reasons married to job-oriented men are most likely to move toward recognition as coproviders (and increase their wage ratio).
5. Couples who are most ambivalent about their definition of the wife's responsibility to provide will be likely to resolve this inconsistency either by having the wife quit work or by accepting her as coprovider.
6. Job-oriented husbands will have an easier time accepting their wives' increased work commitment than will career-oriented husbands.
7. Job-oriented husbands in families with younger children will be most likely to increase their share of household responsibility, whereas career-oriented husbands and fathers of older children will be less likely to.
8. Regardless of her share of the family income, a wife's bargaining power will be improved by gains in self-esteem and increased social support outside the marriage.

In the next chapter we will find out what indeed did happen to the 16 families between the time of the 1975–1976 interviews and the writing of this book. Although the theories of social scientists are never designed to predict outcomes for individual families, it is the ability to predict as opposed to simply describe that is the test of any theory.

NOTES

1. Since Burke and Weir (1976:649) studied industrial engineers and accountants and their wives, this pattern may be limited to professional men. Booth's replication of the Burke and Weir study using a probability sample of Toronto households found that husbands of employed wives were, if anything, *more* satisfied with their marriages than were husbands of housewives.

2. I am endebted to Linda Haas for reminding me of this alternative. In fact, several of the women interviewed mentioned getting up early in the morning so that they could have time for themselves, and time budget studies show that working women have less leisure time than their own husbands, housewives, or husbands of housewives (Robinson, 1977).

3. Olson, et al. (1979) have developed a far more complex model of family systems using "adaptability" and "cohesion" as their two main dimensions. They make a useful distinction between a "healthy" balanced cohesion characterized by interdependence and a "less healthy" extremely high cohesion characterized by dependence.

6
THE FAMILIES
SIX YEARS LATER

Indeed, any mechanical philosophy of human dynamics is inadequate—except when looking backward, because in looking backward, *any* development can be organized into *any* scheme, if it is general enough. (Rose, 1944:1033–1034)

If, just for fun, we were to use the theory presented in Chapter 5 in order to make predictions about specific families, we might doubt that Cynthia Davis would resolve her inconsistency about being a coprovider by taking the factory job her husband wanted her to take. Because Anne Dooley and Joan Collins were each self-motivated women who were increasing their own work commitments in spite of being married to career-oriented men, we might expect their marriages to experience the most strain. Of the two couples, the Dooleys should have most conflict because they are couple- as opposed to child-centered, but the Collinses having a pattern of regulated but unresolved conflict should be the least likely to successfully resolve the strain. Linda Meyers was also increasing her work commitment in 1976, and her husband, who gave his marriage and family first priority, was unhappy about the loss of her companionship. But given their history of conflict resolution, we would expect them to be able to resolve this difference while keeping the relationship intact. We could expect that family-motivated wives such as Bess Holling, Nancy Williams, and Billie King, who had told us in Chapter 3 that they did not intend to continue working longer than they had to, might in fact quit working. We could also expect that husbands who were either career oriented or superproviders and had older families such as Martin Holling, John Devore, Bill Anderson, and Joe Correlli would be unlikely to add any more household responsibilities, whereas husbands who were job oriented and had younger children such as

Mike Schultz, James Mooney, and perhaps even Richard James might be more likely to.

The results of brief follow-up interviews done between November 1982 and February 1983 confirm only some of these predictions. Cynthia Davis did give in to the factory job not long after the 1976 interview and by 1979 she was earning more than half of the family's income. Although the Dooleys, Collinses, and Meyers all experienced considerable strain at least in part as a result of the wives' career ambitions, it was the Dooleys and the Meyers who ended their marriages and the Collinses who resolved the conflict between the demands of their two careers. As expected, Bess Holling, Nancy Williams, and Billie King had all left the labor force by 1982 and, although I was not able to get very complete information on changes in role sharing, I did find out that whereas Martin Holling and John Devore never increased their shares of housework neither did James Mooney. In fact, after James Mooney got onto first shift, he did *less* rather than *more* housework. In this chapter, I will discuss how the results of the follow-up interviews apply to the theory presented in Chapters 3 to 5.

THE FOLLOW-UP INTERVIEWS

A comparative case study such as this normally sets out to develop rather than to test hypotheses. Generally, hypothesis testing is done either in controlled laboratory settings or by means of large surveys that lend themselves to statistically controlled analyses. One way of partially testing hypotheses developed in such research, however, is to find out whether or not predictions based upon one's theory in fact came true. Luckily, having a contract to publish this study provided me with a convenient excuse to recontact the 16 families in the fall of 1982.

In November 1982, I sent letters, a long overdue report on the project, and a two-paged questionnaire to the families at their 1976 addresses. When envelopes came back as undeliverable, I traced the couples by telephone. By February 1983, I had had replies from or had been able to contact by phone all 16 couples. Some wrote long letters in addition to filling out my questionnaire. Others waited for me to call them and then answered all my questions in detail. One sent her résumé to show me how she had moved up in her career since that last interview. Although one couple preferred not to take part in the follow-up, the rest were cooperative and several even bothered to obtain their own copies of the manuscript and read it so that they could include comments on it in their replies to me.

In addition to reading the written replies from both husbands and wives, I spoke with one or both spouses in all 16 families. As I spoke with "my" families, I realized that I, like many field researchers, had begun to feel close to the families I had spent so much time learning and writing about. Having once heard the well-known cultural anthropologist Leslie White condemn those "female anthropologists" for getting too close to "their tribes," the scientist in me shuddered at the thought. Nonetheless, I was gratified that the families had not forgotten me and instead said such things as, "Believe it or not, we were just talking about you the other day," and "We wondered what had happened to you." Rather than shutting me out of their lives as they had every right to, 15 of the 16 welcomed me back as if I were a relative returning from a long trip.

Compared to six hours of taped interviews, a short questionnaire and 15 to 20 minutes on the telephone cannot provide very complete information about changes in a marital relationship over a period of six years. Because of the brevity of the telephone interviews, the stories I heard are more likely to be the stories people wanted to tell me rather than the stories that would give me most insight into what had happened to the family since the last interview. However, I was able to get information about each spouse's gross income in the previous year, work history, reasons for changes in marital status or jobs, and a few clues about how the wives' bargaining positions and husbands' household responsibilities had changed. What I have for 1983, then, may be compared to a polaroid snapshot, which, although far inferior to the family albums compiled in 1975–1976 can be added to the last page of the album to bring it up to date.

THE WIVES AND THEIR WORK IN 1983

Of the four women who had been working for "family" as opposed to "self" reasons in 1976, only Cynthia Davis was still in the labor force by 1983. Of the remaining 13, 10 had either been promoted from their 1976 positions or changed work places in order to find more challenging work. Five of these ten had also improved their incomes relative to their husbands (although sometimes their gain was temporary and due more to a decrease in the husband's income than to an increase in the wife's). Table 6.1 summarizes changes in labor force status, occupations titles, and wage ratio for the 16 families.

Getting Out

Billie King

In July 1976, Billie King had recently left her job as a clerk in order to be home with her 6 year-old daughter for the summer. Billie told me then that, for her, being a mother and a wife were more important than working outside the home:

TABLE 6.1 Changes in Labor Force Participation, Occupational Title, and Wage Ratio, 1976–1983

Provider Role Definition—1976	Husband's Occupation		Wife's Occupation		Wage Ratio		Provider Role—1983
	1976	1983	1976	1983	1976	1982	
Secondary Providers							
Correlli	Engineer (self-employed)		Secretary	Secretary	14	40a	(A)
Devore	M.D.	psychiatrist	Staff benefits clerk	Supervisor (same office)	14	18	S
James	Machinist	machine repair	Church secretary	Administrative secretary			A
Holling	Engineer/administrator		Administrative secretary	Housewife	25		sole provider
King	Fireperson	Fireperson	Clerk	Housewife	22		sole provider
Reade	Engineer	Engineer	Secretary	Administrative assistant	30	45	C
Ambivalent Coproviders							
Collins	Engineer/administrator	Engineer/research and development	Title editor	Computer sales	42	43	C
Davis	General stores clerk in factory both years		Custodial worker	Security guard	40	17b	C

TABLE 6.1 Changes in Labor Force Participation, Occupational Title, and Wage Ratio, 1976–1983 (continued)

Provider Role Definition—1976	Husband's Occupation 1983	Husband's Occupation 1976	Wife's Occupation 1983	Wife's Occupation 1976	Wage Ratio 1976	Wage Ratio 1982	Provider Role—1983
Dooley	CPA and lecturer	Professor (assistant)	Assistant comptroller	Finance analyst	44	c	Divorced
Williams	Factory inspector	Foreman	Housewife	Switchboard operator	30		Husband sole provider
Coproviders							
Anderson	Deceased	Electrician	Data analyst	Data analyst	44	d	widowed
Hutchins	Safety inspector	Foreman	Library clerk	Library clerk	33	30	C
Marx	Jointly ran vacuum cleaner dealership in both years				50	50	C
Meyers	Sales administrator	Hospital administrator	Supervisor	Secretary	33		Divorced
Mooney	Machinist	Machinist	Administrative secretary	Secretary	30	42	C
Schultz	Machinist	Machinist	Administrative secretary	Secretary	33	47	C

Key: A, Ambivalent coprovider; S, secondary provider; C, coprovider.

a. Maria Correlli suggested that she was doing most of the providing in 1982, but gave no information about wage ratio.

b. Cynthia Davis earned 50% of the household income as a factory worker from 1977–1979.

c. Anne Dooley earned over half the family income for awhile between 1979 and 1981.

d. Mary Anderson's share of the family income was somewhat less than 44% at the time of Bill's death in 1981.

> When I feel best about myself is when I'm home taking care of my family and know they feel secure because I'm here and that's why it always bothered me to be away at work. And just seeing them happy . . . . I think that should be the most important thing to any mother and wife.

Then, Billie thought that perhaps when school started again she would return to work. However, when I spoke recently with her husband Forrest, he told me that Billie had never gone back to work after the summer of 1976. Since 1976, the Kings' need for additional income had diminished somewhat. They had bought and sold houses twice since 1975 and made money on each move. Three of their four children are now on their own, and Billie and Forrest have bought a modular home, which they plan to live in when they retire and move to Tennessee. If Billie did not want to work, there was no need for her to. As Forrest said, "she did what she wanted to."

Bess Holling

When I spoke with Bess Holling in February 1983, she had just been grocery shopping on Saturday because, having been typing a manuscript at home all week, she hadn't had time to get her shopping done. After working 14 years, Bess had "retired" (that is how she described it) in July 1982. By January 1983, the older son was almost finished with his PhD, the daughter had hers already, and the younger son had received his law degree. Bess, who was the "kids' scholarship though college," had done her work. Right after retiring she and Martin went on a five-week trip in Europe using the money she had earned in the past few months. Martin summed up Bess' reasons for leaving her job:

> When you interviewed us, we had three children in college. Since the principal reason for her working has ended, she has stopped working.

Bess told me that she had really enjoyed the past few months "now that she can call her time her own." She continues to do typing at home to earn $2000 a year to put into a tax-free IRA. Meanwhile, Martin, who has moved up a notch in an engineering firm, earned $72,000 last year and still works 55 hours a week. For him, the main change now that Bess is not working is that "the guilt is less." When she was working she had a heavy load managing both her job and the household. He told me that he had always felt guilty about her load but "didn't do much about it."

Nancy Williams

Like Billie King, Nancy Williams had been ambivalent about working when I interviewed her in June 1976. She said then that if she stopped working, the money was what she would miss most. Otherwise she would feel more relaxed and would get more accomplished at home and, she said, she "wouldn't be so grouchy." When I interviewed Don Williams a year later, he had been laid off since December 1975, and the family was living on his unemployment insurance and Nancy's wages. Although Don did not seem overly concerned about getting another job or being called back to work, Nancy had been goading him, threatening to quit her job if he didn't find another one. To me, however, he had said,

> If I don't get another job around here, its not going to bother me. There's a
> lot of things you can do to survive . . . . But if you have to have that big
> money, then you might as well forget it.

Already 47 in 1976, he had plans to retire at age 55. As it turned out, after Don had been laid off for a little over a year, the Williamses moved to Tennessee where Don was able to get a job as an inspector at a manufacturing company. A married daughter, her husband, and four grandchildren live nearby and a son is going to college while living at home. Nancy told me that if she had been able to take her job at Datan with her, maybe she would still be working, but since, according to Hanes they can live on "half the income" they needed in the midwest with four children at home, she really does not need to work. Occasionally she works part time at the college bookstore, and last year she earned $2000 while Don earned $17,000. With four grandchildren, the house, and a large yard to take care of, she does not miss her job.

Cynthia Davis

Given that all three of the wives just discussed had expressed ambivalence about working in 1975–1976, it is not surprising that they were no longer working full-time six years later. Cynthia Davis, however, also expressed ambivalence about working in 1976, but instead of leaving the labor force, she took the factory job her husband had been urging her to apply for and stayed there for two years until she was laid off in 1979. During her second year, she was earning more than half the family income (over $20,000) because she was getting more overtime work than Mike was.

Cynthia told me that the adjustment to factory work had been hard for her. The strain of the new job combined with her chronic heart condition (she has a prolapsed valve) led to an ill-afforded weight loss during the first few months at the factory. However, by the time Cynthia was laid off, she was working at a job that was not too taxing and she told me that if they called her back she would go back "in a minute." Now, she is working as a security guard on second shift for $4.25 an hour. She would prefer working days as she did in the factory and of course would like to make more money. However, she continues to work, in spite of the inconvenient hours and low pay, because now she likes working for its own sake. The woman who in 1976 had thought she might enjoy being at home full-time, told me in 1983 that, even if her family did not need her income, she would continue working because, as she said, "I like to dress up and get out with people."

Given what I learned about Cynthia Davis in 1975–1976, I might have expected her to drop out of the labor force as soon as it was possible. She has instead become more self-motivated over the years and now says that she works as much because she wants to as because she has to. However, given her husband's 1976 desire for his wife to both become more independent of him and to earn more money, we are left wondering how much of Cynthia's "conversion" is the result of Mike's prodding and how much of it comes from Cynthia herself.

Conclusion

It should not be surprising that women who are working more for their families than for themselves are likely to leave the labor force when it becomes possible for them to do so. However, the examples of these four women tell us much about the dynamics of a couple's decision regarding a wife's labor force participation as they do about the importance of the wife's individual motivation. The wife's motivation, after all, is only one component of a more complex process involving the original terms of the bargain under which she first went to work, the husband and wife's subsequent changes in attitudes toward her work and her providing responsibilities, and the couple's level of economic need. If neither the husband nor the wife is strongly in favor of the wife working and neither believes that her working is an economic necessity, then we should be able to predict with almost 99% certainty that she will not work. When Bess Holling and Billie King quit their jobs, all of these conditions were true for them. Nancy Williams and Cynthia Davis were more ambivalent about working than either Bess Holling or Billie King and they resolved their ambivalence in opposite ways. In this case, the decisive factors may be the extent to which their husbands are committed to the provider role and the wife's bargaining power.

Don Williams no longer wanted to make a lot of money but he was strongly committed to being a provider. In fact, he had a hard time separating "provider" from "father" and "husband." When asked to assign priorities to these roles, he said, "These have all got to work together to do what you've set out to do. And that's to provide for your family, to take care of your family." Nancy, in addition, had a strong investment in being provided for. Both Don and Nancy are family oriented and want to spend time with their children and grandchildren. Given these values and goals, Nancy probably had little trouble convincing Don to move to

Tennessee where he could get another job and she could be close to her married daughter and grandchildren.

In the Davis family, however, Mike seems to have been more interested in Cynthia's working than Cynthia was. Furthermore, whereas the Williamses had moved to a place where it cost less to live and were approaching the empty nest stage of their marriage, the Davises had bought a larger house and still had two teenaged children at home who may soon have college expenses. This means that if Cynthia drops out of the labor force or decides to earn less, Mike must earn more by working overtime. Although he also says that he thinks it is his responsibility to provide, he does not say that he would prefer to have Cynthia at home. Instead, he was instrumental in getting Cynthia to change her job so that she could make more money, even though, according to Cynthia, this job change was a source of psychological and physiological stress for her. Although I suspect that Nancy won the bargain in the Williams family (if anyone "won"), I think that Mike, at least initially, won the bargain in the Davis family. He said that it would be better for Cynthia if she took the factory job, but she stayed on the job even when it was demonstrated that it was not better for her because she was being paid more money and because Mike wanted her to do it.

Staying In

Of the 13 wives who remained in the labor force in 1983, 10 had either been promoted from jobs they had held in 1976 or had changed work places to accept jobs giving them more responsibility, income, or both. Of the three who did not report promotions or advancements in this period, Maria Correlli gave me little information except to say that she was currently working full-time and that her husband's business was in trouble; Gisela Marx was struggling, along with her husband Peter to keep their vacuum cleaner dealership from going under, and Roberta Hutchins was still working at her job in a small-town library. Of the 10 who did experience some occupational mobility, 5 substantially increased their contributions to the family income for all or part of the six-year period and at least 6 women demonstrated increased work commitment by taking more demanding jobs. Because wives who decreased their work commitment were married to men who supported their wives' desire to be provided for, decreases in work commitment appear to have led to less rather than more stress in the marriage. However, because women who chose to increase their work commitments were more likely to be married to men with competing rather than complementary goals, their marriages did not always fare as well. In this section, I will discuss how the wife's changing work commitments combined with the husband's changing goals, affected the husband's work/family priorities and the marriage as a whole.

Internal Sources of Stress

At the end of Chapter 6, I predicted that couples with competing as opposed to complementary goals would experience the most strain and that increased work commitment by the wife would lead to most conflict in husband- and coupled-centered marriages and least in child-centered marriages. On the basis of this hypothesis, we might have predicted that the more Anne Dooley and Linda Meyers left their husbands at home alone while pursuing their own careers, the more conflict there would be in their marriages. Although we would have been right for the Dooleys and the Meyers, we would have been wrong if we made the same prediction for the Collinses. In this section, I will explain why a wife's spending long hours away from home contributed to the dissolution of two marriages but left a third flourishing.

Bob and Anne Dooley.   When I interviewed Bob and Anne Dooley in 1976, Anne had been working overtime all summer putting in a new data processing system for her department. Bob, meanwhile, had been home caring for the children and feeling guilty about not doing the research and writing projects his academic career demanded of him. He felt resentful of Anne's work and told me, "During that period of overtime, I felt that working was the shittiest thing anyone could ever do." In addition to this apparent conflict in Anne and Bob's career demands, the Dooleys had high standards for all their family roles and had trouble finding adequate household help. At the time, I wondered what would happen as Bob's tenure decision approached.

When I spoke with Bob in 1983, I discovered that the tenure decision had never come. In 1977, discontent with the pressure to both teach and publish and unimpressed with the quality of his colleagues in the business school, Bob began an accounting business. He continued teaching until June 1979, when he left the University and put all of his energies into the business. Unfortunately, 1979 was an exceptionally bad year for small businesses of all sorts, and Bob and his partner found themselves facing client after client who had to be advised to declare bankruptcy.

Meanwhile, Anne Dooley had left Datan a few months after I interviewed her in 1976 and had taken a job with a large company in a city an hour's drive from her home. While Bob was watching his clients' businesses fail and wondering if his own would survive, Anne was being groomed by her company to become the top woman in finance. In the fall of 1979, her company sent her to a 10-week, out-of-town seminar on women in middle management. After she came back, she began putting in even longer days at work, leaving the house at 5:00 AM and returning as late as 9:00 PM. For Bob, this was the beginning of the end of the marriage.

In making the decision to attend the out-of-town seminar, Anne had discussed her plans with the entire family and thought that she had the support of all three of them, including Grace, her 14-year-old daughter, and Tim, her 10-year-old son. However, even though Anne had left a freezer full of prepared meals and Grace was getting dinner on the table every night as well as doing the laundry, Bob described the 10 weeks Anne was away as being "hard, very hard." He said, "She would call, or she wouldn't call. I didn't like that part." For Bob, apparently, what was hard was not being able to depend upon Anne's companionship. Anne told me that after she returned from the seminar, "The more money I made and the busier I got, the more he [Bob] would stay away from the house." Bob said that as he encountered more and more problems with his business, he began doing less at work but drinking more and staying away from home until finally in June 1980 he began to get some psychological counseling.

During this hard year, Bob and Anne did talk about how lucky they were that Anne was earning as much money as she was so that the family was not suffering from the decrease in Bob's earnings. However Bob told me that even when Anne was earning $10,000 to $15,000 more than he was, he still felt that it was his responsibility to provide. Somehow, even though all their money went into the same pot and even though his income did not cover the family's expenses, Bob still thought of the mortgage as his responsibility. Similarly, after reading my research report, Anne described herself as never having been comfortable with the idea of being a coprovider. Even when she was moving up the company ladder and even after she had had her consciousness raised at the seminar for women in management, she still thought that Bob should be the head of the family and was frightened when she realized that he had a lot of inner conflicts. She wanted to see him as a strong person who had "everything settled," but in the fall of 1979, he was not acting like one.

Whereas Bob was upset by Anne's 14-hour workdays, Anne's major complaint was that she could not get Bob to participate in negotiations about how the housework would be done. She was doing all the laundry and all the shopping and would blow up periodically, saying she physically could not do all she was doing at home and work the hours she was working, but then nothing would change. She thinks that Bob resisted responsibility for housework because were he to accept it, he would feel as if he were giving up something. Bob, on the other hand, says that he stopped doing housework after he started his own business, "because he didn't have the time." Given that Anne's workday left her with no more time than Bob's did and given that Bob's business was declining rather than expanding, it appears that the housework issue was part of a larger question of whose work should be considered more important and how the demands of each person's work should fit into the relationship. Neither Anne nor Bob mentioned discussing that. Instead they continued to fight about Anne's being away so much, Bob's drinking, and the housework, and neither felt supported by the other.

Finally, in January 1981, Bob moved out and he and Anne, ambivalent about a divorce, tried a trial separation. Meanwhile, Anne had found a marriage counselor and Bob went with her about eight times until he stopped because he felt that the counselor was not directive enough for him. Anne and Bob agreed to a divorce in October and the divorce was final in May 1982. Not long after that, Bob sold his business, remarried, and moved to another part of the country. Looking back on it, Anne described the divorce as "to some extent part of a midlife crisis." She and Bob were each in their late thirties and had stayed married for the children's sake until they finally decided that it was not good for them to do this. Bob's explanation, however, emphasizes how hard it was for him to have his business going downhill while Anne was away from home for 14 hours at a time.

> Anne was gone a lot. Her top priority was her job. I expected her to be home . . . me being a silly male.

In addition to Anne's failure to meet Bob's expectations of an available (perhaps doting) wife, Bob's failure to meet Anne's expectations of a "sturdy oak capable of handling anything" and the discomfort each was having with the reversal of their provider roles, Anne and Bob had been having trouble dealing openly with conflict. Bob described himself as a "bull in a china shop" who had a need to confront things directly while Anne always wanted to smooth things over. This difference in style may have been partially responsible for each staying away from home for longer and longer hours in 1979. In any case, their difficulties in dealing openly with conflict seem to have prevented the Dooleys from resolving the part of their conflict that resulted from competing work and family priorities.

In spite of these problems, Anne and Bob worked hard on their divorce just as they each had on their marriage and their careers. Anne told me that she and Bob had kept their respect for each other, and Bob described their "working really hard through the divorce" so that the kids could get enough loving and he and Anne could stay friends. When I spoke with Anne on the telephone, she had recently called Bob to get some ideas from him for a talk she had been asked to give.

At the time of this writing, Anne was still living with her son at their old address. Grace was away at college but home on weekends, and both children regularly visit their father during school vacations. Anne describes herself as having grown tremendously and being much happier with herself. Bob is also happier with his life and himself, although he misses his children a great deal. His new wife, also named Anne, is working on her PhD in clinical psychology and has been exposing Bob to some of her thinking about androgyny. Since this is the second marriage for both of them, they are seeing a counselor in order to give this marriage a better chance. Bob and his new wife have what Bob describes as excellent fights. Anne II does not back off. At the moment, Anne II is working on her dissertation and is not employed while Bob is both teaching and running an accounting business. He says that he does nevertheless share the cooking and does all of the ironing and the outside work, which he estimates to be 40% of all the household work. Still, however, he considers providing to be his responsibility.

What will happen when and if Anne II wants to work 60 hours a week? We can only guess, but hopefully Bob and Anne II will have developed the skills to more clearly negotiate each of their work commitments than was possible in Bob's first marriage. As many family sociologists have observed, breaking with tradition often deprives one of the luxury of being able to proceed through life unconsciously. Perhaps this is why Holmstrom (1972) found that the professional women in her study were better able to balance their work and family lives in their second marriages than they had been able to in their first ones.

David and Linda Meyers.   When I interviewed the Meyers in 1976, Linda, like Anne Dooley, had been working overtime at her job. Meanwhile, David had been home full-time recuperating from back surgery. Not only did David resent Linda's putting more time into her work when he was available to spend more time with her, but he also needed and wanted her attention. Instead, he found himself managing the household while waiting for Linda to get home late from work.

Although David had said then that when he finally understood how important Linda's work was for her, he had been able to be more sympathetic. When I spoke with him in 1983, he traced the decline of their marriage to the time of the back operation. Linda moved out and filed for divorce in June 1979. (David said he could not bring himself to do it.) The divorce was final in December and now Linda and David live in separate apartments across the street from each other. The youngest son lives with David and helps keep the house while a daughter away at college stays with Linda on school vacations. Linda and David have both been dating other people since the divorce but neither has remarried.

As with Bob and Anne Dooley, competing goals and violated expectations played a part in the Meyers' divorce. However, in contrast to Bob Dooley who had been career oriented throughout his marriage, David Meyers had given his family top priority and had always been supportive of Linda's work. He is the one man in the managerial-professional category whom I considered to be job as opposed to career oriented. Given the emphasis David placed on his family and his history of sharing household responsibility, we might have expected David Meyers to adjust more easily to Linda's increased work commitment than Bob Dooley did to Anne's. However, as the following description shows, the loss of their wives' companionship and attention at a time in their marriage when they were expecting and needing more rather than less of it made both men less satisfied with their marriages (cf. Rubin, 1983).

As Linda Meyers became more and more involved in her middle-management job at Datan, she also continued her struggle to become a more independent person as opposed to the "child-wife" she had been in the earlier part of her marriage. The death of her mother in the year following David's back surgery also contributed to her struggle for autonomy. In addition, she got some help from a psychological counselor. Comparing her marriage to the marriage of other professionals described in my research report, Linda wrote

> David was different from other professional people mentioned in your article in that he shared in housework and shopping even before I went to work. His income was twice mine and although he gave me gifts, he had a difficult time "allowing" (how I hate to use that word now!) me to make spending decisions. I was gradually accepted as a coprovider and our incomes did go jointly into the pot. I let him do all the worrying, to "take care of me." When I finally wanted to be responsible and assertive (when I grew up), I forced him to change the role into which I'd thrust him . . . one factor contributing to the divorce.

Whereas, for Linda, the central issue was her own personal growth and autonomy, for David, the major difficulty was not getting back what he had been giving. He said that Linda's independence was not a problem for him. He had been frustrated with his job in hospital management and felt that he was holding himself back so that he could spend more time with the kids and allow Linda to put more energy into her career. He would have been willing to do this if Linda had had more time to spend with him. Instead, she was giving more time to her work and, from David's point of view, did not have time to do things with him or to take vacations. Just when the children were getting old enough so that David and Linda could take vacations without them, Linda was no longer available to do this. Having made what he considered a sacrifice for Linda's career, David did not think that this was fair. As he told me, "I wasn't getting it back."

David mentioned one or two other factors that he thought contributed to the divorce. Among these were differences in the ways Linda and David deal with conflict and anger. David complained that Linda was uncomfortable with anger and did not give him enough room for his angry feelings and said that this difference was especially noticeable in a conflict

THE FAMILIES SIX YEARS LATER / 155

he and she had about how to deal with their oldest son. No doubt there were many other issues that I did not learn about; however, if we are to accept their accounts on face value, conflicting work/family priorities and different styles of dealing with anger played a part in the Meyers' divorce as they did in the Dooleys'.

Like Anne and Bob, however, both Linda and David view their divorce positively. For David, it was "the best thing that ever happened to them." After the divorce, he had "all these energies freed up," and, in January 1980, he left his hospital job to take a job in a small company that sells and maintains hospital equipment. Perhaps as a result of the intensity with which he worked in that first year, he had a heart attack and had to have bypass surgery in March 1981. However, he is now president of his company and is earning over $100,000 a year. He told me that he still loves Linda and that they are best friends. Furthermore, he thinks that they have a better relationship now than they did when they were married to each other. For a new spouse, though, David wants someone who is not tied down to either career or family so that he and she can together enjoy the condominium in Florida he can now afford and take some time off every month to have fun. Linda, meanwhile, has continued to move up in her job and has had three promotions since 1980. She earned $30,000 a year in 1981 and she sounded happy and enthusiastic when I spoke with her on the telephone.

For both the Dooleys and the Meyers, the wife's increasing work commitment at a time when the husband was experiencing dissatisfaction with his own work and expecting more companionship from his wife led to increased conflict and marital dissatisfaction. In each case, the wife wanted more autonomy at the same time that the husband wanted more togetherness. However, whereas Bob Dooley was able to give Anne very little support in her rise to the top, David Meyers held his career back and expected something in return, which he did not get. For these couple-oriented marriages, companionship was an important goal. When personal goals shifted and began to conflict, husbands resented the loss of their wives' companionship. At this point, conflict resolution strategies broke down. The wife's need to avoid angry exchanges combined with the husband's need to get things out in the open pushed each partner further away from the relationship rather than closer together. However, the mutual respect and long history of attempting to work things out led each couple to continue working on their relationship throughout the separation and divorce and end up with an intact relationship of which they feel proud. Although the marriages "failed," their relationships "succeeded."

Ted and Joan Collins. The reader will remember Ted and Joan Collins as the couple who sparred over Joan's career advancement ("Too bad they don't give a rating for 'bitch,' because you'd get a six on that one, too.") and could not agree about whose job really came first. Their relationship had been child- as opposed to couple-centered and although Joan's work had provided them with more common ground, I was not optimistic about their ability to resolve the subterranean guerilla warfare in which they seemed to be engaged. Something happened, however, in the six intervening years that has resulted in a closer marriage and the adoption of complementary and joint, as opposed to competing, career goals.

When I called the Collins home in January 1983, one of their daughters told me that her parents were out for a walk and would be returning in an hour. The next evening Joan said that during their walk, they had been discussing what their business card would look like when and if they established a joint consulting business. Perhaps they would use the phrase, "Call-in the Collinses." In the years since I had interviewed her, Joan had moved up to a managerial position at Datan and was making $35,000 a year in 1981. In the fall of 1982, she left Datan and started working for a computer firm in sales. Like Anne Dooley, she was commuting nearly an hour each way to work, leaving at 6:00 AM and returning at 8:00 PM. Before she was laid off in December, she was expecting to gross $50,000 for the year matching Ted's income. When I called, she and Ted were planning a one-week Caribbean tour (without the children), and Joan planned to look for a similar job in computer sales after they returned. She is excited about the prospects of continuing to advance in this fast-moving field.

For a couple who once told me that they had returned from a vacation because they missed the kids and had nothing to say to each other, plans for a business partnership and a Caribbean cruise came as a surprise. In separate telephone interviews, Ted and Joan explained what had happened.

In 1981, Ted had begun to feel overstressed at work. As manager at an engineering firm he was constantly being asked to do things he did not want to do and found himself agreeing to do things without thinking about what they would mean to him or to his family. When he realized that he was spending half his time in a city 300 miles from home and still could not say "no" to additional job demands, he sought professional counseling. Joan went with Ted for six months, and once Ted understood that Joan did not need him to stay in management, Ted was able to decide to move out of his overly demanding job into a research and development position, which he likes much better, even though it meant forgoing a salary increase for that year. In addition to helping Ted understand that he had Joan's "permission" to take a detour on his career ladder, the counseling helped Joan resolve some underlying issues in her family history that had been having an impact on their relationship.

After Ted and Joan had resolved Ted's "midcareer crisis" and Ted had been working in research and development for the summer, Joan decided to make her move. She left her job at Datan and took a new job in computer sales in a firm an hour's commuting distance away. Now that Ted was not traveling as much and now that he was feeling less stressed, he was willing to do what needed to be done at home in order to allow Joan to leave the house at 6:00 AM and return at 8:00 PM. The same man who had, in 1976, told me that "everyone had to have responsibilities that were theirs" and that cooking was one thing he did not do was now telling me that he had been doing all of the cooking during the week. Although he himself would not have chosen to do the driving that Joan was doing, he thought that the knowledge she was gaining would help her advance in the field and was, therefore, worth the sacrifices each of them was making. After the children finish college (two will be in college next year), Ted thinks that maybe he and Joan can take the risk of starting a consulting firm together. The same husband who used to joke about giving his wife a "bitch" rating now wants to work with her as a partner, and they seem to equally enjoy fantasies about the "Call-in the Collinses" consulting firm. From Joan's point of view, "things have never been better."

Analysis

One striking difference between the way in which career changes happened for the Collinses as compared to the Meyers and the Dooleys is that Joan did not make a dramatic change in her career (although she had been making incremental changes all along) until after Ted had resolved his own career crisis. Each one of them was, therefore, able to provide support for the other as the changes happened. The Dooleys and the Meyers, however, were not blessed with such timing. The wives were going full-speed ahead at the same time that the husbands were feeling frustrated and dissatisfied with their own work. Furthermore, whereas Ted and Joan Collins had a child-centered marriage that was only beginning to be more companionate, the Meyers and the Dooleys had more couple-centered marriages and higher expectations for companionship. For Ted and Joan, then, whatever time they spent together was a bonus, whereas for Bob Dooley and David Meyers, the time apart was deprivation. I suspect also that the idea of using Joan's new experience as the basis for even more companionship in the future makes the time she must now spend away more palatable. For David Meyers and Bob Dooley, however, each new level of commitment their wives made to their work kept their wives still further away from them with no hope of a reunion in the forseeable future.

External Sources of Stress

In the previous section we saw how wives' career ambitions combined with husband's career frustrations can sometimes contribute to divorce. Couples in which both spouses were family oriented or one family and one work oriented were less likely to report internal conflict over work/family priorities and more likely to describe external sources of stress such as work-schedule changes, layoffs, and business failures. In this section, I will describe how the recession and changes in work schedules affected the Davises, Mooneys, Hutchinses, Reades, and the Marxes.

Work Scheduling.   When Cynthia Davis was working in the factory, she and Mike each worked days, and this fit in well with their school-aged children's schedules. Now Cynthia works second shift and sometimes works on weekends. Mike cooks dinner for the children and the children do the dishes. Cynthia gets home after everyone is in bed and gets up after they leave in the morning. Her family would like to have her home in the evenings and on weekends, and she is trying to get the midnight shift instead. Meanwhile, because Cynthia's income as a security guard is less than half what she earned on the assembly line, Mike is working as much overtime as he can in order to make up the difference. This means that even on the weekends when Cynthia is home, Mike may not be. When I called, Cynthia told me that it had been quite awhile since she and Mike had been able to go out with each other on the weekend.

In contrast, James Mooney's problem was a result of getting *off* second shift rather than *onto* it. For several years, James had been working afternoons so that he could care for his boys during the day. Before they reached school age, he would wake up with them in the morning, feed them breakfast, and care for them until he left for work at 3:00 PM. While he was with the children, he would also do housework, repairs, and errands so that Jill had less to do when she got back from work in the late afternoon. Four years ago, when the boys were 9 and 10, James Mooney decided to move to the day shift. Although this gave him the opportunity to participate in the growing number of sports events in which his children were now involved, his new schedule initially posed an adjustment problem. For a man who had been used to returning home at midnight to a sleeping family, coming home physically and mentally tired in the late afternoon was a shock. Jill and boys were already home and as James describes it, he found himself suddenly "right in the middle of the family." He told me that he did not know how this had worked out for Jill (they had not discussed it), but for him, it was "quite an adjustment."

Ultimately, James' first-shift schedule has given Jill and James more time together. They go out on weekday evenings to take their boys to soccer and baseball games and have gotten to know other parents as a result. In addition to becoming much less socially isolated than they were as a "two-shift" family, they have become closer now that they can all be together at the same time. Although working the day shift has made it easier for James to be a father to school-aged children and companion to his wife, working days has made it harder for James to share the housework. After he has worked all day long programming and operating computer-controlled machines, he does not feel like doing much of anything when he comes home. In fact, he says that he is doing even less of the repair work and "other things that are considered men's jobs" since he began working the day shift. Jill also reported that James was doing less housework but did not complain about it. For her, housework was relatively unimportant compared to the time they now have together and the achievements of their two teenaged boys.

Tom and Roberta Hutchins also had a temporary problem due to the demands of Tom's new job. After being laid off from his job as a foreman for awhile in 1976, Tom Hutchins found a new job as a safety compliance officer. During the first few months, he had to travel a great deal and would often be away from home for the whole week. This, he and Roberta both say, put a greater burden on Roberta, but the problem was resolved when Tom was able to decrease the amount of traveling he did. He stills travels once in awhile, but neither of them see this as a problem now. Because moving up a career ladder is considerably less important for Tom Hutchins than it was for Ted Collins, it was easier for Tom to say "no" to excessive demands at work than it had been for Ted.

The Recession.   Other externally caused changes in family life resulted from the recession. Because the blue-collar men who had not been laid off by 1976 were the ones who then had over 10 years of seniority, none of them were laid off subsequently even though as much as 40% of the work force in their plants was out of work. It was instead the small business people and white-collar workers who felt the impact of the recession between 1976 and 1982. I have already described how the decline of Bob Dooley's business at the same time that Anne's career was flourishing contributed to their divorce. In contrast to the Dooleys, the Reades and the Marxes experienced parallel rather than opposing changes in their work lives. In this section, I will describe how losing jobs at the same time brought Harold and Paula Reade closer together, whereas the strain of dealing with their floundering business led to a hard period in Peter and Gisela Marx's marriage.

Harold and Paula Reade.   Harold and Paula Reade have had complementary rather than conflicting work/family priorities. Harold was career oriented, devoting an average of 55–60 hours a week to his research at an engineering institute. Nonetheless, when Paula took a job as a secretary for the local board of realtors, Harold was willing to help more in the household. Paula, meanwhile, tailored her work commitment to the needs of her family by leaving meetings promptly at 5:00 PM even when she was the one responsible for taking notes. In 1976, Paula had told me that she returned to work at least partly in order to provide "backup" in case Harold should lose his job at the institute. Dependent as it was upon large research grants, the funding for Harold's work was always precarious.

As the two boys at home became more independent, Paula began to move up from her secretarial position, becoming an administrative secretary in 1978, an assistant to the vice-president in 1979, and an executive director in 1980. She enjoyed the challenge of accepting more and more responsibilities, but in 1981, due to the decline in the real estate market, her position was eliminated. At the same time, the funding for Harold's position disappeared and both the Reades were out of work at the same time. Because two of their three sons were economically independent and because of severance pay from each of their jobs, the Reades did not suffer financially, but Paula describes the emotional toll on both of them as "devastating." In her letter, Paula wrote about how the way in which her termination had been handled made her feel as if she "had done something awful."

In spite of the blows Paula and Harold had each suffered, they were able to support each other during the time they were both unemployed. When asked to describe changes in his marriage since 1976, Harold wrote

Depending upon one another during our respective periods of unemployment strengthened our appreciation of each other, I believe.

Paula concurred, adding "Our already solid marriage was made more solid by the emotional upheaval of both of us losing our jobs at the same time."

Within the next three months Harold found a rewarding job doing biomedical engineering and Paula found a job as an executive assistant for another organization. She has to commute and does not like having to work her way up another organization. She realizes, however, that without a college degree, she has little hope of starting near the top. For this reason she is going to school nights in order to complete her BA so that she will have an easier time starting at the management level should she make future job changes.

Because the college-student son living at home does a lot of the housework and cooking, Paula's commuting causes little disruption in the household. When the boys were younger and taking turns helping with meal preparation, Harold had found the commotion in the kitchen rather nerve-wracking. Now, however, he does not have to do as much of the cooking himself, although he does all the dishwashing, and neither Harold nor Paula consider the rest of the housework to be much of an issue. They think of their division of labor as something that "just happened," and Harold described their bargaining as having "no structure". Apparently, they have both forgotten the time nearly 10 years ago when Paula sat the family down and delegated tasks. Then, Harold took the bathroom "because it was the smallest!"

Peter and Gisela Marx   When I interviewed them in 1976, Peter and Gisela Marx were partners in a vacuum cleaner dealership. By 1982, they were in danger of losing the business even though each of them was still working 50 hours a week in an attempt to save it. In 1979, they expanded their dealership to include carpet sales, installing, and cleaning. Relying on large loans, they acquired inventory and paid for local television advertisements. In September and October 1979, they began to get orders from several car dealers and other local businesses. Then, in November, interest rates went up, car dealerships began to go out of business and cancel their orders, and the Marxes were left with their inventory and interest to pay on their loans but few sales.

In the following three years, the business did not improve greatly and although they have not lost money, they cleared only $14,000 in 1981. In order for them and their two children to live on this income, they have had to eliminate eating out and most forms of entertainment as well as vacations. Their children make life a little easier by doing a lot of the housework, but still Peter and Gisela have found it hard to continue working as hard as they are when, as Gisela said, at the end of the week, "there is no place to go but home."

Worrying and working together constantly and then going home without the promise of escape to dinner or a movie began to wear on the Marxes. They became less patient with each other at work and at home. For awhile, they thought that their personal relationship was deteriorating. Having prided themselves upon their ability to communicate with each other and their mutual respect, they were surprised and disappointed at what appeared to them to be a failure of the relationship. The mutual withdrawal that followed the increase in tension level was bewildering to both of them. Finally, they began to talk about what was happening and eventually came to the conclusion that their short tempers had more to do with the recession than with any underlying problem in their relationship. Then, once they had been able to externalize the "enemy," they began to work out a survival strategy. This year they are making what they described as "a last ditch effort" to keep the shop open. If they fail, they will either look for other jobs locally or consider moving the business to another state. They would prefer to remain business partners if they can because they like to work together, but meanwhile they are considering whatever alternatives may be necessary. Like the Reades, the Marxes have been able to use their mutual misfortune as an impetus for joint problem solving. This became possible, however, only after they were able to locate the problem outside rather than inside their relationship. When at least part of the couple's conflict results from competing goals and priorities, as was true for the Dooleys and the Meyers, then joint problem solving is more difficult.

NEW WAGE RATIOS AND CHANGED BARGAINING POSITIONS

In a two-paged questionnaire and a 15- to 30-minute telephone interview, one cannot learn a great deal about six years of role bargaining. One can, however, learn about some of the factors affecting bargaining discussed in Chapters 3 through 5. I know, therefore, about changes in wage ratio, jobs, and labor force status. In addition, I have each spouse's estimation of how the division of labor has changed between 1976 and 1982 and some accounts of how personal changes have improved the wife's bargaining position. This section, then, addresses hypotheses 4 through 8 listed at the end of Chapter 5 and focuses on changed wage ratios, role definitions, and bargaining power.

Secondary Providers

In 1976, women I described as secondary providers were earning 30% or less of the family income and were seen as "pinch hitters," whose income was either not necessary at all or would be needed only temporarily. Their husbands told them that they could quit "whenever they wanted to," and if anything went wrong at home, they were expected to quit. Most were married to career-oriented or superprovider husbands who, although they sometimes helped a little more around the house, did not expect to make major changes in their own lives in order to support their wives' work efforts. Since they did not "really need" their wives to work, they did not expect that their wives should "really need" them to share household responsibilities. Because the women in this study had been working for two or more years by the time of the second interview, several already gained recognition as coproviders in 1976. Of the six who remained in the "secondary provider" category, Bess Holling and Billie King did not intend to continue working indefinitely; Jane Devore and Maria Correlli were not only in low-paying and dead-end jobs but also were married to men earning relatively high incomes; and both Theo James and Paula Reade were married to men who had made it clear that they had a stake in being considered the "main provider" even though their wives were at the time contributing 30% of the income.

If it is true that wage ratio and each spouse's role attachments are the best predictors of provider role definition, Jane Devore and Maria Correlli who are both self-motivated had a chance of becoming coproviders only if their husbands' incomes decreased. As secretaries without college degrees, they had little hope of equaling their husbands' $50,000-and-above incomes. (In 1981, John Devore was earning $75,000.) We would have expected family-oriented women such as Bess Holling and Billie King to become permanent secondary providers or to leave the labor force. The only women who had a good chance of moving toward coprovider status were Theo James and Paula Reade, and then only if something happened to either their wage ratio or marital relationships to improve their bargaining positions. After all, their 30% share of the family income in 1976 was similar to the 30–33% shares that four of the six coprovider wives were earning.

As we now know, Bess Holling and Billie King did leave the labor force, and Paula Reade did gain new recognition from her husband by providing emotional and financial support during their joint unemployment. Jane Devore, although she stayed at her job and did get a promotion, still makes only 18% of the family income because Dr. Devore earns so much. However, Maria Correlli appears to be bearing more of the responsibility to provide than she used to due to a decline in her husband's business. Since she did not want to talk to me, all I know is that she is working full-time while his business is floundering. In the next few pages we will take a closer look at how Theo James and Paula Reade have changed their bargaining positions while Jane Devore has not.

Theo and Richard James

Richard James was the factory worker who had told me in 1976 that although his wife's 30% contribution to the family's income was a "big help," *all they did* with her paycheck was to make house payments. Because Richard objected to having to look after his two young sons after he got home from work, Theo was thinking of taking a job as a school secretary so that she could be home when the children returned from school. Instead, after spending one more year as a church secretary, she quit for the summer because she did not like the job: "Everyone there thought I was working for everyone and I had to work on Sundays. I was 'yes' person." In the fall, she found another job, not as a school secretary, but rather as a clerk in a hospital working 8:00 to 4:30 and getting home at 5:00 PM. The boys get home before Richard does and have to call her at work as soon as they get in. Richard, if not working overtime, gets home at 4:00 and, when he was attending evening classes to qualify for a machine repairman's job, would have dinner ready when Theo came home. Normally, he and Theo do the dishes together after dinner so that they have time with each other.

For Theo, the major change in her bargaining power has resulted not from a change in the proportion of the income she contributes (33% now as opposed to 30%) but rather as a result of assertiveness skills she has learned on her job. She told me that although she really does not like working for women bosses, the eight nurses whom she serves in the outpatient clinic have provided role models for her. She hears them talking about standing up to male doctors and administrators and says that this gives her the idea that she can stand up at home also. In addition, she has taken two assertiveness training classes offered at her workplace. Overall, she thinks that her work has made her feel like "more of a person." This was, in part, demonstrated by her seeking a competitive offer from a hospital closer to her home and using this to win a new title as administrative secretary and a raise in pay after a year and a half on her job.

One incident Theo chose to share with me suggests that although Richard still holds the purse strings, those strings are getting looser. In April 1981, Theo decided that she wanted her own two-seater sports car. She found a second-hand Datsun 280Z for $5500. Since Richard was a UAW member, he was not happy about his wife buying a foreign car and wanted her to get a Corvette instead. When she took him with her to test-drive the car, he would not drive it. She told him that she would buy it anyway and he said, "Just go ahead and try. You won't be able to get a loan without my signature." (He had used a similar strategy when she wanted to return to work, saying "I doubt you can find a job.") Ten years ago, Richard would have had the finance companies on his side, but in 1983 Theo had no trouble getting a loan on her own income and signature. A male friend from work came along for moral support, encouraging her to be independent and do what she wanted to. (Several of Theo's friends are men, and Richard appears to have no problem with this.)

Richard did not like the fact that Theo had bought the car over his protest, but, faced with a *fait accompli*, he "let" Theo use some of their "joint money" in addition to her already depleted private savings to help finance her car. However, he did not want her to drive the car to his workplace when she met him for lunch. After a year, however, Richard agreed to take the Datsun on their annual anniversary trip, and according to Theo, he "absolutely loved" it. Still, he hopes that the next time Theo wants a sports car, she will buy a Buick. She says she will buy American *when and if* American sports cars become competitive. Theo's independent income as well as her separate base of social support strengthen her *bargaining position*. At the same time, assertiveness training and exposure to new role models have helped her adopt a more individualistic *bargaining strategy*. Rather than plead with Richard that he should allow her to have the car she wants "because it is only fair," Theo combined the unilateral action of buying the car with the simple assertion that she could buy herself a car with her own money, regardless of what Richard wanted (cf. Scanzoni and Szinovacz, 1980:67). He did not *have* to "let" her use joint money, but since he does love her and does want to live in harmony with her and she is not totally dependent upon him for either financial or emotional support, he gave in. Richard is also doing a lot more cooking, laundry, and housework of all sorts since the last interview, although I cannot tell whether or not this is also the result of Theo's improved bargaining power.

Harold and Paula Reade

Harold and Paula Reade whom I have already discussed have also changed the balance of power in their family. In their case, the change stems from their experience of being unemployed at the same time. It helped each of them (and perhaps especially Harold) to see how they were both financially and emotionally interdependent. In addition, because of Harold's unemployment and Paula's promotions in her former job, Paula's share of their 1981 income was 45% as opposed to 30% in 1976. This may change for 1982 and 1983 given that Harold moved to a higher-paying job and Paula took a pay cut, but as Paula writes, being a two-job family is a way of life for them now. Paula Reade is no longer a secondary provider who can quit whenever she wants:

> A two job family is a way of life for us now, both economically and emotionally. I know that when I retire I will still be involved somewhere. I can't sit at home and watch the world on television. I want to be a part of it.

Far from "watching the world on television," Paula Reade at 54 is still adding skills and accomplishments to her résumé.

Jane and John Devore

The Devores were one of the couples kind enough to read the entire manuscript and comment upon it. They found my description of them accurate and Jane comments that the description fits as well in 1982 as it did in 1976:

> I believe it's accurate. I am married to a professional man who seems to consider my job in a more positive light than he did in the past. However, it should require no change in his own contribution to the caring of the family or household.

John remains as active as ever in his career, and at age 55 is completing a residency in psychiatry so that he can work in the substance abuse area. Nonetheless, now that their children are on their own (with occasional returns from not-quite-adults who need help) Jane and John report that their relationship has continued to improve, with John's recovery from alcoholism continuing to play a major part in what feels to both of them like a "new marriage."

Ambivalent Coproviders

According to Hypothesis 5 at the end of Chapter 4 the couples who were most ambivalent about being coproviders in 1976 but who were in fact dependent upon the wife's income should be more likely than either secondary-provider or coprovider couples to make a change that would reduce the inconsistency. Wives who were in fact coproviders but who were having trouble accepting themselves as such could either drop out of the role altogether or become more committed to it. Becoming more committed to the role would be hardest in cases in which the husband was also having trouble accepting the wife as a coprovider and easiest when he was more enthusiastic than she about her contributing to the family income.

Although it may be fortuitous, all four couples considered to be ambivalent coproviders did make dramatic changes, all of which have been discussed earlier in this chapter. Joan and Ted Collins have become less ambivalent about Joan's coprovider role as a result of Ted's resolving his own work conflicts. Nancy Williams solved her ambivalence by moving to Tennessee so that her husband could find a job and she could be close to her family. Don Williams, who saw his wife as "just helping out for awhile," is satisfied with this arrangement. Only Anne and Bob Dooley were unable to resolve the inconsistency within the context of the relationship. Thus, of the four ambivalent wives, one has become a permanent housewife, working part-time when she feels like it, two others have become more recognized as coproviders, although Theo James still struggles for her financial autonomy, and the fourth left her marriage before she was able to completely accept her self-sufficiency.

Coproviders

Couples who were already comfortable with the idea of being coproviders in 1976 might be expected to stay that way. Since all of them included wives who were self- as opposed to family-oriented, these wives would also be good candidates for increasing their incomes relative to their husbands. As predicted, all of the coprovider wives remained in the labor force, all continued to earn 30% or more of the family income, and two did substantially increase their shares. Self-motivated women who did not increase their wage ratios had husbands who earned a great deal of money (Jane Devore and Linda Meyers) or were themselves in low-paying dead-end clerical jobs, such as Roberta Hutchins' $12,000-a-year library job and Theo James' administrative assistant job.

In 1976, Jill Mooney was an ambitious woman who looked forward to getting more training so that she could get more interesting and responsible work and advance in her career. For Jill, "work was a haven from home and home was a haven from work." Although she would have liked her husband James to earn more money, she was content to earn it herself as long as he was willing to help at home. James, as we saw, grew attached to his parent role and had no problem with Jill earning more money. They were hoping to buy land and maybe a larger house as a result of Jill's earnings.

Jill did get a promotion in 1977 and has become manager of the office in which she was working in 1976. In 1982, she was earning $21,400. She was given on-the-job training and took seminars at the university. For awhile she worked as a systems analyst. However, she said that the systems analyst position "was taking too much of [her] personal time and was frustrating." For that reason she moved back to her old job as office manager. Now she characterizes herself as less ambitious than she used to be. Money is not that important any more, and whatever extra money they have goes toward the boys' education. Next year both boys will be in private school, and since both are excellent students, the Mooneys are already saving for college. Jill says that she and James are not spending money on themselves and never did buy the larger house. The boys are the first priority for their money as well as time.

James' income as a machinist has steadily increased but did not make the qualitative leap that Jill's did when she moved into a managerial position. This means that she now earns 42% of the family income compared to the 30% she earned in 1976.

Cathy Shultz is in a very similar position. Married to a machinist whose income has plateaued, she had been able to increase her share by getting a promotion to executive secretary. Because Mike was laid off for a few weeks last year, he grossed only $20,000 compared to Cathy's $18,000 making her share 47% of the family income. Mike is taking courses in electronics and thinks he might like to get into television repair work eventually and get out of what he describes as a "little dirty job" repairing machines.

Mike still feels grateful that Cathy is working, and with her income, they have been able to take expensive vacations and visit relatives in Germany. He, like other coprovider husbands, still says, "I wish she could quit, but . . . ." After the kids finish college, then, he told me, Cathy can "do whatever she wants." Until then, it is really necessary for her to work.

The only self-motivated woman who might have increased her share of the family income but did not was Mary Anderson. In 1976, Bill Anderson was laid off from one of his two jobs and was considering giving up his second job when and if called back to his permanent one. Had he done that, Mary would have been earning more money than he. Since their children were becoming financially independent and since Bill had finally decided that Mary needed him for more than just his paycheck, he was seriously considering working only one job. Instead, he continued to work at his second job after being called back to the other one, and ironically, the second job provided the circumstances that led to his death in February 1981. The company he worked for sent him to Nigeria where he contracted a form of malaria for which there is no cure. He returned home and died a few weeks later. Mary told me that, at the time of his death, he was making nearly as much money on his permanent job as she was at her job as a group leader at Datan. She also said that in the years just before Bill died, "things were just beginning to get really good" for her and Bill. They were spending more time with each other and enjoying the independence of the "empty nest" stage of their marriage. One wonders, however, if Bill Anderson ever really did give up being a superprovider as I thought he had in 1976.

The six women who were coproviders in 1976 remained coproviders as long as they were married and two increased their shares of the family income. In addition, two ambivalent coproviders had become less ambivalent and at least one secondary provider had been recognized as a coprovider. By 1982, provider role definitions had shifted so that only Jane Devore could still be considered a secondary provider. Theo and Richard James could perhaps be considered ambivalent coproviders, whereas the Reades, Collinses, and Davises may all be added to the coprovider list. The more the wife becomes committed to continue working and the more her husband acknowledges that her income counts, the further the wife moves toward being defined as a coprovider. Nonetheless, Mike Davis and Mike Schultz each continue to insist that providing is more their responsibility and still tell the interviewer that they "wish [their] wives could quit, but . . . ." Even when a man has become willing to rely on his wife for 40 to 50% of the household income, he still finds it necessary to acknowledge that the responsibility for earning the family income is really his. The role of the good provider may be dying, but it is not dying easily.

ROLE BARGAINING AND ROLE SHARING

As they improved their wage ratios and/or gained in self-esteem, several wives appear to have increased their bargaining power. Theo James stands up for what she wants now both at home and at work and demonstrated her ability to make and carry out a decision unilaterally when she bought her own car. Harold Reade has a new appreciation of the ways in which he and Paula are financially and emotionally interdependent, and Ted Collins has not only stopped putting his wife down for doing well on her job but is now making sacrifices so that she can continue to advance in her career. Although I had expected that wives' increased bargaining power might lead to more household work being done by husbands, this relationship was not as clear in the 1982 follow-up as it had been in the 1975–1976 interviews. The James, Collinses, Marxes, and Schultzes all did report that husbands were now doing more than they used to, but James Mooney and Harold Reade were doing somewhat less. In addition, all couples who had teenaged children at home reported that the parents were doing less housework, while children were doing more. Although some husbands may have been doing a larger share of the total than they once did, that total has decreased and the children are doing more. Because husbands and wives were asked only to give their impressions of who was doing more and who was doing less since the last interview, this longitudinal glimpse of changes in the division of labor is admittedly impressionistic. However, it does help to corroborate what our cross-sectional comparisons in 1976 as well as large-scale surveys have found: life cycle status is an important determinant of household division of labor, and husbands of young children do more household work than do fathers of older children still at home but less than fathers whose children have left home (Model, 1981). In the next section I will discuss briefly the ways in which life cycle status changes and work scheduling affected division of labor.

Life Cycle Changes

In 1979, I conceived of role sharing as a progression toward more and more equality. The more the wife is recognized as a coprovider, the more household roles will be shared; and the more these roles are shared, the more symmetrical the companionship will be, which in turn will further the wife's recognition as coprovider. The 1982 interviews have shown me that although the wife's increased income and husband's dependence upon that income may improve her bargaining power, this does not always lead to more sharing of household roles, especially if the work to be done is diminishing as a result of children becoming older and, therefore, not only requiring less energy from their parents but also making more of their own contributions to household work. Theo James told me that her oldest son enjoys doing housework and will call her at the office to find out what he can do for her. She doesn't pay him for it, but in exchange for his help, it is understood that his parents will buy him things that he wants, within reason. Similarly, the Marxes' two children will often have dinner cooked for their parents and sometimes will have cleaned the family room or done another chore without having been asked. Then, Gisela told me, the kids will say, "Well, all the work is done, so why don't we all go to a movie." (Given the Marxes' stringent budget, going to a movie is not often possible, but they will think of something fun that the family can do together.) Mike Schultz does not like to ask his children to help much since they have their homework, but they do pick up after themselves and his son will drive to pick Cathy up at work. Mike Davis says that he is able to get his two children to do quite a bit, although Cynthia maintains that she still does a lot of housework on the weekends because she "doesn't trust" the children to do it correctly. In general, however, the total burden of parenting and housework had substantially declined as the children got older and as this happened, housework became much less of an issue for the 16 families.

Work Schedule Changes

Work scheduling, meanwhile, continued to affect division of labor in 1982. At midlife, however, work schedules have more of an impact on meal preparation and housework than they do on child care. Mike Schultz, for example, is still working the midnight shift. He gets home in the early morning and sleeps until 3:00 PM. After the children get home from school, he gets dinner ready so that they can all eat after Cathy gets home at 4:30. Mike Davis, whose wife is working the second shift, is in a similar position and cooks dinner for the children and himself on Cynthia's workdays. Because Richard James gets home earlier than Theo, it makes sense for him to cook on the days on which he has class so that the family can finish eating in time for him to get to his 7:30 class. Ted Collins was also cooking dinners when Joan was commuting. Although cooking, like child care, is something that must be done daily and cannot be effectively postponed, housecleaning may either wait or not be done at all. Thus, because James Mooney feels less like doing housework at the end of his workday than he did on his mornings at home before going to work, he has stopped doing housework and Jill does whatever housecleaning that gets done.

CONCLUSION

Since theories developed from comparative case studies are closer to the real lives of the people studied than are conclusions drawn from statistical analyses of survey data, it is not surprising that the hypotheses listed at the end of Chapter 5 do fairly well when "tested" against the actual changes taking place in the lives of the 16 families. Three of the four women who were self as opposed to family motivated did leave the labor force. Couples with competing as opposed to complementary goals did suffer more strain, but with the help of a good marriage counselor and either judicious or lucky timing, some potentially severe conflicts were turned to the couples' advantage. This was especially the case when the problem could be defined as external to the relationship as opposed to being a function of it. Husbands responded differently to wives' increased work commitments depending both upon their expectations for companionship and the ways in which their wives' work affected the marital companionship. Whereas Bob Dooley was uncomfortable about both the long hours Anne spent away from home and her usurping the role of provider, David Meyers expressed less concern about his wife's career advancement than he did about her being unavailable to him. Job-oriented husbands did have less trouble accepting wives' increased incomes than did professional husbands, but changes in the marital relationships of professionals such as Ted Collins and Harold Reade made it easier for such men to rely on their wives' incomes. Although the couples have moved toward increased emotional and financial interdependence, they have not necessarily increased the sharing of housekeeping. Here life cycle status and work scheduling appear to be at least as important as role bargaining in determining the husband's share. As the children grew older, they both created less work for their parents and did more of it themselves. When a wife's increased work hours left a gap in household maintenance, husbands would step in and cook dinner or see to it that the children did their chores. However, unlike "becoming a parent," becoming a housekeeper appears, for men at least, to be reversible. Although a child's smiles and tears may lock a man into a cumulative and ongoing relationship, a gleaming kitchen floor simply gets dirty and a cooked dinner is eaten.

7

CONCLUSION: ROLE BARGAINING AND ROLE SHARING REEXAMINED

Up to this point, I have developed the role bargaining model outlined in Chapter 1 with only passing reference to the work of other sociologists. By avoiding copious references to research findings, I hope I have made the book more readable for those who do not share the misfortune of having learned "sociologese." This chapter, however, is addressed primarily to family scholars and practitioners, and deals in somewhat more depth with the issues raised in Chapter 1. First, I will discuss the utility of the bargaining model and examine some of the problems associated with inferring family process from division of labor. Next, I am going to reexamine the relationship among social class, role sharing, and role bargaining and finally discuss the question: "Is becoming a two-job family good for marriages?" Although most of this chapter is addressed to family scholars, the last section should be of interest to the general reader as well.

THE BARGAINING MODEL

Because the term, "bargaining" carries with it marketplace connotations of short-term individual gain, some sociologists find theories based on notions of bargaining or exchange to be inapplicable to primary relationships. Basing their understanding of exchange theory on Homans (1961), Simpson and England contend that bargaining theory emphasizes the individual interests of each spouse. Since bargaining power depends upon the resources each spouse can offer or withhold, they argue that bargaining theory requires that, "A gain in resources and resulting bargaining power for one entails a loss for the other (1982:151)."

Conceived of in such narrow terms, the bargaining model is clearly inappropriate for many, if not most, exchanges between spouses, lovers, or close friends. As I pointed out in Chapter 5, exchanges between spouses are often not of the *quid pro quo* variety. In fact, this has long been recognized by exchange theorists, especially those who, following Thibeaut and Kelly, define rewards so broadly as to include all kinds of gratifications (see Nye, 1979). In primary relationships, the relationship itself is a source of gratification and therefore, as several authors point out (Nye, 1979: 9; Blau, 1964), partners are unlikely to sacrifice the long-term benefits of the relationship for a short-term gain. This is why husbands in this study were in a double bind when faced with their wives' growing commitment to work. Although the wife's employment gave the couple more common ground and made the wife a more interesting companion, the wife's growing autonomy and competing demands for her time made it less likely that the husband could enjoy her companionship whenever he wanted to. Furthermore, the more the husbands subscribed to such egalitarian principles as, "It is only fair that I should allow my wife to enjoy occupational achievement if that is what she wants," the more of a bind he was in. Far from either a *quid pro quo* (give me this and I'll give you that) or a zero-sum (if you get more, I get less) sort of situation, the bargains described in this book often involve a complex balance of gains and losses, both individual and mutual. When Jane Devore gained bargaining power by gaining enough self-esteem to increase her demands for autonomy, (thus improving her bargaining *strategy*), John Devore lost the prerogative to expect Jane's company whenever he wanted it regardless of her needs. However, because of the new respect he has for Jane, he has gained a more equal companion and a more enjoyable relationship. John's short-term loss, therefore, has become a long-term gain for him, Jane, and the relationship.

Another criticism of exchange theory has been that such theory often assumes that there is general agreement among actors about what is a reward and what is a cost. In his earlier work, for example, Scanzoni argued that the more ably the husband fulfilled his provider role, the more his wife would reward him by performing her household duties (1970). On this basis, Scanzoni outlined a "web of reciprocity" involving a chain of rights and duties. A key assumption underlying the whole model, however, is that "one of the expectations inherent in the wife role is that the husband will provide as much status as possible (1970:32)." While some of the wives described in this book had this expectation, others, given the choice between their husbands' occupational achievements and more family time, would choose more family time. In fact, one might argue that, the higher the husband's income, the less likely it is that his wife will be willing to trade still more income for family time (i.e. income has decreasing marginal utility). Indeed, it is this sort of criticism which has led Aldous and others to suggest a curvilinear relationship between husband's occupational achievement and marital satisfaction (Aldous, 1969). While low income husbands withdraw from the family because they cannot fulfill their provider roles, upwardly mobile and high-income husbands often sacrifice their family relationships in the interest of occupational mobility (Dizard, 1968; Young & Willmott, 1973; Seidenberg, 1975). Aldous labels this perspective "success constraint theory" (Aldous, 1979:244). Although it may have been safe to assume that in American society prior to 1970, wives in general expected that their husbands would provide for the family as well as they could, it was not true that the husband's provider role was equally central in all households (see Komarovsky, 1940) or that all wives would sacrifice whatever was necessary in order to increase their husbands' incomes.

In answer to the criticism that exchange theory does not take into account differential valuing of rewards and costs, several writers have combined a symbolic interaction perspective with exchange theory (Singelmann, 1972; La Rossa, 1977). Symbolic interaction stresses the meanings people attach to events or interactions and argues that these meanings or definitions have consequences of their own (Burr et al., 1979:47). Thus, even if Anne Dooley did not believe that she was violating her marriage contract by being away at work fourteen hours at a time, her husband, Bob, defined it that way and was angry about her failure to fulfill what he thought were mutual expectations. Similarly, husbands used to a husband-centered companionship experienced more feelings of loss when wives returned to work than did those in child-centered families, because their definitions of what marriage is and should be were different. Throughout this book, meanings people attach to actions, events, or other peoples' words have been given special attention. As Komarovsky discovered in her study of unemployed men (1940), husbands who believe that being the main provider is essential to being a husband have a harder time relinquishing the provider role than those for whom other family roles such as father, companion, and caretaker are equally important. Role bargaining of the sort described in this book cannot be understood without reference to the subjective meanings people give to their own and each other's behavior.

Given all of these qualifications, is it still useful to conceive of what happens when wives return to work in terms of bargaining or exchange? Clearly, the husbands and wives I have described were bargaining only in the broadest sense of the word. In retrospect, they were likely to say, as Harold Reade did, that "there was no real structure" to their bargaining. Things just evolved. However, as I mentioned in Chapter 6, Harold Reade did agree at one point to clean the bathroom "because it was the smallest."

This, I would argue, is an excellent example of bargaining. His wife, Paula, had reasoned that because she was working, it was only fair that she should get more help with the housework from both Harold and the boys. Harold had agreed that "it was only fair" but sought to minimize the extra time housework would cost him by choosing "the smallest room." (Obviously, he had never cleaned a bathroom!) Looking back on it nearly eight years later, however, Harold sees no "structure" to their bargaining and instead describes their division of labor as having evolved naturally. Because family process involves a long chain of hundreds and hundreds of negotiations and exchanges, many of which become institutionalized, family process appears to "just happen" and family structure to "just grow."

As a sociologist, I have chosen to describe family process as a series of exchanges and have assumed that a generalized "norm of reciprocity" governs such exchanges even when the norm is not made explicit and even when neither spouse verbally acknowledges that an exchange is taking place. The bargains described in this book are similar to the silent bargains Strauss describes in Chapter 14 of his book *Negotiations*, (1978):

> Some negotiations may be very brief, made without any verbal exchange or obvious gestural manifestation; nevertheless, the parties may be perfectly aware of "what they are doing" . . . . they may not call this *bargaining*, but they surely regard its product as some sort of worked-out agreement. Other negotiations may be so implicit that the respective parties may not be thoroughly aware that they have engaged in or completed a negotiated transaction (1977:225).

Strauss then goes on to say that families are an excellent setting for this kind of implicit agreement which is made tacitly and is visible when it is violated, but invisible when honored.

As we have seen, spouses sometimes assumed that they knew what the other spouse wanted and then were surprised when a course of action resulted in unanticipated consequences. For example, when Anne Dooley was working such long hours, she complained she could not work the hours she was working and still be responsible for all of the housework. That complaint assumes that her husband has agreed to her working such long hours and should be prepared to support Anne's work commitment by helping more with the housework. Bob, however, does not appear to have made such an agreement (although he did agree to her attending the out-of-town seminar discussed in Chapter 6). In fact, he resented the time she was putting into her work and thought she should be spending more time with him. However, he did not say this in so many words. He simply refused to do housework, saying he did not have time and then began to spend more time away from the house himself. This pattern of action and reaction, incorrect assumptions, partial negotiations, and silent bargains was repeated many times in the 16 families. If the couple was fortunate, successive approximations led to a clearer definition of the problem and more explicit agreements about a solution (such as the Marxes' plan to try to save their business). Otherwise, tension could persist indefinitely in the form of regulated conflict such as the guerilla war the Collinses were having in 1976 about whose work was most important. Thus, although the bargaining described here rarely fits the formal bargaining model, it could be argued that when couples do have conflicts of interest, those who are able to make their expectations explicit and then negotiate the differences fare best. Unfortunately, in a time of rapidly changing gender role expectations, internal confusion and ambivalence are often part of the problem. Not only do people not know what their *spouses* want, they are not really sure what *they* want either. It is precisely in such times that it is least advisable to assume that marital relationships will "just evolve."

Far from being a way in which one spouse can triumph over another in a zero-sum game, bargaining between spouses is a means for husbands and wives to clarify their wants and needs to themselves and each other and then to agree upon a way in which both can get most of what they need. Role bargaining typically involves implicit disagreements about the work and family priorities of one or both partners. The couples in this study found that as the balance of power in their marriages became more equal, their companionship generally improved. However, when each of them wanted to put work before family, bargaining was most difficult. Common ground, therefore, is an insufficient basis for marital stability. Only through clear negotiation can spouses with competing interests find a mutually satisfactory solution.

Outcome vs. Process

In the first chapter, I argued that bargaining power was a better indicator of marital equality than was division of labor. Even in a study such as this one, however, bargaining power is harder to measure (or define "operationally") than is division of labor. Family sociologists have had a long and continuing debate over both the concept of power in marriage and the best way of measuring it on surveys (Bahr, 1974; Safilios-Rothschild, 1970). While many researchers have relied on indices of decision-making (Blood & Wolf, 1960), others have attempted to measure "the ability to have one's way despite opposition" (Olson & Ryder, 1970). Decision-making measures involving six or more pre-defined decision-making areas have the advantage of being easy to administer and analyze, and the disadvantage of being difficult to interpret. If the wife decides about what new furniture to buy, does that mean she has more power than the husband in that area, or does the husband just not care about the furniture and so choose to delegate this responsibility for deciding to his wife (cf. Bahr, 1982)? Laboratory studies involving real couples responding to projective measures (i.e. faced with such a decision, what would you do?), and open-ended interviews asking couples to list areas of disagreement and then describe what happened, are limited to small samples, making their results more difficult to generalize. Survey researchers are therefore left to draw on what can be learned from small scale studies using open-ended questions and then to devise measures of process. One example is Scanzoni's measure distinguishing among six different types of bargaining strategies used by wives in discussions with their husbands (1978).

Leaving aside the question of what power is and how to measure it, I will reconsider here some of the issues raised in Chapter 1. Can one infer bargaining power from the division of labor or from the outcomes of decisions made in families? Does increased wage ratio always lead to increased bargaining power? What about the contributions of bargaining skills, choice of strategy and self-esteem independent of wage ratio?

Resource-Based Power Models Re-examined

Most surveys which have measured wage ratio have found that the more money the wife makes relative to her husband, the more he helps with the housework (Farkas, 1976; Ericksen et al., 1979; Model, 1981; Haas, 1981). Several studies have also found employed women to have more decision-making power than do non-employed women (Blood & Wolfe, 1960; Lupri, 1969; Bahr, 1974). However, the connection between decision-making power and husbands' household help is less clear. When decision-making power is measured by asking who decides about X and when X involves (as it usually does in such studies) the decision to use money, then it is not surprising that employed women have been found to have more input on such decisions than do non-employed women. Furthermore, as I suggested earlier, having the power to decide about something about which one might prefer not to decide is an empty victory. Nancy Williams decided which bills were to be paid when, because she balanced the checkbook, but she really would have liked her husband Don to do this and goaded him with the taunt, "Ain't you man enough to pay the bills?" Nonetheless, to the extent that employed women both have more decision-making power and get more help from their husbands than non-employed women, it is possible that decision-making power and husband's share of household help are related. Unfortunately, most studies use relative resources as proxies for power, making it difficult to know whether or not the more "equitable" division of labor reported is really the result of a more equal balance of power. Given that women vary in the extent to which they *want* and *need* help from their husbands, researchers seeking to establish a link between balance of power and division of labor in marriage would do well to include measures of *wants* and *needs* as well as a measure of "ability to get one's way despite opposition."

While studies of resource-based power in marriage have failed to establish a clear link between power and division of labor, studies measuring the responsibility to provide have fared better. Both Haas (1981) and Scanzoni (1978) found that wives defined as coproviders were more likely to get help from their husbands than employed wives who were not so defined. Scanzoni explains this by arguing that "women who succeed in bringing their provider role into negotiations about housework are the more effective bargainers" (1978:78).

In this study, however, I have given several examples of women who did not choose to use their bargaining power in order to get more household help. Perhaps, then, women who get the most help have the most bargaining power, but those who have the most bargaining power do not always get more help because they do not always ask for it.

If power is defined as the "ability to get someone to do what they would not otherwise do" (Dahl, 1957), then we might ask whether wives who are doing the least desirable half of the household chores have as much power as their husbands do. The husbands in this study chose child care, cooking and shopping over housecleaning. Husbands tended to do what they liked doing or what absolutely had to be done in their wives' absence. Since housecleaning is most postponable and least preferred, it was most often left for wives who then either passed it on to the children, did it themselves, or hired someone to do it. Since neither Jill nor James Mooney like to do housework, it is significant that Jill is being left with it. However, since Cynthia Davis has high standards and does not trust her children to do cleaning (which their father is willing to insist that they do) the housework she does is more the result of choice than it is of her power position.

It therefore appears that a causal chain leading from relative resources to bargaining power to division of labor is over-simple. The crucial intervening variables are role attachments (role priorities) and role overload. Increased bargaining power results in more help from husbands only when 1) wives want help and ask for it, and 2) husbands would not otherwise have given this help spontaneously. Furthermore, tangible resources are not the only determinants of either provider role definition or bargaining power. Role attachments affecting both the wife's desire to be seen as coprovider and the husband's willingness to relinquish part of the provider role and bargaining power is affected by dependency balance, each spouse's self-esteem and their relative (and joint) bargaining skills. Jane Devore gained bargaining power, as did many other wives, because working made her feel like "more of a person." Theo James gained bargaining power both by valuing herself more highly and by taking an assertiveness training class, while Paula and Harold Reade each gained more ability to influence the other as a result of increased mutual respect and interdependence. The Reades' example suggests that: The more respect each spouse has for the other, the more able they are to listen to each other, making each more able to convince the other to bend in a desired direction.

Hopefully, creative uses of laboratory studies and well-conceived survey measures will allow future researchers to explore in more detail the relationship among: conflict, communication, and division of labor in dual worker families. Such studies should use either the couple or the whole family as the unit of analysis and should include measures of role attachments, bargaining strategies, role definitions, situational contingencies and a measure of power which is not linked to predefined decision-making areas.

LIFE CYCLE STATUS

The concept of family life cycle as commonly used is a series of stages each of which is typified by an earning potential, marriage cohort, age, presence or absence of children, and age of children. Recently Spanier et al. (1979) have questioned some of the assumptions underlying the life cycle concept. They argue that each of components of family life cycle has a somewhat different relationship to different dependent variables and suggest a "multiplicity of developmental stratification schemes" (1979:37). For example, as increasing numbers of professional women have their first children after 30 it is less easy to assume a relationship between age of mother, marriage cohort, and birth of first child.

Among the 16 families, however, the components of family life cycle followed the commonly made assumptions, the major difference being that wives of professionals went back to work later when their children were older, whereas wives of blue collar workers went back to work early when their children were younger. In the following discussion, therefore, I am using family life cycle as an heuristic device with the understanding that all the pieces may not fit together quite as nicely as I have suggested.

Life cycle status is related to division of labor in families independently of the balance of resources or power within the marriage. Therefore, a wife's employment status, wage ratio, provider role definition, and bargaining skills are probably better predictors of husband's household help at some stages of the life cycle than they are at others. Several studies have shown that division of labor is most equal at the honeymoon and retirement stages of marriage and becomes less equal after the birth of the first child (Blood & Wolfe, 1960; Haas, 1981; Model, 1981). In a study of Swedish couples under age 65, Haas found considerable support for the "honeymoon hypothesis," according to which domestic role sharing is most likely to occur at the early stages of the family life cycle. Using measures of shared responsibility for daily care of the home as well as a more detailed measure based on division of responsibility for each of seven task areas, Haas found that life cycle status accounted for about a third of the variance in division of household responsibility with young, childless couples sharing most (Haas, 1981). Model's analysis of 1978 Detroit Area Survey data (1981), however, finds that retired men (not included in Haas's study) do the largest percentage of total household work, although role segregation does increase over the life cycle, making retired people more likely than newlyweds to do tasks alone (cf. Blood & Wolfe, 1960:70-71). Model makes important distinctions among: 1) the percentage of work done by husbands, 2) the total amount of work done (in hours), and 3) the extent to which tasks are done alone or together. (She does not, however, distinguish between responsibility for the task and the doing of it.) Each measure is distributed differently over the life cycle (1980:231).

Given the well established relationship between life cycle status and division of labor and the probable relationship between bargaining power and division of labor, at least at some life cycle stages, I would like to suggest some hypothetical relationships among role overload, bargaining power and role priorities at each life cycle stage:

1) Because women's wages peak at age 30 and men's at age 45 (Barrett, 1979:37), *newlyweds* between 18 and 25 would have more equal wage ratios, than would couples at midlife. Prior to the birth of the first child, couples are likely to have both a high proportion of shared tasks and a more equal division of labor and bargaining power than at any time other than retirement.

2) *Birth of the first child* is often preceded by a shift in the dependency balance with the wife becoming more dependent upon the husband and expecting more help from him. Husbands at this stage may be solicitous of their wives (La Rossa, 1977). After the birth of the child, roles become considerably more segregated with husbands often taking on overtime and extra work (D.O.L., 1975) and wives specializing in childcare and housework. If the wife is also working outside the home, role overload is at its maximum in the early child-rearing stage. How much bargaining power the wife will have at this point depends upon the family bond structure, the husband's role priorities and the wife's employment status and provider role definition. In a couple-centered family, the husband may be motivated to share childcare regardless of his wife's employment because "it is good for the family" (Defrain, 1979). However, a work-oriented husband in a husband-centered family will expect his wife to get up in the middle of the night because "it is only fair" that she do so, especially if she is not working. If she is working, then she may still be expected to get up because his work is more important than hers. Only if both spouses recognize the

wife as a coprovider at this stage, will the wife have enough bargaining power to insist that a reluctant husband share the responsibility of parenting. Mothers of young children who work because they want to have least bargaining power due to the expectation that women should stay home while children are young unless they need to work.

3) In families with *only children under 12*, I would expect the wife's bargaining power to be most related to division of labor. Depending upon how much help is available from relatives or paid housekeepers, this is the stage at which wives need the most help from their husbands. After the children are old enough to help and need less care themselves, the wife's bargaining power becomes less related to division of labor and more to other outcomes in the relationship such as shared companionship and decisions about careers and vacation plans.

4) At *midlife*, other changes take place both in women's estimations of themselves and in marriages which are at least partially independent of employment status. Studies of women at midlife find that as their children grow up, women begin to form identities independent of their husbands (Reese, 1982; Rubin, 1979). Feeling like "more of a person" gives a woman more bargaining power at this stage, especially if she is also recognized by her husband as a more autonomous being entitled to more personal space. Although in this study employment was shown to facilitate this process, a more independent identity at midlife may be a stage of development common to all women. In the follow-up study, we saw that when the midlife "flowering" for the wife is combined with a midlife "fading" for the husband, the marriage may suffer. Some family scholars suggest that strict adherance to male sex role stereotypes is most dysfunctional at midlife (cf. Cohn, 1979). Men like Ted Collins and Harold Reade who are able to relinquish their role as sole provider may fare best.

4) *At retirement*, couples sometimes experience a few years in which the wife is still working after the husband has retired. At this stage, husbands sometimes assume such tasks as cooking, shopping, and errands in an effort to fill their lives (cf. Keith & Brubaker, 1979). If Model is right, it is also the stage at which husbands do the largest share of the housework. (There is some controversy about this. See Szinovacz, ed., 1982.) However, because role overload is least at this point, wives' bargaining power may have rather little to do with the increased amount of work done by retired husbands. In fact, some wives may wish their husbands would not attempt to infringe on "their" kitchens. It would be interesting to find out whether or not couples who enjoy several years of retirement together eventually begin to reduce role segregation and enter the "second honeymoon" phase of division of labor. This, together with most of the above hypotheses, remains to be explored in future research.

SOCIAL CLASS, ROLE BARGAINING, AND ROLE SHARING

Much of the writing on dual-career couples in both the popular and academic literature has focused on dual-career "super-couples" (cf. Bird,

1979) in which each spouse has a highly demanding career. When this study was begun in 1975, only 14% of all working couples included two managerial or professional workers (see Appendix J). Furthermore, since this 14% includes school teachers and lower level management workers, the precentage of working couples with what have come to be known as absorptive or "greedy" occupations (Kanter, 1977; Handy, 1978) is probably smaller. Thus, dual-career super-couples probably account for less than 10% of the total distribution of dual-worker couples while two-job and one-job/one-career couples occupy most of the rest of the space under the curve (see Table 7-1). As unusual as they are, however, these dual-career couples are the prototypes for the image of the egalitarian or semi-egalitarian (sometimes called neo-traditional) couples which emerged from case studies done in the 1970's (Holmstrom, 1972; Rapoport, 1971; Poloma & Garland, 1971). Although no researchers found husbands sharing housework and childcare equally with their wives in such families, most did find that men married to career-committed women did help with the housework more than did professional men married to housewives.

Side by side with the egalitarian super-couple image are a rapidly increasing number of surveys which show that the more money a husband makes, the less housework he does and the more education a wife has, the less housework she does (Ericksen et al, 1979; Pleck 1983). Because few of these studies use the couple as the unit of analysis, we do not know how many of these highly educated wives are married to men with high incomes. Nonetheless, many researchers continue to assume that career-oriented women will be married to egalitarian men. In this section, I will discuss the probable relationship between social class and each of the variables previously shown to be related to bargaining power, role sharing, or both.

Although several of the variables which affect role sharing are also related to social class, the variables which directly influence the redefinition of provider roles and work/family priorities are better predictors of role sharing than is SES. This discussion, therefore, will consider separately the probable relationship between SES measures and each of the following determinants of role sharing:

1. Each spouse's work/family priorities,
2. proportion of the family income earned by the wife (wage ratio),
3. the age of the children at the time the wife returns to work, and
4. the family bond type.

Work/Family Priorities and Social Class

When asked which is more important to them, work or family, only 10% of the employed husbands responding to a 1977 national survey placed work first while 50% said that their families were more important and 30% gave them an equal emphasis (Pleck and Lang, 1978). Employed wives, while giving greater priority to the family, showed a similar pattern with 7% of them placing work above family, 73% putting the family first and 20% saying that work and family were of equal importance to them. Furthermore, if given a chance to redistribute work/family time, only 12% of the husbands and 5% of the wives would choose to put more time into their work, while the remainder would either devote more time to their families (40% and 47%) or keep their present balance (46% and 48%). Thus, on surveys at any rate, working men and women alike give their families top billing.

However, analyses of work/family priorities by social class find that lower-middle class men are more family-centered than upper-middle class men (Rainwater, 1965: 304; Aldous, et al. 1977; Young and Willmott, 1973). Young and Willmott, for example, found that when asked where they got their primary satisfactions, managing directors were more likely than middle management or other classes of workers to cite work and far more likely to say that work interfered with their homes and families (Young and Willmott, 1973: 252-253). Managing directors gave responses such as, "In this job, the work always comes first. The family has to wait" (Ibid: 251). Perhaps, then, Pleck and Lang's percentages correspond roughly to the occupational structure of the U.S. with the 10% of the men who are work oriented being in highly absorptive occupations, the 30% "equal emphasis men" in less absorptive middle management and skilled positions, and the 60% placing family first in the least absorptive occupations such as low level clerical, production or service work. If this is also true for women, then a distribution of couples' work/family priorities might look something like the hypothetical one presented in Table 7.1 with upper and middle class couples above the diagonal and lower middle and working class couples below it.

The sixteen couples correspond to this pattern with some important qualifications. Some manual workers such as Forrest King and Bill Anderson placed work first even though they did not have "professional" orientations to their work. They were superproviders who regularly worked one and a half to two jobs and who considered providing to be their most important family responsibility. They have lost themselves in the provider role in the same way that some top level executives lose themselves in their work, and the effect on their families is similar. They are rarely at home and they have insulated themselves from other family demands. On the other hand, some professional men such as David Meyers treat their occupations as jobs and use their autonomy and flexible work hours to spend more time with their families. Other professional men like Bob Dooley and Ted Collins find themselves pulled between their family and work responsibilities.

**TABLE 7.1   A Hypothetical Distribution of Dual Worker
Families by Work/Family Priorities**

	Wife's Work/Family Priority			
	Work	Work & Family	Family	Total%
Husband's Work/Family Priority				
	Dual Career and One Career/One Job			
Work	3%	2%	5%	10%
Work & family	2%	10%	18%	30%
		Two Job		
Family	2%	8%	50%	60%
Total Percentages based on Pleck and Lang (1978)	7%	20%	73%	100%

On balance, I would say that there is a relationship between social class
and the relative emphasis people give to work and family, but that this does
not mean that we can substitute measures of occupational prestige or
education for measures of work/family priorities or role attachment.
Furthermore, to the extent that family-oriented husbands are less resistant
than others to helping their working wives and sharing more family
responsibilities, we could also expect social class to be related to role
sharing. Lower-middle class couples in the bottom half of Table 7.1 should
have less difficulty working out role sharing agreements than those in the
top half. However, given a dual-career marriage between an ambitious wife
and an equally ambitious husband, shared responsibilities may result from a
long and tough bargaining process in which the wife wins the struggle to
have her work taken seriously.

Wage Ratio and Social Class

As we saw in Chapter 4, the proportion of family income contributed
by the wife is an important determinant of the redefinition of the provider
role (see Table 4.1). Without exception, wives earning 25% or less of the
family income were defined as secondary providers, whereas all wives
earning 40% or more were defined as providers, albeit sometimes in an
ambivalent fashion. Wives earning around 30% of the family income were
defined either as secondary providers or coproviders depending largely

upon each spouse's role attachments and bargaining power. Given that wage ratio partially determines provider role definition, and that provider role definition in turn affects role sharing, we can hypothesize a relationship between wage ratio and role sharing.

There is already considerable evidence that the higher the husband's absolute income, the less housework he does (Pleck, 1983; Ericksen et al, 1979). In addition, studies using wage ratio as an independent variable have found a relationship between relative income and husband's housework (Scanzoni, 1978; Haas, 1981; Farkas, 1976). The more money women make relative to their husbands, the more help they get with the housework. While, in this study, the women earning the highest proportions of family income were as likely to be wives of professional men as they were to be wives of blue collar workers, in the general population this is not the case. In fact, in 1977, full-time working wives with family incomes under $15,000 contributed 47% to 62% of that income while wives with family incomes of $25,000 and over contributed an average of 33% of the total (Hayghe, 1978: A-42). Model found in a 1978 Detroit area analysis that the majority of equal-income households were also low-income households (1981: 233). In general, therefore, it is the wives of poorly paid workers who earn most money relative to their husbands and not the wives of professional and managerial workers. Therefore, to the extent that wage ratio is related to husbands' housework contributions, we would expect that families in the lower half of the income distribution would be more likely to share housework than those at the upper end.

Marital Companionship and Social Class

In Chapter 1, I argued that the measures of marital companionship used by Blood and Wolfe (1960) are both class and sex biased because they consider marriages to be companionate when husband and wife attend the same organization meetings, and when the wife listens to her husband talk about his work. If a companionate marriage is defined as one in which companionship is important to both spouses and the needs of each receive equal priority, then only couple-centered marriages can be called companionate.

Among the 16 families, the blue collar workers were slightly more likely to have couple-centered marriages than were professionals before the wives returned to work. While professionals tended to have husband-centered marriages in which husbands' needs came first, the blue collar workers were more likely to have child-centered relationships in which husband and wife rarely did anything without the children.

Since Rainwater (1965) and Bott (1957) describe conjugal role segregation among lower class couples in terms similar to the child-centered marriages in my lower-middle class families, I would hypothesize the following relationship between family bond type and social class: husband-centered marriages will be predominant in the upper and upper-middle class. Couple-centered ones in the middle and lower-middle class while child-centered marriages will be more typical of the lower class (who were not included in my study).

What this study suggests is that simple measures of satisfaction with companionship are inadequate indicators of the inequality of companionship and that both the emphasis the couple places on companionship and the symmetry of the exchange should be taken into account. If this is done, it is possible that many middle and upper-middle class marriages once thought to be companionate will be classified as husband-centered and that couple-centered marriages may be found at all class levels.

If professionals are more likely than others to have husband-centered marriages, then wives who return to work will find the dependency balance shifted in their favor, giving them added leverage to gain recognition as coproviders by their work-involved husbands. If lower-middle class couples are more likely than others to have couple-centered marriages, then they should find it easier to share household roles without extensive bargaining.

Wives' Work Commitment

While upper-middle class husbands are more likely than lower-middle class husbands to have absorptive occupations and earn substantially more money than their wives, upper-middle class working wives are probably more likely than lower-middle and lower class wives to have jobs which provide them with an opportunity for advancement and which are psychologically rewarding (Ericksen et al., 1979: 304). However, high job satisfaction and a strong commitment to her work do not always increase a wife's bargaining power. In a study of American working wives, Scanzoni found that women who considered their work to be just as important as their husbands' work were more likely than those who did not to define themselves as coproviders and to get help with household chores (1978: 56). Safilios-Rothschild, however, found that Greek wives who had low commitment to their work got more help from their husbands than did those with high work commitment (1970). Although Greek wives who were highly committed to their work were also women who could afford to hire (and did hire) maids, it is also possible that the women with low work-commitment were more able to induce their husbands to help them by threatening to quit work if their husbands did not help. Safilios-Rothschild's results, however, suggest that this strategy was most likely to be successful with husbands who had a relatively good education but not very high incomes. Husbands with low incomes who presumably needed their wives to work, withdrew from housework altogether when their wives' incomes were as high or higher than theirs (1978: 67). What, then, can we say about the relationship between social class, wives' work commitment, and bargaining power?

In the two-job family study, upper-middle class women were more likely to find rewarding jobs than were lower-middle class women. Joan Collins has been able to work her way into a managerial level position without a college degree and, after fifteen years at home full-time, Bess Holling has been able to combine her volunteer organizational experience and training as a journalist to get a job as an administrative assistant. Cathy Schultz, a wife of a factory worker, would like to have a more interesting job, but needed both more training and better connections to find one. Only a few were as fortunate as Mary Anderson who, after several years of on-the-job training, has a well paid and interesting job as a data analyst at Datan. If a woman's level of job satisfaction affects how much she is willing to fight to stay in her job, we might then expect that upper-middle class women will be more tenacious than will lower-middle class and lower class women. Job satisfaction, however, is an elusive quality. Jill Mooney had a dull job (1976), but found it preferable to staying home and fought just as hard to keep her routine clerical position as Joan Collins did to continue in her salaried managerial post. It is, therefore, difficult to say whether or not upper-middle class women who, on the whole, get more rewards from their jobs, have a greater psychological investment in keeping them. However, if it is true that they will fight harder to keep their jobs, it is also true that they *have to* fight harder because they are more likely to be married to professional men who would prefer that their wives devote a larger share of their attention to them and the children.

A wife's work commitment, therefore, can increase or decrease her bargaining power depending upon how much her income is needed and how skillfully she is able to bring her coprovider status into the bargaining. As as an upper-middle class woman's work is considered not really necessary and less important than her husband's (cf. Poloma & Garland, 1971), she will remain a "junior partner" no matter how strongly she is committed to her work. However, because strong work commitment may be coupled with upward mobility (cf. Paula Reade), growing self esteem, and new bargaining skills (cf. Theo James), such women may also be able to win the battle to have their work taken seriously, thereby earning more bargaining power in future negotiations.

Age of Children

The lower the husband's income, the more probable it is that a wife will return to work before her children reach school age (Bednarzik and Klein,

1977). This means that lower-middle class women are more likely to return to work while their children are young than are middle and upper-middle class women. However, the smaller the family income, the less the family can afford to hire childcare help and the more likely it is that spouses will work alternate shifts so that one parent can be with the children at all times. Fathers in double-shift families such as James Mooney may be alone with their children for as many or more waking hours than the mothers. This makes sharing of parental responsibility as well as childcare tasks more workable for them than for men who are rarely alone with their chidren (Hood & Golden, 1979). Furthermore, as I stated previously, since younger children increase the wife's overload, husbands whose wives return to work while the children are young will be under more pressure to share household tasks. In fact, Pleck and Lang (1978) found that fathers of preschool children spend more time in both childcare and household chores than do fathers of older children, and that fathers of preschool children whose mothers work spend even more time.

Although the proportion of time husbands spend doing household tasks is different from the amount of responsibility husbands and wives share for them, the two are probably correlated well enough for us to accept one as an indicator of the other. Thus, the lower the husband's income and the younger the children at the time his wife returns to work, the larger the proportion of childcare and household responsibilities he is, therefore, likely to share with his wife.

THE FAMILY-CENTERED LOWER-MIDDLE CLASS MARRIAGE

If husbands give family priority over work, if wives return to work soon after the birth of their children and earn close to half of the total household income, and if both partners value time spent alone with each other, a couple has a much higher probability of sharing a large proportion of parenting and housework responsibilities than if the reverse is true. Thus, the Devores, an upper-middle class couple discussed in Chapter 3, shared no additional responsibilities after Jane returned to work when her youngest child was 11, and she was earning only 15% of the family income. Although their relationship had become less husband-centered than it had been previously, Jane was unable to convince John to accept more of the household responsibility. Since he does not need her to work, she should not need him to do dishes or mow the lawn. The Davises, the lower-middle class couple contrasted to the Devores in Chapter 3, share a wide range of responsibilities. Both consider the family more important than work. Cynthia stayed out of work for only two years, returning when her youngest child was one, and she contributed 40% of the family income. Their relationship is more couple- than child-centered and they do what they can to accommodate each other's needs.

In this study, the professional husbands who shared roles with their wives all had children under 12 at the time their wives returned to work and, with one exception, all had wives who earned 40% or more of the family income. Thus, they are not typical of professional husbands of working wives in general. However, to the extent that lower-middle class two-job couples are more like the Davises than they are like the Devores with regard to role attachments, wage ratio, and age of children at the time the wife returns to work, there may indeed be a relationship between social class and role-sharing. If there is, it is probably curvilinear with lower-middle class couples having the highest incidence of shared household responsibility and very poor working couples and very rich ones have the least. Model, for example, found that high income husbands contributed more to housework when married to equal earning wives, but otherwise ranked lowest in housework (1981: 234). However, the most important conclusion to be drawn from this discussion is that socioeconomic status (SES) is not the best predictor of either division of labor or role sharing in two-job couples. The work/family priorities of each spouse, wage ratio, age of children at the time the wife returns to work, and perhaps some measure of family bond type together should explain more of the variance in role sharing in any large sample of dual-worker families than will any single measure of SES.

IS BECOMING A TWO-JOB FAMILY GOOD FOR A MARRIAGE?

If the research on social class and division of labor is muddied by poor conceptualization and inadequate measures, research on marital satisfaction and wives' employment suffers from as many or more problems. Most of these problems have been discussed in other reviews of the literature (Nye, 1974; Staines et al, 1978). Firstly, too many studies lump working wives together in a single category by asking such questions as, "Are working wives really more satisfied?" (Wright, 1978). Although recent studies are less likely than previous ones to stop with zero-order correlations, many authors still assume that "working wives" is a meaningful category. Given the fact that the demographic characteristics of working wives have become increasingly similar to those of housewives (Smith, 1979), we might expect that, in many ways, working wives today would be at least as different from each other as they are from housewives. Since the wife's motivation to work, her work satisfaction, age of children and attitudes of her husband towards her work have all been found to condition the relationship between wives' employment and marital satisfaction, subsequent studies would do well to control for at least some of these variables in their analyses.

Secondly, studies of marital satisfaction employ measures which range from a single Likert scale item asking how happy one is with one's marriage to complex multidimensional scales of marital adjustment. Studies which measure more than one aspect of marital adjustment and satisfaction often find that different aspects of marital adjustment vary independently of each other. For example, Staines et al. (1978), found that although working wives were more likely than housewives to report both thinking of divorce and wishing they had married someone else, they were similar to housewives on global measures of marital satisfaction. As Nye points out, it is the balance of satisfactions and rewards which is crucial (1979). A different balance of rewards may exist for different categories of people at different stages of the life cycle. In addition, measures of satisfaction (marital satisfaction , work satisfaction, life satisfaction) typically lack a benchmark. Lillian Rubin interviewed blue collar wives who were satisfied with their marriages if their husbands brought home the paycheck, did not drink and did not beat them (1976). Unskilled blue collar workers sometimes tell interviewers that they are satisfied with their work because, "this is about all a guy like me can expect" (Strauss, 1974). Thus, in order to reach any conclusions about how such things as role sharing and wives' work commitment are likely to affect marriages, we need to know something about each spouse's marital role expectations. In this study, work/family priorities and family bond type mediate the relationship between wife's employment and marital satisfaction.

Lastly, if any topic demands studies of couples and relationships as opposed to studies of individuals, it is this topic. Researchers who have used the couple as a unit of analysis have been rewarded with interesting and useful results. For example, Mirra Komarovsky found that the extent to which a man lost authority due to unemployment depended upon how much his authority was derived from his provider role. Men whose wives and children valued them for all their family roles lost less authority then those whose respect had been based more narrowly on their paychecks (1940). Similarly, in a study of British college graduates and their husbands, Bailyn found that the happiest marriages paired family-oriented men with either family-oriented or work- and family-oriented women. The least happy marriages involved career-oriented men married to career-oriented wives (1970). Becoming a two-job family, then, is neither good nor bad for marriages. This study and those of other researchers cited here suggest that, "it all depends . . . ."

A NOTE TO TWO-JOB FAMILIES, POLICY MAKERS, AND PRACTITIONERS

Although this is not a "how-to-do-it" book, the families in this study do describe several changes in their lives which made it easier for them to cope with becoming a two-job family. They also mention aspects of industrial and social policy which make it difficult for them to combine two jobs and family responsibilities. In this final note, I would like to distinguish between coping strategies available to individuals and families, and institutional changes which need to be made in work places as well as in society as a whole. Two-job families have enough of a burden without assuming responsibility for problems which belong to the whole of society. However, the growing movement for "management initiatives for working parents" (Baden & Friedman, 1981) and innovative ways of restructuring work to fit family needs has come about only because people have begun to look outside families for solutions to some of the problems experienced by working couples.

Coping Strategies

Although the couples described here used several strategies in learning how to live as a two-job family, the three most important ones are: 1) reducing role overload by learning to be satisfied with dirtier houses and simpler meals and/or delegating work to paid housecleaners and older children, 2) coming to terms with ambiguity about the relative priorities of each spouse's work and family roles, and 3) making each spouse's wants and needs clear to the other and discussing the implications of each person's wants and needs for the other's wellbeing (and the family's). Although James Mooney does not clean house now that he is on day shift, Jill Mooney has decided to place lower priority on how the house looks, making housework less a source of conflict than it might otherwise be. Because Nancy Williams resisted sharing the provider role with her unemployed husband, Don, she would neither "let go" of the housework and trust Don to do it, nor be content to let him do as he liked. (He described her as getting after him to do this or that and then doing all the housework over again on the weekend.) Paula Reade, however, knew what she wanted, asked for it and got it when her sons and husband each took a room to clean.

Asking for what one wanted was hardest for most of the families described in ths book. In intimate relationships, we often want those who love us to "prove" their love by guessing what we need. If the person fails to guess, it just shows that they never really did understand anyway. In my own life, I have found that I am least likely to ask for what I want and need when I am most ambivalent about my right to have it. Who am I to expect my husband to take over most of the household duties while I am finishing a book? In this study, as wives gained self-esteem and became more clear about what they wanted, they were able to ask for it more directly. Some of them (like Joan Collins in 1982) easily got what they asked for because their husbands and children, like other husbands and children everywhere, were only waiting to be asked. Others, like Jane Devore, asked their husbands to share more responsibility and were met with resistance, but asking is the first step. Although a clear request may be refused, it is more likely to be granted than an unclear, unvoiced expectation coupled with silent resentment. Probably the most important service a family counselor can do for couples dealing with shifting work/family priorities is to help each identify what he or she wants and then learn how to ask for it.

SOCIAL CHANGE

While some changes can be had just for the asking, others require legislation, new union contracts, and a redefinition of the relationship between work and family in society. Rigid work schedules, the lack of permanent part-time jobs, difficulty in finding adequate and affordable childcare help, mandatory overtime work for blue-collar workers, and excessive expectations for managerial and professional workers all create obstacles for dual worker couples. James Mooney, the machinist who cared for his children during the day, did not want to work 70 hours a week, but faced disciplinary action if he did not. Anne Dooley and Linda Meyers each worked extra hours in order to meet their employers' expectations and advance in their careers. What Arlie Hochschild has called "the clockwork of the male career" (1975) does not leave much time for families, and women who compete with men in what have traditionally been male occupations often find themselves faced with even more conflict between work and family demands than do other working women (cf. Heins, 1976, Philliber and Hiller, 1983).

One of the major obstacles to change in the work place is what I call the "one family/one job assumption." It is best exemplified by the following quotation from Arnold Packer who, in 1977, was a Department of Labor assistant secretary for policy evaluation and research:

> One can think of the traditional American family structure with two parents and children in which the family head goes out to work and makes enough of a living to keep the family together. The major thrust of any program ought to be to support this as the predominant situation for Americans . . . Moreover, secondary workers are coming into the labor force at a rapid rate, and these could take the poorer paid jobs that are left open as family heads move on to better positions (WIN, 1977:17).

Since the document quoted was an internal Labor Department memo and not a public policy statement, it would be unfair to hold Mr. Packer accountable for it. However, the thinking espoused in that statement has also been published in the report made by the Carnegie Council on Children (Keniston, ed., 1977). In their chapter, "Jobs and a decent income," the Carnegie Council argues that full employment should mean one job per household:

> To be realistic, and since heads of household are the one group of earners most relevant to families with children, we have limited our proposals to that group (Ibid: 86).

I do not take issue with the Council's contention that our society must first guarantee all families at least one full-time job or the equivalent before we can think of providing more than that. However, I am concerned with the bias against working wives implied in both Mr. Packer's and the Council's statements. By assuming that all working wives married to working husbands are "secondary workers," policy makers justify both low wages and lack of job training programs for women, and make it very difficult for role sharing families to exchange the wife's market work for the husband's family work. It is therefore important to be clear about the definition of "secondary worker."

I like the definition which Congresswoman Martha Griffiths offered to Willard Wirtz after he had explained that the unemployment situation was not as bad as it seemed because of "all those secondary workers in the statistics":

> Well, I think when you come before this committee as the Secretary of Labor, you should have an objective definition of secondary workers, because I think the Secretary of Labor should treat all workers alike. Therefore, I would like to make a suggestion for a definition of secondary worker. The primary worker is the one who buys the children's clothes, the groceries, and pays for the music lessons and the books; and the secondary worker is the one who buys the fishing tackle, the outboard motors and the booze. (Griffiths, 1976:97).

Although Martha Griffiths' statement was tailored to impress male members of Congress who would find it difficult to consider booze and fishing tackle to be anything but a necessity, her point is well taken. Just what is it about the incomes of "secondary workers" which makes them "secondary"? As we saw in Chapter 4, both husbands and wives no longer considered the wife's incomes secondary after they had become dependent upon them, and the larger the share of the income earned by the wife, the harder it was not to become dependent upon her earnings. Given that women in my study who earned one-third or more of the family income were not considered secondary providers by their families, I would say that most wives who work full time are not secondary providers at all but coproviders. In March 1975 they earned an average of 40% of their total family incomes and comprised more than 40% of the 24 million working wives (Hayghe, 1976:16).

If full-time working women are not considered secondary providers either by themselves or by their families, then perhaps the Department of Labor is justified in labeling them "secondary workers" on the grounds that their families can get along quite well without their incomes. If "getting along quite well" means living according to the Department of Labor's intermediate budget for a family of four, then a family earning $14,333 in 1974 could afford a trip to the movies by the husband and wife together three times a year and by one of them alone once a year and could allow only $3.78 per person per week for all leisure time activities (Keniston, 1971: 28-29). In 1974, the median income for multiworker husband-wife families was $14,885 while that for single worker families was $12,360 (Hayghe, 1976:18). By this standard, therefore, many two job families could not keep up without the second income.

Although most of the blue collar workers in my study were earning incomes above the median even before their wives returned to work, some, like Mike Davis and Richard James were earning only $12,000 a year in 1975. Without a second income, their families would be living below the Department of Labor intermediate budget.

As Howard Hayghe points out, the dual earner household has become the family's answer to inflation (1982:34-36). In 1980, the median income for dual earner households was $27,741 compared to $20,470 for households supported by husbands only (Ibid; 36). Since 1971, inflation, underemployment and unemployment have so undermined the family wage that it is no longer reasonable to assume that the average family can live adequately on a single income. Families provided for by husbands only are three times as likely to live in poverty as are dual earner families (7.2% vs. 2.1%). Until and unless our society can provide wages adequate to support a family on 40-60 hours of work a week, American families will continue to be faced with difficult choices about the allocation of time and money.

RECOMMENDATIONS

My most important message to policy makers, therefore, is: "Rethink the term 'secondary worker' and stop assuming that all 50% of the married women now working do not 'really need to work.' Start thinking instead of how families with young children can be assured an adequate income without working a total of 80 or more hours per week outside the home." If policy makers do begin to take seriously the needs of two-job and single parent families, they will undoubtedly begin to pay more attention to suggestions already made by writers such as Rosabeth Kanter (1977), Rosemary Ruether (1977), Archibald Evans (1977), Joseph Pleck (1977), Jean Renshaw (1976), James Levine (1976), Rhonda and Robert Rapoport (1978) and Mary Rowe (1978). All of these writers address the work/family conflicts which are created by the one family/one job assumption for dual worker and single parent families.

The recommendations being made by this growing number of work/family scholars include:

1. A commitment by our society to reduce occupational segregation and the resulting gap between men's and women's wages.
2. More options for working parents made possible through permanent part-time jobs, shared jobs, parental leave for both parents, sick leave for parents of sick children and on-site child care.
3. Expansion of the use of flextime, personal holidays and other alternative work scheduling which would give dual worker couples more flexibility in adapting to each other's work schedules.
4. New ways of combining work and family roles. These might involve:
   a) giving working parents priority in choosing shifts so that they can more easily arrange child care and family time;
   b) offering a variety of career paths or job ladders which would allow workers to devote less time to their work during early child rearing years without losing seniority or opportunities for advancement;
   c) family leaves for up to a year for men or women who choose to drop out of labor force in order to devote time to their children and/or spouses;
   d) an end to mandatory overtime work in all occupational categories.

If such recommendations were put into practice, it would be possible for fathers like Don Williams to attend their children's basketball games and for husbands like James Mooney to take time off on week-ends when their working wives are home. Tampering with the "clockwork of the male career" (Hochschild, 1975) might also reduce the pressure put on upwardly mobile professional men and women so that they would not have to make hard choices like those faced by Linda Meyers and Anne Dooley.

Before any of these suggestions can gain wide acceptance, some basic cultural assumptions about the relationship between work and family need to be reexamined. As Rosabeth Kanter argues in her essay, *Work and Family in America* (1977), work has never been as separate from family as the mythology of industrialized societies has made it seem. With the growth of dual-worker families, the two spheres overlap even more. As more and more women return to work shortly after childbirth, it can no longer be assumed that child care is a problem which must be solved by the nuclear family alone. Although insurance companies are allowed to exclude pregnancy from their policies for women workers "because it is a matter of personal choice" (Bird, 1979: 18), at some point soon, we as a society will have to decide whether or not we choose to reproduce and how we propose to care for the children if we do. We no longer have an unpaid labor force of ready-made care givers large enough to do the job (Rowe, 1978).

A CONCLUDING NOTE

In this book, I have argued that a woman's entry into the labor force will most likely result in her husband's assuming more housekeeping and parenting responsibility when some combination of the following are true:

1. she is work-commited
2. she chooses (by preference or necessity) to relinquish some of her housekeeping and parenting responsibility
3. she earns 30% or more of the household income *and* is defined as a coprovider
4. he is family-oriented and sees his work as a job rather than as a career
5. he is willing to relinquish part of his provider role
6. she has acquired more bargaining power due to her provider role rights, increased self-esteem and decreased emotional dependence upon her husband.

Readers who are looking for a blueprint for an egalitarian marriage should not be discouraged by the discovery that none of the 16 husbands in this book shared the housework equally with their wives and that even those husbands who did take on additional responsibilities tended to choose the ones they most enjoyed. After all, none of the couples in this book decided to become coproviders *in order to* adopt a more equal division of labor. Instead they became two-job couples either because the wife needed to get out of the house or the family needed money, or both. In the process of becoming a two-job family, some couples also developed a more equal balance of power in their marriages and a more equal division of labor in the household. This move towards equality was, however, an unforeseen and unintended consequence of becoming coproviders. As James Mooney said:

> Whereas, the situation we have . . . I never really thought . . . it might be just the way the situation was out of necessity . . . I was brought closer to my kids.

In contrast, couples who start out with the goal of sharing roles may fare quite differently. In her study of 31 role-sharing couples, Linda Haas (1980) found that three-fourths of the couples who had developed an equal division of labor had done so because they wanted to eliminate the wife's overload and over half said that they wanted to reduce the husband's burden as provider. Given such goals, they were able to work out a division of labor in which each spouse spent about 16 hours a week doing housework and each had between 26 and 27 hours a week of leisure, with mothers doing slightly more childcare and fathers doing a bit more housework. Haas had to look hard to find these couples and the couples worked hard to achieve equal role-sharing. Haas writes that over half reported that one or both spouses resisted doing non-traditional tasks, and often found it easier to revert to a more traditional division of labor until the overworked spouse threatened to stop doing the task in question forcing the "lazy spouse" to reform (1980: 293). Although this strategy may appear similar to Joan Collins' decision to "go on strike" until Ted Collins planned the children's summer schedules, it is different. Since Haas's role-sharing couples had already agreed to share roles equally, the protesting spouse could refer to a *mutually agreed-upon standard* when role sharing broke down. Ted and Joan Collins, however, were in the process of negotiating such a standard when Joan, without announcing it, went on strike.

Couples who purposefully decide to share roles are like couples who begin to share roles "without really thinking about it" in at least one important respect, however. Most find that the new common ground created by role sharing and the increased communication necessary to maintain role-sharing relationships brings them closer together.

APPENDIX A

Wife Interview Checklist (January 1976)

1. Rapport building. How day has been so far.
2. Permission to use tape recorder.
3. Background information: Residence history, marital history, job history, births of children, and plans for more children.
4. Period before returning to work: Feelings about self. What were friends doing, what was going on in husband's life? What was a typical day like before returning to work?
5. Decision to go back: What prompted the decision, husband's attitudes at the time, with whom did she discuss the decision? What did her friends think? Relatives? What was it like to hunt for a job?
6. Going back: How did it feel at first? What was hardest? What did she like, not like about working?
7. After being back: self-image, child care, relationship with husband, relationship with children, division of labor, family recreation, friendships and social network, time to self, decision making.
8. Any changes in: Time husband spends with children? Time couple spends together? How does typical day (weekday and weekend) look now?
9. Other background information: Ethnic and religious identification, parents' occupations on both sides, number, sex and ages of siblings.
10. Her feelings about work/family roles:
    Children: How does she feel about parenting? What does she like most, least? Ages at which she enjoys children most?
    Housekeeping: How does she feel about housewife role? What is important to her about it? What does she need the house to look like? How much does it bother her if it is not clean?
    Providing: Would she want to quit her job? In what circumstances would she quit? What kind of job would she like if she does not like present one? At whose cost/gain does she work? How is her money used? How much money does she make?
11. Marital relationship: How should decisions be made? What does she think about women's lib? Examples of major disagreements and the ways in which they were settled. How did her returning to work affect her husband's life?
12. End of Interview: Anything important that we have not covered? Questions she has for me? Explanation about use of data, possibility of callbacks, pay, possible references to other women who have returned to work.

APPENDIX B

Transcribing the Interviews

Complete transcriptions are both costly and unwieldy and take enormous amounts of time both to type and to analyze. Therefore, after experimenting with several methods of note taking and partial transcription, I settled on a two-step procedure for transcribing interviews. This involved my sitting down at the transcribing machine and typing the tape location of each topic, my question to the respondent, and a summary of dialogue and information for which I did not need direct quotations. After this, I went through these notes and drew arrows pointing to sections I wanted trascribed verbatim. Using these notes as a guide, an assistant would transcribe portions of the tape indicated, typing my questions on the left side of the page and the respondent's answers on the right (see Appendix F). This method allowed us to keep a record of all information that could be found on each tape; summarize dialogue about what things happened, when, and where, and transcribe verbatim accounts of how and why things happened and how people felt about what was going on at the time. It also saved a great deal of time and made each case record easier to use.

APPENDIX C

Developing Grounded Codes

Using indexed transcriptions, my assistants and I developed codes for the variables used in this study. Although the conceptual basis for the codes is clear from the text. I would like to outline the coding process from start to finish, using "changes in provider roles" as an illustration. The reader is then invited to use the materials included in Appendixes H and I for more information on how codes were constructed for marital roles, family bond type, parenting, and housekeeping.

The development of code categories proceeded in zig-zag fashion alternating between note taking and category construction until we arrived at the general theoretical categories used in this analysis and felt confident about our judgments. In the course of the analysis, three different assistants helped with coding, and each assistant checked the previous coder's judgments. In the process, we refined decision rules for bounding the categories: All of this was done in the following six steps:

1. Note taking on all interviews to assess the range of information available on given topic.
2. Organization of these notes into categories and subcategories associated

with the topic, and development of a data sheet systematically recording notes under each of these categories for each case.

3. Thorough examination of each case for information in each category and subcategory, and the recording of information on data sheets together with reference to the field note pages where the information was found.
4. Development of detailed codes for each role analyzed.
5. Development of general theoretical categories from the detailed codes.
6. A final check on role change coding and reexamination of general category boundaries.

Using the indexed case notes, we developed data sheets indicating topics about which we wished to make more detailed observations. For example, among the things Richard James spoke of when questioned about providing responsibilities were his attitudes toward women making more money than their husbands, how he viewed his own provider role, and how he and Theo used their second income (see Appendix F). After noting types of information available about provider roles in all interviews, we developed data sheets for recording detailed observations. For example, on the Provider Role Data Sheet, assistants were instructed to take notes on (1) husband's definition of his provider role, (2) the priority he gave the provider role over other family roles, (3) the husband's definition of the wife's role, (4) the wife's definition of both his and her roles and what her money is used for, (5) putdowns of either spouse by the other of the other's provider role performance, (6) feelings of own inadequacy as a provider expressed by either spouse, (7) each spouse's income, (8) any questions, comments, or general observations the coder had after reviewing the case. The data sheet and entries for Richard and Theo James are included in Appendix G.

Using these data sheets, we then developed more detailed codes for provider roles. These reflected the range of responses for each category of observation. For example, subjective evaluations of the use of the wives' money ranged from "we don't need her money at all" to "we do it together, her money is necessary. We couldn't get along without it" (see Appendix H). After reviewing data sheets for each case and placing each couple into the coding categories developed from the data, we were then ready to decide on more general theoretical categories.

As we reviewed the code sheets, patterns began to emerge. Couples who pooled incomes and/or used the wife's money for ongoing expenses often agreed that they "did it together" and that the wife's money was necessary, whereas couples who earmarked the wife's money for specific purposes thought of the second income as "extra." Furthermore, some couples who were dependent upon the wife's income had positive attitudes about this, whereas others who were also dependent on the second income expressed ambivalent feelings about their present division of providing responsibilities.

Based on this information, I then decided that provider roles could be described in three general categories: (1) main/secondary providers, who earmarked the wife's money and thought of it as extra, assuming that the wife "could quit whenever she wanted to," (2) coproviders, who pooled incomes and/or used the wife's money for ongoing expenses, assuming that the wife would always work, and (3) ambivalent coproviders, who agreed that the wife's income was necessary to maintain their present standard of living but were not comfortable with the situation. In addition, I took note of changes in husbands' attitudes as reported by their wives as well as husband's self-reports of such changes. This information helped to trace changes in provider role definition over time. For example, Mary Anderson reported that her husband Bill had not always been happy with the idea of her earning money. He was afraid that she might become too independent and leave him. However, when she was still with him after working for 10 years, his objections subsided.

Similar procedures were followed for the development of family and bond type, marital companionship, parenting, and housekeeping codes. Finally, after couples were placed in the general theoretical categories that we constructed, I had one assistant who did not know about these decisions to go back over each case and take notes on role changes using a shortened form of the code sheet (see Appendix I). This assistant was instructed to make judgments about the division of responsibility in each couple before and after the wife returned to work and to summarize, in writing, evidence for changes in this division of responsibility. I then compared my evaluations with his and made final decisions when there were discrepancies.

APPENDIX D

Reliability

Although data sheets became more detailed each time an assistant went back through the field notes scouting for more information, judgments about how to code each case on the detailed code sheets were remarkably similar. Unfortunately, I did not have each assistant recode the data independently but instead had each one check the previous one's work. However, given the large amount of information we had on which to base our decisions, we generally found that we could substantiate each coding decision with several quotations from the field notes. I suspect, therefore, that detailed code decisions are highly reliable because they are not far removed from the data themselves.

The general theoretical categories were more of a problem. Here I had to make decision rules that would produce the same results regardless of who followed them. Sometimes, in trying to follow such rules, we found that they were not specific enough and had to modify them. However, when we found ourselves wavering about whether a specific couple were coproviders or main/secondary providers, it meant that the decision rules were not specific enough. For example, in coding the Jameses for provider roles, one assistant (Ann Joachim) noted that Richard James felt that they could get along without Theo's money but that Theo felt her income made her independent of her husband, saying, "I don't need him financialwise." She also noted that the Jameses used Theo's money for house payments and health insurance as well as improvements in the quality of life.

When another assistant (James Brown) reexamined the data on provider roles and made specific notes about changes in attitudes, he observed that Theo seemed to be accepted as a provider but not a main provider and that Richard now wanted Theo to work as it made it easier for him. Jim Brown thought that Richard considered Theo's money necessary. We then had to decide whether the Jameses were coproviders or main/secondary providers. The Jameses earmarked Theo's money for house payments and health insurance. Richard said that he was the "main" provider and that providing came first among his three family roles (provider, companion, father). Had we been working with 1600 couples rather than 16, we could have constructed a provider role sharing scale from our detailed code sheet and then divided the sample into halves or quartiles based on the median score. In this instance, however, we needed a decision rule. Thus, the category of "coproviders" became limited to couples who pooled their incomes, used the wife's extra money for a variety of ongoing expenses, and agreed that her money was necessary. Since the Jameses earmarked Theo's money for house payments, I decided that they were main/secondary providers.

APPENDIX E

Labor Force Characteristics

Population	Characteristic	Percent of Population with Characteristic	Date	Source
1. Husband-wife (H-W) families	Multiple earner	49	March 1975	Hayghe (1976:13)
2. H-W families	One earner (male)	34	March 1975	Hayghe (1976:16)
3. White wives, husband present	In labor force	42.2	March 1974	Hayghe (1975: A-14)
4. Working wives married to full-time year-round workers	Working full time, year round	45	1974	Hayghe (1976:18)
5. H-W, multiple-earner families	Wife is one of additional earners	84	1974	Hayghe (1976:18)
6. Full-time, year-round working wives, husband present	Children under 18 at home	46	1974	Hayghe (1974:291)
7. Full-time, year-round working, wives, husband present	Children under 6 at home	27	1974	Hayghe (1974:291)
8. Employed husbands	Professional-technical	16	1975	Hayghe (1976:16)
9. Employed husbands	managerial	17	1975	Hayghe (1976:16)

APPENDIX E

Labor Force Characteristics (continued)

Population	Characteristic	Percent of Population with Characteristic	Date	Source
10. Employed husbands	Craft workers	23	1975	Hayghe (1976:16)
11. Employed husbands	Operatives	17	1975	Hayghe (1976:16)
12. Working wives of professionals	Clerical workers	35	1975	Hayghe (1976:17)
13. Working wives of craftsmen	Clerical workers	38	1975	Hayghe (1976:17)
14. Working wives of operatives	Clerical workers	32	1975	Hayghe (1976:17)
15. Dual-worker couples	Both spouses managerial or professional workers	14	1975	Extrapolated from Hayghe (1976: 16–17)
16. Male workers, wife present	Working afternoon or night shifts	12	May 1977	U.S. Department of Labor (1978)
17. Manufacturing workers	Working afternoon or night shifts	17	May 1977	U.S. Department of Labor (1978: Table I)
18. Women workers	Working day shift	87	May 1977	U.S. Department of Labor (1978:2)

APPENDIX F

SAMPLE TRANSCRIPTION

Notes to Transcriber: Richard James Case

370 HOW WOULD IT FEEL IF SHE EARNED MORE MONEY THAN YOU?

(Basically, doesn't feel it would bother him. Can't relate to King's way of looking at it. Can see that society is set up that way, but it wouldn't bother him if she earned more.)

391 DO YOU THINK OF YOURSELF AS THE PROVIDER?

409 HER PAYCHECK FOR HOUSE PAYMENT

421 SAVING MONEY

Doesn't save money because doesn't have credit union. Wishes he had a better one. Other means of saving don't appeal to him. Used to used tax rebate as means for savings. Changed dependent status when laid off. Just changed it back now.

448 DOES HE DO STUFF AUTOMATICALLY IN CONNECTION WITH KIDS, ETC?

(I explain difference between delegated to one vs. doing things on own.)

Theo comes in and offers us iced tea.

(I explain some typical division of labor.)

467 THEIR DIVISION OF LABOR

(and how she spends money)

Partial Transcription

#16   Richard James

Interviewer	Tape Location	Respondent

How would it feel if she earned more money?

370

I don't know if that would bother me or not . . . I don't think it would bother me. I'd just feel that we had more purchasing power . . . I don't think it means anything if a woman makes more than her husband.

It's interesting, different views on this . . . (cites King case)

Oh. I don't know why that would have anything to do with it . . . that was funny.

The thing was, why would she stay with him? If she didn't need his paycheck, I guess . . .

I can't even relate to that. (OTHER GUYS SAY, "SHE'S STILL TWO THOUSAND DOLLARS BEHIND ME.") (Something about feeling inferior because of the way society is set up.) But I don't think it'd bother me.

So you think of yourself as the provider?

Now that we both work I think . . . I used to think of myself as the provider because I was, and now I think I'm the main provider. (BECAUSE YOU MAKE PROPORTIONATELY TO HER . . .) Oh yeah. But . . . (YOU MAKE TWICE AS MUCH AS SHE DOES?) Probably more than that. Course she's just working parttime now. When she's working full-time I make at least twice.

Does it ever give you the feeling of you can sort of relax a little? Because she's contributing like you don't have to worry as much . . .

406

Yeah, that comes into it. (IT'S NOT QUITE THE PRESSURE . . .) Right. Like now we just use her paycheck to pay the house payments. So that's about all we do with hers—just pay the house payments. So that's a whole lot of money I don't have to worry about paying. And it used to—we set aside so much so that when it came due I'd know that I had—whereas I don't worry about it now because she gets paid at the end of the month.

APPENDIX G
PROVIDER ROLE DATA SHEET: RICHARD JAMES

Case # 16	Name: James	Provider Role
1. a. Husband's Definition of a. His role	"I used to think of my self as the provider because I was, and now I think I'm the main provider (F-20).*	
b. Role priority	1. provider 2. companion 3. father "Is that odd?" (F-22).	
c. Her role—why she works	Use her checks to make house payments. "That's a whole lot of money I don't have to worry about paying" (F-20).	
2. Wife's Definition of a. His role	"I feel like if Richard doesn't want to stay here, I don't ne . . . , I need him, but I don't need him financialwise. I think I could get along without him" (0-41).	
b. Relationship of hers to his	Wife thinks of husband as not only being her husband, but also as a friend and a helper. Provider role not emphasized in her evaluation of him (0-41).**	
c. Her role—what money is used for	Spend more money now that wife works. Go to dinner, parties, to the show more. Spend more money on clothes (0-31). Better quality things (0-40). Paid health insurance (0-21).	
3. Attitudes and Putdowns	See story about Theo's car (F-23).	
a. Her putdown of his provider role.	I really felt superior over him because I was making the house payment because I went to work. Like without me, Richard couldn't survive."	

Case #	Name:	Provider Role

3. Attitudes, cont.

b. His feelings/
attitudes re
adequacy,
inadequacy

Husband says it wouldn't bother him if wife made more money than he. "I'd just feel that we had more purchasing power" (F-20). "Don't think it means anything if a woman makes more than her husband." (*Note*: How do we interpret this? At face value?)

c. His putdowns of
her provider role

"All we do with her check is make house payments" (F-20).

4. Objective Data

a. Salaries

R c. $4800 yr

H c. $11500 yr

b. Employment
status and
history

R: sales clerk while in high school; secretary in engineering department; private secretary for city planner, now also a secretary (at church).

H: Tool and dye setup; used to work in a bookstore.

c. Ages of kids

Two boys: 6 and 8.

**5. His willingness
to take on other
chores and roles**

If R has a bad day, H will have dinner ready and table set. "I feel that anything in the house as far as housework or dishes is ot taboo territory for either one, but it should be more her" (F-21).

COMMENTS

Missing data
Ideas

---

* The numbers in parentheses refer to page number on either the original (O) or the follow up (F) field notes in 1975 and 1976.

** R = respondent; H = husband.

APPENDIX H

DETAILED CODE CATEGORIES

Provider Roles

Case # _____

Name: _____

Coder:_____ Date:_____

1. Wage ratio: W/H _____

2. Subjective evaluation of wife's financial contribution:

Husband   *Wife*

_____ a)   We don't need her/my money at all.   a) _____
            We use it for what she/I want(s).

_____ b)   Her money goes for extras, icing on the cake.   b) _____

_____ c)   Her money helps. Without it we'd have to tighten   c) _____
            our belts, but we could get along without it if
            necessary (but H still sees himself as the major
            breadwinner).

_____ d)   We do it together. Her money is necessary. We   d) _____
            couldn't get along without it.

_____ e)   Usually her money goes for extras, but in a crisis   e) _____
            we need it for backup. It takes the pressure off.

3. Actual use of wife's money:

_____ a)   Support of family in time of crisis.

_____ b)   Pooled with husband's for all expenses.

_____ c)   Used for specified ongoing expenses: _____

_____ d)   Major capital investments (education, house, car, etc.).

_____ e)   Improvements in quality of life (appliances, recreation, better
            clothing, extra vehicles, etc.).

_____ f)   Things for herself and/or to keep her job.

(check all that are applicable and try to rank in order of importance.)

4. Husband's attitudes toward wife working:

Before   *After*

_____ a)   Her return felt as an attack on his manhood, etc.   a) _____
_____ b)   I decided to let her work since that is what makes   b) _____
           her happy, but I wish she wouldn't.
_____ c)   It's O.K. It makes her happy and I wouldn't have   c) _____
           it any other way.
_____ d)   I want her to work. It would be a lot more pres-   d) _____
           sure on me if she didn't.

5. Attitude toward wife earning more money than she is now earning (actual or hypothesized); i.e., what if she gets (got) a raise? What if she could support you both?

Actual   *Hypothesized*

_____ a)   Fear he won't be needed.   a) _____
_____ b)   Fear that he can no longer support family in the   b) _____
           accustomed style.
_____ c)   Happy that he doesn't have to earn as much, but   c) _____
           wouldn't want to give up his role, i.e., quit
           working.
_____ d)   Would love to quit if she made enough money.   d) _____

Note tone: _____

6. Husband's stated role priority now:

Provider _____ Husband _____ Father _____ Other: _____

7. Job commitment and overtime work:

Husband   *Wife*

_____ a)   Wants to advance as far as possible.   a) _____
_____ b)   Would like to advance within limits imposed by   b) _____
           family and other interests.
_____ c)   Not interested in advancement or job change.   c) _____
_____ d)   Interested but feels it is unlikely.   a) _____
_____ e)   Other: _____   e) _____

SPOUSAL ROLES

Case # _____
Name: _____
Coder: _____Date: _____

1. Desire for spouse's companionship:

Wife   *Husband*

1   High   1   Notes: _____
2   Medium   2   _____
3   Low   3   _____

Discrepancy score: _____

2. Companionship experienced (check if yes for each spouse):

Husband   *Wife*

_____ a)   Shares the other's experiences.   a) _____
_____ b)   Listens to the other about the events of the day.   b) _____
_____ c)   Shares the other's friends.   c) _____
Husband total _____   Wife total _____
Extent of reciprocity: _____
Notes: _____

3. Expressed satisfaction with companionship (quotes expressing satisfaction/dissatisfaction):

Wife: _____

Husband: _____

Is wife getting as much companionship as she wants? _____

Is husband getting as much as he wants? _____

4. Intimacy rating:

	High	Medium	Low
a) Amount of emotional support exchanged	1	2	3
b) Ability to resolve conflicts	1	2	3
c) Do activities together without children:	Often	Sometimes	Rarely/never

Total _____

5. Satisfaction index _____

6. Total score _____

Parental Roles

Case # _____

Name: _____

Coder:_____ Date:_____

1. Sex based division of labor:

Husband   *Wife*

_____ 1. a) Boys go to this parent.   1. a) _____
_____   b) Girls go to this parent.   b) _____
_____ 2. a) Seen as disciplinarian.*   2. a) _____
_____   b) Seen as nurturant, gentle, supportive, etc.   b) _____
_____ 3. a) Concerned with long-range planning (educa-   3. a) _____
                      tion, shaping lives, etc.)
_____   b) Concerned with daily care.   b) _____

Note: Is father described as more of a disciplinarian than our other data
suggest is in fact true? _____
_____

2. New parental roles added by husband since wife returned to work:

_____ a)   None (Note at bottom is he was always active).
_____ b)   Helps when asked on an irregular basis.
_____ c)   Has new period each day or week when he is alone with
                      children on a regular basis.
_____ d)   Is responsible for children most of the time wife is working
                      and/or during summers and school vacations.
_____ e)   Has added psychological responsibility as well as custodial
                      care since wife returned. (Evidence: thinking about children
                      on a day-to-day basis, making provisions for their daily
                      activities, thinking about how they feel, etc.)

Circle of extent of this: One area only.   Two.   Several.

Describe: _____
_____

Other notes:

3. Outside help? (When children were under 16, if known.)

	When?	How regular?
Older Children		
Relative		
Neighbor/friend		
Hired person		
Summer camp		

4. Attitudes toward parental control:

_____ a) A parent should be with children at all times.
_____ b) It's OK to leave children with relatives.
_____ c) It's OK to leave children with nonrelatives or send them to camp.
_____ d) Children under 16 are old enough to be on their own some of the time.

Note: If attitudes of parents differ, please indicate: _____
_____
_____

5. Major emphasis in child care:

_____ a) Parents should see to it that their children stay out of trouble (they should control behavior).
_____ b) Give children enough love and attention and they'll turn out OK later on.
_____ c) Mixed (describe): _____

Note of emphasis is different for each parent: _____
_____

Other notes:

Housekeeper Roles

Case # _____

Name: _____

Coder: _____Date: _____

1. Stereotypes of roles after wife's return:

MALE	Who does it?	Code	Who decides?	Code	Note on changes since return
Yard					
Car maintenance					
Garage					
Basement					
FEMALE					
Cleaning					
Cooking					
Dishes					
Groceries					
Pet Care					
Social planning					
Clothes shopping					
Sewing					
Laundry					
NEUTRAL (common)					
Gardening					
Garbage					
Bill Paying					
Interior decorating					
Furniture/appliance shopping					

H = husband usually does it

h = husband helps

H/W = husband and wife do it equally

C = children do it

c = children help

O = outside help

F = whole family does it together

If wife says she has to tell H to do yard, then code "who decides?" with W and H for "who does it?"

2. Role Flexibility: ease with which roles can be exchanged in times of crisis or otherwise (i.e., resistance to role sharing; areas which either spouse will either not give up or take over, if physically capable).

Wife will not give up: _____

_____

Wife will not take over: _____

_____

Husband will not give up: _____

_____

Husband will not take over: _____

_____

3. Extent of shared responsibility (i.e., extent to which H shares housekeeper role *after* return to work).

a) H does little outside of provider role. _____
b) H does traditional masculine tasks. _____
c) H accepts delegated tasks from W. _____
d) H takes on responsibility for one or more area(s) (other than child care) after return. _____
e) H and W are joint managers of all household work. _____

Note: To what extent does pattern *after* return represent a change?

Describe: _____

_____

4. Has husband taken over additional responsibilities when he was out of work? _____ Which ones? _____

APPENDIX I

ROLE CHANGE EVALUATION SHEETS

1. *Evaluation of Changes in Provider Roles (from cases and notes)*

A. Before:

    1. Wife not assigned any economic responsibility by:
        herself   husband   both   NA (not ascertained)

    2. Wife seen as possible pinch hitter in time of need by:
        herself   husband   both   NA

    3. Wife seen as important source of income over an indefinite period of time by:
        herself   husband   both   NA

B. After

    1. Wage ratio _____

    2. Subjective evaluation _____

    3. Actual use _____

    4. Husband's fear of loss of role: _____

_____

_____

_____

Summary of changes inferred from above: To what extent his wife become established as a provider for her family? Do both spouses define her role similarly? Has there been a change in this definition since she began working?

2. *Parental Role Changes*

Case # _____

Name: _____

BEFORE wife returned to work:

1. Were parental roles sex-typed along any of the following dimensions?

    _____ a) Boys go to father; girls go to mother.
    _____ b) Mother deals with young children and infants;
              father deals with older children.
    _____ c) Mother is seen as nurturant; father is seen as disciplinarian.
    _____ d) Mother does daily care; father is concerned with long-range
              planning.

    Is there any evidence of change in sex typing after return to work? ___

    _____
    _____
    _____

2. To what extent was father involved in daily care of children before wife
   returned to work?

    _____ a) Little contact with children except as whole family.
    _____ b) Father plays with children in his leisure time.
    _____ c) Father helps with children at request of mother.
    _____ d) Father has regular, delegated responsibilities for the
              children, daily or weekly.
    _____ a) Father assumes psychological as well as custodial
              responsibility for children. (See AFTER code sheet)

    What changes have been after wife's return to work? To what extent are the
    changes due to wife's return? _____

    _____
    _____
    _____

3. *Housekeeper Role Changes: Before Return to Work*

Case # _____

Name _____

1. a) Husband does little in house-not even traditional male tasks_____
   (does not assume responsibility for the house).
   b) Husband does traditional male tasks (assumes responsibility_____
   for the house).
   c) Husband helps when asked. _____
   d) Husband assigned specific delegated responsibility. _____
   e) Husband assumes responsibility for housekeeping. _____
   f) Total sharing. _____

2. Was husband *willing* to do traditional female housekeeping tasks even
   if he actually did not do them? _____

   _____

   _____

   _____

3. Evaluate role changes due to wife's return to work. _____

   _____

   _____

   _____

   _____

   _____

BIBLIOGRAPHY

Albrecht, S. L., D. L. Thomas and B. A. Chadwick, 1980, *Social Psychology*. Englewood Cliffs, N.J.: Prentice-Hall.

Aldous, J., 1969, "Occupational characteristics and males' role performance in the family." *Journal of Marriage and the Family* **31**:707–712.

Aldous, J., M. Osmond, and M. Hicks, 1977, "Men's work and men's families." In W. Burr, R. Hill, I. Nye, and I. Reiss (eds.), *Contemporary Theories about the Family*, pp. 227–258. New York: Free Press.

Anderson, S. A., C. S. Russell and W. R. Schumm "Perceived marital quality and family life-cycle categories: A further analysis" *Journal of Marriage and the Family* **45**:127–140.

Baden, C. and D. E. Friedman (eds.), 1981, *New Management Initiatives for Working Parents: Reports from an April, 1981 Conference*. Boston, MA: Wheelock College.

Bahr, S. J., 1982, "Exchange and control in married life." In F. I. Nye (ed.), *Family Relationships: Rewards and Costs*, Beverly Hills, Calif.: Sage.

Bailyn, L., 1970, "Career and family orientations of husbands and wives in relation to marital happiness." *Human Relations* **23**:97–113.

Barrett, N. S. 1979, "Women in the job market: Occupations, earnings, and career opportunities." In R. E. Smith (ed.) *The Subtle Revolution*. pp. 31–61. Washington, D.C.: The Urban Institute.

Bednarzik, R. W., and D. P. Klein, 1977, "Labor force trends: A synthesis and analysis." *Monthly Labor Review* **100**:3–15.

Berk, R. A., and S. F. Berk, 1979, *Labor and Leisure at Home: Content and Organization of the Household Day*. Beverly Hills, Calif.: Sage.

Bernard, J., 1972, *The Future of Marriage*. New York: Bantam.

Bernard, J., 1981, "The rise and fall of the good provider role." *American Psychologist* **36**:1–12.

Bird, C., 1979, *The Two Paycheck Marriage*. New York: Rawson, Wade.

Blau, P., 1964, *Exchange and Power in Social Life*. New York: Wiley.

Blood, R. O., Jr., 1972, *The Family*. New York: Free Press.

Blood, R. O., and D. M. Wolfe, 1960, *Husbands and Wives: The Dynamics of Married Living*. New York: Free Press.

Booth, A., 1977, "Wife's employment and husband's stress: A replication and refutation." *Journal of Marriage and the Family* **39**:645-652.

Bott, E., 1957, *Family and Social Network*. London: Tavistock.

Braverman, H., 1974, *Labor and Monopoly Capital*. New York: Monthly Review.

Brown, B. W., 1978, "Wife-employment and the Emergence of Egalitarian Marital Role Prescriptions: 1900-1974." *Journal of Comparative Family Studies* **9**:5-17.

Burgess, E. W., and H. Locke, 1953, *The Family: From Institution to Companionship*. New York: American.

Burke, R. J., and T. Weir, 1976, "Relationship of wives' employment status to husband, wife and pair satisfaction and performance." *Journal of Marriage and the Family* **38**:279-287.

Burr, W. R., G. K. Leigh, R. D. Day and J. Constantine, 1979, "Symbolic interaction and the family." In W. Burr et al. (eds.) *Contemporary Theories About the Family*. New York: The Free Press.

Clark, R. A. and V. Gecas, 1977, *The Employed Father in America: A Role Competition Analysis*. Paper prepared for presentation at the 1977 Annual Meeting of the Pacific Sociological Meet.

Clark, R. A., F. I. Nye, and V. Gecas, 1978, "Work involvement and marital role performance." *Journal of Marriage and the Family* **40**:9-22.

Cohen, J. F., 1979, "Male roles in mid-life." *The Family Coordinator* **28**:465-471.

Dahl, R. A., 1957, "The concept of power." *Behavioral Science* **2**: 201-218.

Davis, M. R., 1982, *Families in a Working World: The Impact of Organizations on Domestic Life*. New York: Praeger.

DeFrain, J., 1979, "Androgynous parents tell who they are and what they need." *The Family Coordinator* **28**:237-243.

Dizard, J., 1968, *Social Change in the Family*. Chicago: Community and Family Study Center.

Engels, F., 1954 (1884), *The Origin of the Family, Private Property and the State.* Moscow: Foreign Language.

Ericksen, A., W. L. Yancey, and E. P. Ericksen, 1979, "The division of family roles." *Journal of Marriage and the Family* **41**:301–313.

Evans, A., 1977, "Alternative work schedules in Europe." Paper presented at the National Conference on Alternative Work Schedules, Chicago.

Farkas, G., 1976, "Education, wage rates, and the division of labor between husband and wife." *Journal of Marriage and the Family* **38**:473–484.

Friedan, B., 1963, *The Feminine Mystique*. New York: Norton.

Gillespie, D., 1975, "Who has the power? The marital struggle." In M.J. Freeman (ed.), *Women: A Feminist Perspective*: 64–87.

Gilman, C. P. S., 1898, *Women and Economics*. Boston: Small, Maynard.

Glaser, B. G., and A. Strauss, 1965, *Awareness of Dying*. Chicago: Aldine.

Glaser, B. G., and A. Strauss, 1967, *The Discovery of Grounded Theory*. Chicago: Aldine.

Goffman, E., 1961, *Encounters: Two Studies in the Sociology of Interaction*. Indianapolis, Ind.: Bobs–Merrill.

Goode, W. J., 1963, *World Revolution and Family Patterns*. New York: Free Press.

Gowler, D., and K. Legge, 1978, "Hidden and open contracts in marriage." In R. Rapoport and R. Rapoport (eds.), *Working Couples,* pp. 47–61. New York: Harper & Row.

Griffiths, M. W., 1976, "Can we still afford occupational segregation?: Some remarks." In M.Blaxall , and B. Reagan, (eds.), *Women and the Workplace*, pp. 7–14. Chicago: University of Chicago Press.

Grønseth, E., 1975, "Work-sharing families: adaptations of pioneering families with husband and wife in part-time employment." Paper presented at the Biennial Conference of the International Society for the Study of Behavioral Development, University of Surry.

Haas, L., 1980, "Role-sharing couples: A study of egalitarian marriages." *Family Relations* **29**:289-296.

Haas, L., 1981, "Domestic role-sharing in Sweden." *Journal of Marriage and the Family* **43**:957-965.

Haas., L, 1982[a], "Determinants of rolesharing behavior: A study of egalitarian couples." *Sex Roles* **8**:747-760.

Haas, L., 1982b, Wives' commitment to breadwinning Sweden. Paper presented at 10th World Congress of Sociology, Mexico City.

Handy, C., 1978, "Going against the grain: Working couples and greedy occupations." In R. Rapoport and R. Rapoport (eds.), *Working Couples*, pp. 36-46. New York: Harper & Row.

Hartman, H., 1976, "Capitalism, patriarchy and job segregation by sex." In M. Blaxall, and B. Reagan, (eds.), *Women and the Workplace*, pp. 137-169. Chicago: University of Chicago Press.

Hayghe, H., 1975, "Marital and family characteristics of the labor force, March 1975." Special Labor Force Report 183, U.S. Department of Labor, Bureau of Labor Statistics.

Hayghe, H., 1976, "Families and the rise of working wives: an overview." *Monthly Labor Review* **5**:12-19.

Hayghe, H., 1978, "Marital and family characteristics of workers, March 1977." Special Labor Force Report 216, U.S. Department of Labor, Bureau of Labor Statistics.

Hayghe, H., 1982, "Dual earner families: Their economic and demographic characteristics." In J. Aldous (ed.), *Two Paychecks: Life in Dual Earner Families*. Beverly Hills, Calif. Sage, pp. 27-40.

Heins, M., S. Smock, J. Jacobs, 1976, "Productivity of women physicians." *Journal of the American Medical Association* **236**: 1961-1964.

Herbst, P.C., 1952, "The measurement of family relationships." *Human Relations* **5**:3-35.

Hill, R., 1949, *Families under Stress*. New York: Harper.

Hochschild, A. R., 1975, "Inside the clock work of male careers." In Florence Howe (ed.), *Women and the Power to Change*. pp. 47-80. New York: McGraw Hill.

Hoffman, L. W., 1958, *Some Effects of the Employment of Mothers on Family Structure*. Ph.D. dissertation, Department of Sociology, University of Michigan, Ann Arbor.

Hoffman, L. W., 1963, "The decision to work." In I. Nye (ed.), *The Employed Mother in America*, pp. 18–39. Chicago: Rand McNally.

Holmstrom, L., 1972, *The Two-Career Family*. Cambridge, Mass.: Schenkman.

Homans, G. C., 1961, *Social Behavior: Its Elementary Forms*. London: Routledge & Kegan Paul.

Hood, J. C., 1980, *Becoming a Two-Job Family*. Ph.D. dissertation, University of Michigan, Ann Arbor.

Hood, J., and S. Golden, 1979, "Beating time/making time: the impact of work scheduling on men's family roles." *Family Coordinator* **28**:575–582.

Huber, J., and G. Spitze, 1981, "Wives' employment, household behaviors, and sex-role attitudes." *Social Forces* **60**:150–169.

Hunt, P., 1980, *Gender and Class Consciousness*. London: Macmillan.

Kanter, R. M., 1977, *Work and Family in the United States: A Critical Review and Agenda for Research and Policy*. New York: Russell Sage.

Keith, P. M. and T. H. Brubaker, 1979, "Male household roles in later life: A look at masculinity and marital relationships." *The Family Coordinator*. **28**:237–243.

Keniston, K., and the Carnegie Council on Children, 1977, *All Our Children; The American Family under Pressure*. New York: Harcourt Brace Jovanovich.

Komarovsky, M., 1940, *The Unemployed Man and His Family*. New York: Dryden.

Kreps, J., 1971, *Sex in the Marketplace: American Women at Work*. Baltimore: Johns Hopkins.

Kuhn, T., 1962, *The Structure of Scientific Revolutions*. Chicago: University of Chicago Press.

LaRossa, R., 1977, *Conflict and Power in Marriage: Expecting the First Child*. Beverly Hills, Calif.: Sage.

Lein, L., 1979, "Male participation in home life: Impact of social supports and breadwinner responsibility on the allocation of tasks." *The Family Coordinator* **28**:489–495.

Lein, L., M. Durham, M. Pratt, M. M. Shudson, R. Thomas, and H. Weiss, 1974, "Final report: Work and family life." National Institute of Education Project No.3-3094. Wellesley, Mass.: Wellesley College Center for Research on Women.

Levine, J. A., 1976, *Who Will Raise the Children?* Philadelphia: Lippincott.

Lupri, E., 1969, "Contemporary authoritarian patterns in the West German family: A study in cross-national validation." *Journal of Marriage and the Family* **31**:134–144.

Marks, S. R., 1977, "Multiple roles and role strain: Some notes on human energy, time and commitment." *American Sociological Review* **42**:921–936.

Mason, K. O., J. Czaka, and S. Arber, 1976, "Change in U.S. women's role attitudes, 1964–1975." *American Sociological Review* **41**:573–596.

Miller, J. B., 1976, *Toward a New Psychology of Women.* Boston: Beacon Press.

Miller, J., and H. Garrison, 1982, "Sex roles: The Division of labor at home and in the workplace." In R. Turner and J. F. Short (eds.), *The Annual Review of Sociology*, pp. 237–262. Palo Alto, Calif: Annual Reviews Inc.

Mitchell, J., 1977, "Women: the longest revolution." In N. Glazer and H. Y. Waehrer (eds.), *Women in a Man-Made World*, pp. 169–180. Chicago: Rand McNally.

Model, S., 1981, "Housework by husbands: Determinants and implications." *Journal of Family Issues* **2**:225–237.

Mortimer, J. R., Hall, and R. Hill, 1978, "Husbands' occupational attributes as constraints on wives' employment." *Sociology of Work and Occupations* **5**:285–313.

Mowrer, E., 1932, *The Family, Its Organization and Disorganization.* Chicago: University of Chicago.

Norwood, J. L., and E. Waldman, 1979, "Women in the labor force: some new data series." Report 575, U.S. Department of Labor, Bureau of Labor Statistics.

Nye, F. I., 1974, "Husband-Wife Relationship," Chapter 8 in L. W. Hoffman and F. I. Nye, *Working Mothers.* pp. 207–225. San Francisco: Jossey-Bass.

Nye, F. I., 1979, "Choice, exchange and the family." In W. Burr et al. (eds.) *Contemporary Theories About the Family.* pp. 1–41. New York: The Free Press.

226

Nye, F. I., V. Gecas, H. M. Bahr, S. J. Bahr, J. E. Carlson, S. McLaughlin, and W. L. Slocum, 1977, *Role Structure and Analysis of the Family*. Beverly Hills, Calif.: Sage.

Oakley, A., 1974, *The Sociology of Housework*. New York: Pantheon.

Olson, D. H. and R. G. Ryder, 1970, "Inventory of marital conflicts (IMC): An experimental interaction procedure." *Journal of Marriage and the Family* **32**:443–448.

Olson, D. H., D. H. Sprenkel, and C. S. Russell, 1979, "Circumplex model of marital and family systems. I: Cohesion and adaptability dimensions, family types, and clinical applications." *Family Process* **18**:3–18.

Papanek, H., 1973, "Men, women and work: Reflections on the two person career." *American Journal of Sociology* **28**:852–872.

Philliber, W. W. and D. V. Hiller, 1983, "Relative occupational attainments of spouses and later changes in marriage and wife's work experience." *Journal of Marriage and the Family*. **45**:161–170.

Piotrkowski, C. S., 1979, *Work and Family System: A Naturalistic Study of Working-Class and Lower-Middle-Class Families*. New York: The Free Press.

Pleck, J., 1977, "The work-family role system." *Social Problems* **24**:417–427

Pleck, J., 1979, "Men's family work: three perspectives and some new data." *Family Coordinator* **28**:481–488.

Pleck, J., 1983, "Husbands' paid work and family roles; Current research issues." In J. H. Pleck, and H. Z. Lopata (eds.), *Research on the Interweave of Social Roles: Families and Jobs*, Vol. 3. Greenwich, Conn.: JAI Press.

Pleck, J. H., and L. Lang, 1978, "Men's family role: Its nature and consequences. Unpublished manuscript, Wellesley College Center for Research on Women.

Pleck, J. H., and H. Z. Lopata (eds.), 1983, *Research on the Interweave of Social Roles: Families and Jobs*, Vol. 3. Greenwich, Conn.: JAI Press.

Pleck, J. H., and J. Sawyer (eds.), 1974, *Men and Masculinity*. Englewood Cliffs, N.J.: Prentice–Hall.

Pleck, J. H., and G. L. Staines, 1982, "Work schedules and work-family conflict in two-earner couples." In J. Aldous (ed.), *Two-Earner Couples*. Beverly Hills, Calif.: Sage.

Polatnick, M., 1973, "Why men don't rear children: A power analysis." *Berkeley Journal of Sociology* **18**: 45–86.

Poloma, M. M., and T. N. Garland, 1971, "The myth of the egalitarian family." In A. Theodore (ed.), *The Professional Woman*. Cambridge, Mass.: Schenkman.

Presser, H. B., and V. S. Cain, 1983, "Shift work among dual-earner couples with children." *Science* **219** (February 18):876–878.

Rainwater, L. 1965, *Family Design: Marital Sexuality, Family Size and Contraception*. Chicago: Aldine.

Rapoport, R. and R. Rapoport, 1971, *Dual-Career Families*. Middlesex, England: Penguin.

Rapoport, R., and Rapoport, R. with J. Bumstead (eds.), 1978, *Working Couples*. New York: Harper & Row.

Reese, R. S., 1982, A Process-Oriented Study of Psycho-Social Development in Women Aged Thirty-Two to Forty-Five. Unpublished Doctoral Dissertation, School of Education, University of Wisconsin–Milwaukee.

Renshaw, J. R., 1976, "An exploration of the dynamics of the overlapping worlds of work and family." *Family Process* **15**:143–165.

Robinson, J. P., 1977, *How Americans Use Time*. New York: Praeger.

Rose, A., 1944, Appendix 1 in G. Myrdal, *American Dilemma*. New York: Harper.

Ross, H. L., and I. V. Sawhill, 1975, *Time of Transition: The Growth of Families headed by Women*. Washington, D.C.: The Urban Institute.

Rowe, M., 1978, "Choosing child care: Many options." In R. Rapoport and R. Rapoport (eds.), *Working Couples*. New York: Harper & Row.

Rubin, L. B., 1976, *Worlds of Pain: Life in the Working-Class Family*. New York: Basic.

Rubin, L. B., 1979, *Women of a Certain Age*. New York: Harper & Row.

Rubin, L. B., 1983, *Intimate Strangers: Men and Women Together*. New York: Harper & Row.

Ruether, R., 1977, "Toward new solutions: Working women and the male workday." *Christianity and Crisis*, February 7, 1977.

Safilios-Rothschild, C., 1970a, "The study of family power structure: A review 1960–1969." *Journal of Marriage and the Family* **32**:539–552.

Safilios-Rothschild, C., 1970b, "The influence of the wife's degree of work commitment upon some aspects of family organization and dynamics." *Journal of Marriage and the Family*. **32**:681–691.

Safilios-Rothschild, C. and M. Dijkers, 1978, "Handling Unconventional Asymmetries." In R. and R. Rapoport (eds.) *Working Couples*. New York: Harper & Row, pp. 62–73.

Scanzoni, J., 1970, *Opportunity and the Family*. New York: Free Press.

Scanzoni, J., 1972, *Sexual Bargaining: Power Politics in the American Marriage.* Englewood Cliffs, N.J.: Prentice–Hall.

Scanzoni, J., 1978, *Sex Roles, Women's Work and Marital Conflict*. Washington, D.C.: Lexington Books.

Scanzoni, J. and M. Szinovacz, 1980, *Family Decision-Making: A Developmental Model*. Beverly Hills, Calif.: Sage.

Seidenberg, R., 1975, *Corporate Wives: Corporate Casualties?* New York: Doubleday.

Sennett, R. and J. Cobb, 1973, *The Hidden Injuries of Class*. New York: Random House.

Shea, J. R., R. Spitz, and F. Zeller, 1970, *Dual Careers: A Longitudinal Study of Labor Market Experience of Women*, Vol. I. Washington, D.C.: U.S. Department of Labor.

Sieber, S. D., 1974, "Toward a theory of role accumulation." *American Sociological Review* **39**:567–578.

Simpson, I. H. and P. England, 1982, "Conjugal Work Roles and Marital Solidarity." In J. Aldous (ed.), *Two Paychecks: Life in Dual Earner Families*. pp. 147–171. Beverly Hills, Calif.: Sage.

Singlemann, P., 1972, "Exchange as social interaction: convergences between two theoretical perspectives." *American Sociological Review* **37**:414–424.

Smith, R. E. 1979, "The Movement of Women into the Labor Force." In R. E. Smith (ed.) *The Subtle Revolution*. Washington, D.C.: The Urban Institute, pp. 1–29.

Spanier, G. B. and W. Sauer, 1979, "An empirical evaluation of the family life cycle." *Journal of Marriage and the Family* **41**:27–40.

Sprey, J., 1969, "The family as a system in conflict." *Journal of Marriage and the Family* **31**:699–706.

Sprey, J., 1971, "On the management of conflict in families." *Journal of Marriage and the Family* **33**:722–731.

Sprey, J., 1975, "Family Power and Process: Toward a Conceptual Integration." pp. 61–79 in R. E. Cromwell and D. H. Olson, *Power in Families*: New York: John Wiley.

Staines, G., J. Pleck, L. Lang, and P. O'Connor, 1977, "Wives' employment and marital satisfaction: yet another look." *Psychology of Women Quarterly* **3**:90–120.

Strauss, A., 1978, *Negotiations: Varieties, Contexts, Processes, and Social Order.* San Francisco: Josey–Bass.

Strauss, G. 1974, "Workers: Attitudes and Adjustments." In Rosow, J. M. (ed.) *The Worker and the Job.* pp. 33–46. Englewood Cliffs, N.J.: Prentice-Hall.

Sussman, M. B., 1975, "The Four f's of variant family forms and marriage styles." *The Family Coordinator* **24**:563–577.

Sweet, J. A., 1974, Returning to work after child-birth: national natality survey." Working Paper 74–31 of the Center for Demography and Ecology, University of Wisconsin-Madison.

Szinovacz, M. (ed.), 1982, *Women's Retirement.* Beverly Hills, Calif.: Sage.

Thornton, A., D. F. Alwin, and D. Camburn, 1983, "Causes and consequences of sex-role attitudes and attitude change." *American Sociological Review* **48**:211–227.

U.S. Bureau of Census, 1976, *A Statistical Portrait of Women.* Current Population Reports, Special Studies: Series P-23, No. 58. Washington, D.C.: Government Printing Office.

U.S. Department of Labor, Women's Bureau, 1969, "Handbook on women workers," Bulletin 294. Washington, D.C.: Government Printing Office.

U.S. Department of Labor, 1978, USDL News 78-188, March 16.

U.S. Department of Labor, 1979, USDL NEWS 79-747, October 31.

U.S. Department of Labor, 1980, USDL NEWS 80-767, December 9.

U.S. Department of Labor, 1982, USDL NEWS 82-276, August 10.

Waite, L. J., 1980, "Working wives and the family life cycle." *American Journal of Sociology* **86**:272-294.

Walker, K., 1970, "Time spent by husbands in household work." *Family Economics Review* **4**:8-11.

Waller, W., 1938, *The Family: A Dynamic Interpretation*. New York: Cordon.

Walster, E. and G. W. Walster, 1975, "Equity and social justice." *Journal of Social Issues* **31**:21-43.

Westcott, D. N., 1975, Trends in Overtime Hours and Pay, 1969-74. Special Labor Force Report, Bureau of Labor Statistics.

WIN Magazine, Women's Washington Representative, 1977, "None of This is anti-feminist." WIN, **18**(August): 17.

Wolff, K. H., 1950, *The Sociology of Georg Simmel*. New York: Free Press.

Wright, J., 1978, "Are working women really more satisfied?" *Journal of Marriage and the Family* **40**:301-314.

Young, M., and P. Willmott, 1973, *The Symmetrical Family*. New York: Pantheon.

INDEX

centered marriage, 76-77; power of wife's salary and, 65-66, 69
Detroit Area Survey (1981), 181
"discounting process," 22
distant father, 98
division of labor (*see* housekeeping responsibilities; role bargaining; role sharing)
divorce, 152-155
Dizard, J., 175
dual-career super-couples, 182-183
dual earner household, 195

egalitarian marriage 8-12; biases in, 9-12; coprovider roles in, 64; elements in, 8; role bargaining in, 118
emotional interdependence, 83
employment, full, 194
England, P., 173
Ericksen, A., 9, 178, 183, 186, 187
Evans, A., 196
exchange theory: criticism of, 174; and provider role redefinition, 116-117; limitations of, 117

family bond types, 24-29; child-centered families, 25-27, 28; in companionate marriage, 71, 72; couple-centered families, 27-29; husband-centered families, 24-25, 28; husband's response to wife's decision to work and, 123
family-centered marriage, lower-middle class, 189-190

family-motivated women, 32-33, 48-51, 55-57
family process, 176
family role performance, role overload and, 130
family roles, definition of, 5
family systems, model of, 136, 139n
Farkas, G., 178, 186
fathers: distant, 98; secondary, 87-92
feminist biases in marriage, 9
field notes, analysing, 20-21
financial independence of wives, 64, 78 (*see also* dependency balance)
follow-up interviews, 142-171; ambivalent coproviders, 166; coproviders, 166-168; labor force status, 143-162; left work force, 143, 146-149; marital stress, 150-162; remaining in labor force, 149-162; secondary providers, 162-165; wage ratios, 162-168

Garland, T. N., 183, 188
Garrison, H., 13n
gender-modern women, 11
Gillespie, D., 12
Glaser, B. G., 15, 21, 22
goals (*see also* work/family priorities): competing, 150-153; complementary, 155-157, 159
Goffman, E., 6
Golden, S., 130
good provider role, alternatives to, 2
Gowler, D., 119
Griffiths, M., 194

Gronseth, E., 5
"grounded categories," 21
guilt and parenting roles, 96

Haas, L., 5, 8, 13n, 14n, 112n, 139n, 178, 179, 180-181, 186
Handy, C., 183
Hayghe, H., 186, 195
Heins, M. S., 193
Herbst, P. C., 5
Hiller, D. V., 193
Hochschild, A., 193, 196
Hoffman, L. Wladis, 5
Holmstrom, L., 153, 183
Homans, G., 173
honeymoon hypothesis, 181
Hood, J. C., 130, 189
housekeeping responsibilities, 43-45; age of children and, 107; changes in, 59, 60, 99-108; in child-centered marriages, 103-106; of children, 102-106, 169; clearly defining, 118, 121; in couple-centered families, 50-51, 53-55, 106-107; double standard for, 107; family reorganization for, 103-106; in husband-centered marriages, 43-45, 100-101; inside/outside distinction, 104, 107; life cycle status and, 109-110, 111, 169-170; no change in 100-103; provider role status of wife and, 110, 111; residual territoriality, 105; sharing equally, 106-107; work schedule changes and, 170
Huber, J., 14n

husband(s): career frustrations of, 150-155; career-oriented, 38-40; dependence of, on salary of wife, 120; job orientation of, 69-71; job oriented, 36-37; occupational prestige of, 69-71; superproviders, 37-38; supportive, 33-36; surpried, 36; work/family priorities, 39-40 (*see also* goals)
husband-centered marriage, 24-25, 28-29; communication in, 72, 73-76; dependency balance in, 76-77; development of, 41-47; housekeeping responsibilities in, 100; main issue in, 56; parenting, 85, 87; traditional, 81-82; transition to couple-centered, 41-47
husband/child-centered families, 27
hypotheses, two-job family, 138

income of wife in bargaining process, 64, 115 (*see also* dependency balance)
interactionist theory, 118
interdependence bargaining power and, 165
interview procedures, 20
interview transcription, 200

job orientation vs. occupational prestige, 70-71
job-oriented men, 56; work/family priorities, 40
joint obligations, 118

Kanter, R. Moss, 183, 196
Keith, P. M., 182
Keniston, K., 194
Komarovsky, M., 21, 175, 191

labor, division of (*see* housekeeping responsibilities)
labor force characteristics, 204-205
Lang, L., 184, 189
LaRossa, R., 7, 175, 181
Legge, K., 119
Lein, L., 5
Levine, J., 196
life cycle status, role sharing by, 109-110, 111, 169-170; division of labor and, 180-182
listening (*see* communication)
lower-middle class marriage, 189-190
Lupri, E., 178

marital companionship, 59, 10 (*see also* companionate marriage)
marital equality, working definition of, 12-13 (*see also* egalitarian marriage)
marital role changes, 59-112; companionship, 71-85; housekeeping, 99-108; parenting, 85-99; provider roles, 60-71; summary of, 109
marital satisfaction, 128, 190-191
marketwork/housework bargain, 1
Marks, S. R., 130
Mason, K. O., 11
midcareer crisis, 156
middle class biases in marriage, 10-12

Miller, J. B., 8, 13*n*
Miller, S. M., 11
Model, S., 169, 178, 180, 181, 190
Mortimer, J. R., 72
Mowrer, E., 10

Negotiations, 177
neo-traditional couples, 183
Nye, F. V., 5, 174, 190, 191

occupational prestige of husband, 69, 70
Olson, D. H., 139*n*, 177
one family/one job assumption, 193-194
open conflict, 135-136

Packer, A., 193, 194
Papanek, H., 72
parenting roles (*see* coparenting): changes in, 59, 60, 87-99; in couple-centered marriages, 50-51; as joint responsibility, 117; life cycle status and, 109-110, 111; no role changes in, 85-87; provider role status of wife and, 110, 111; secondary fathers, 87-92; teenagers, 85-87
patriarchal biases in marriage, 9-10
Philliber, W. W., 193
Pleck, J., 1, 11, 13*n*, 112*n*, 183, 184, 186, 189, 196
Poloma, M. M., 183, 188
position of most interest, 115
power, defined, 179
Pressner, H. B., 112*n*

productive conflict, 8
provided for status, retaining, 127
provider role(s), 2, 44; ambivalent coproviders, 65-69; changes in, 59; 60-71; coproviders, 63-71; in couple-centered marriages, 49-50, 53-54; in husband-centered marriages, 42; occupational prestige of husband and, 69-70; vs. parenting, 90; protection of, 82-83; redefining, 60-71; renegotiating, 124-127; secondary, 60, 62-63, 162-165; superprovider, 71; wage ratio definition, 65, 69, 70
provider role data sheet, 208-209

quid pro quo, 174

Rainwater, L., 184, 186
Rapoport, Rhonda, 183, 196
Rapoport, Robert, 183, 196
recession, 159-162
Reese, R. S., 182
religious conversion, 80
remarriage, 153
Renshaw, J., 196
repetitive conflict, 136
residual territoriality, 105
Reuther, R., 196
Robinson, J. P., 139*n*
role attachment, 6, 24, 55-56; and division of household labor, 179; life cycle stage and, 181-182; and role bargaining process, 116

role bargaining, 1-4, 6-7; bargaining power in, 7, 14*n*; competing vs. complementary goals, 6-7; conflict and equity in, 7-8; in couple-centered marriages, 56-57; equity in, 8-12; goals of, 6-7; in husband-centered marriages, 56; life cycle changes and, 169-170; work schedule changes and, 170
role bargaining process, 113-139; bargaining power in, use of, 115-116; components of, 114, 117; conflict and conflict resolution, 134-137; defined, 117-119; in egalitarian marriages, 118; exchange theory and, 117-118; goals of wife and, 115-116; illustration of, 119-121; marital relationship and, 127-129; position of most interest, 115; prior agreements, 122-123; provider role, renegotiating, 124-127; role overload and, 130-134
role change(s), 59-112; in companionate marriage, 71-85; coparenting, 85-99; in housekeeping, 99-108; in provider roles, 60-71
role change evaluation sheets, 217-219
role commitment, 6
role definition, 7
role distance, 6
role overload: dealing with, 131; description of, 130; and division of household labor, 179; factors in, 130; life cycle stage

and, 181-182; and role relinquishment, 130-134
role redefinitions, 6
role relinquishment, 6, 130-134; cutting back, 132-134; striking, 131-132
role-segregated couple, 57
role sharing, 5, 13n; age of children and, 189; in couple-centered marriages, 51-55; definition of, 5; in family-centered lower-middle class marriage, 189-190; life cycle changes and, 109-111, 169-170; social class and, 71; wives' work commitment and, 187-188; work schedule changes and, 170
Rose, A., 141
Rowe, M., 196, 197
Ryder, R. G., 177
Rubin, F., 127
Rubin, L. B., 16, 154, 182, 191

Safilios-Rothschild, C., 177, 187-188
sampling procedures, 15-19
Scanzoni, J., 7, 9, 10, 11, 14n, 59, 115, 128, 129, 134, 174, 178, 179, 186, 187
school, finishing, 48
secondary fathers: in child-centered marriage, 90-91; in couple-centered marriage, 88-92
secondary providers, 2-3, 60, 62-63; bargaining power of, 124-125; family role of, 62-63; follow-up studies of, 162-165; housekeeping responsibilities

and, 110; parenting responsibilities and, 110; wage ratio among, 69, 70, 162-165
secondary workers, 194-196
Seidenberg, R., 175
self-esteem of wives, 46, 128-129
self-motivated women, 30, 32; follow-up studies of, 166; in husband-centered marriage, 41-47
Sennet, R., 12
Shea, J. R., 33
Sieber, S. D., 130
Simpson, I. H., 173
Singelmann, P., 175
Smith, R. E., 190
social change, 193-195
social class: marital companionship and, 186-187; and role sharing, 71; wage ratio and, 185-186; wive's work commitment and, 187-188; work/family priorities and, 183-185
social networks, 120
sole-provider role, 6
Spanier, G. B., 180
Spitze, G., 14n
Sprey, J., 13, 14n
Staines, G. L., 112n, 190, 191
Strauss, A., 15, 21, 22, 118, 176, 191
stress, marital: external sources of, 157-162; internal sources of, 150-157; recession and, 159-162; work scheduling and, 158-159
strike, household, 131-132
success constraint theory, 175
super-couples, 182-183

superproviders, 37-38, 71; renego-
    tiating role of, 126;
    work/family priorities, 39-40
Sussman, M. B., 118
symbolic interaction, 175
symbols of commitment, 118
Szinovacz, M., 7, 14*n*, 129, 182

task specialization, 8, 9
teasing, 82-83
theoretical sampling, 15
time budgeting, 131, 139*n*
tradition: and companionate mar-
    riage, 81-82, 84; housekeeping
    responsibilities, 100-102
transcription, sample, 206-207
two-person career, 72

urbanist biases in marriage, 9-10

wage ratios, 120, 162-168; and
    bargaining power, 116,
    162-168, 178; among
    coproviders, 65; and provider
    role definition, 69, 70; and
    social class, 185-186
Walker, K., 1
Waller, W., 115
Walster, E., 8

Walster, G. W., 8
web of reciprocity, 174
White, L., 143
wife interview checklist, 199
Willmott, P., 175, 184
Wirtz, W., 194
Wolfe, D. M., 5, 10, 177, 178, 181,
    186
work, wife's decision for: and fami-
    ly bond type, 24-29; husbands'
    attitudes toward, 33-41, 123;
    motivation for, 29-33, 123
Work and Family in America, 196
work commitment of wife, 187-188
work/family priorities, 40; com-
    plementary, 159; family-
    centered lower-middle class,
    189-190; social class and,
    183-185
work motivation: family, 143-149;
    and remaining in labor force,
    148
work scheduling, 158-159; role shar-
    ing and, 170
work-sharing couple, 71
Worlds of Pain, 16
Wright, J., 190

Young, M., 175, 184

Zero-sum bargaining, 174, 177

ABOUT THE AUTHOR

Jane C. Hood is an assistant professor of sociology at University of Wisconsin-Milwaukee. Prior to coming to Milwaukee in 1978, she taught a wide variety of undergraduate courses at The University of Michigan while completing her graduate training.

Dr. Hood has written several articles on work and family roles. Her most recent research concerns shift work, psychological stress, and substance abuse.

She holds a BA in social history from The University of Wisconsin-Madison and a PhD in sociology from the University of Michigan.